D1525761

RATIONING THE CONSTITUTION

RATIONING THE CONSTITUTION

How Judicial Capacity Shapes Supreme Court Decision-Making

ANDREW COAN

Harvard University Press

Cambridge, Massachusetts & London, England

2019

First printing

Library of Congress Cataloging-in-Publication Data

Names: Coan, Andrew, author.
Title: Rationing the Constitution : how judicial capacity shapes Supreme
    Court decision-making / Andrew Coan.
Description: Cambridge, Massachusetts : Harvard University Press, 2019. |
    Includes bibliographical references and index.
Identifiers: LCCN 2018042062 | ISBN 9780674986954 (alk. paper)
Subjects: LCSH: Constitutional law—United States. | United States. Supreme
    Court. | Judges—Workload—United States. | Judicial process—United States.
Classification: LCC KF4550 .C557 2019 | DDC 347.73/26504—dc23
    LC record available at https://lccn.loc.gov/2018042062

For my family—
Lori, Sonali, Sabina, and E-Z-R-A

Contents

RATIONING THE CONSTITUTION

Introduction

The past decade ranks among the most controversial in the history of the United States Supreme Court. In 2010 the Court invalidated key provisions of the Bipartisan Campaign Reform Act, paving the way for the most expensive presidential campaign in American history. Two years later, the Court came within a single vote of striking down the most significant social legislation in two generations. In the process, the justices neutered the Affordable Care Act's Medicaid expansion, effectively denying health insurance to millions of low-income citizens. The following year, the Court struck down the federal Defense of Marriage Act and a crucial provision of the Voting Rights Act, both passed relatively recently by overwhelming majorities of Congress. As an encore, the Court in 2015 struck down the same-sex marriage bans of more than thirty states, most adopted by sizable popular majorities within the past ten years.

Together, these decisions have triggered a major swell of outrage over perceived judicial arrogance and overreach. Leading commentators across the political spectrum have decried the Supreme Court's "disdain for democracy." Even the justices themselves have joined the scrum. The late Justice Antonin Scalia found "jaw-dropping" the Court's pretension of "judicial supremacy over the people's representatives in Congress and the Executive." The Court, he suggested, had "enthroned" itself and placed democratic politics in "permanent judicial receivership." While temperamentally more restrained, Justice Ruth Bader Ginsburg echoes Scalia when she laments the Court's "hubris" in over-ruling a democratically elected Congress. With an expanded conservative majority eager to flex its muscles, these concerns are only likely to grow in the coming years.[1]

The critics are right about one thing. The Supreme Court is capable of issuing occasional decisions that reshape major areas of public policy and thwart the will of democratic majorities. Some recent cases certainly fit this description. The critics are wrong, however, to worry—as Justice Scalia did—about "a Supreme Court standing . . . at the apex of government, empowered to decide all constitutional questions, always and everywhere primary in its role." Compared to the vast machinery of Congress, the President, and the state governments, the Supreme Court is a tiny institution that can resolve only a small fraction of the constitutional issues generated by the American government. Excluding military outlays, the United States executive branch alone had a 2017 budget of $3.5 trillion—larger than the gross domestic product of all but two other countries in the world. By comparison, the 2017 budget of the federal judiciary was just $7.6 billion—less than the gross domestic product of Sioux City, Iowa.[2]

By now this is something of a commonplace among constitutional scholars. But it is a commonplace of a peculiar sort. It receives frequent lip service but is almost never taken really seriously. Advocates for more expansive constitutional protections routinely brush aside, or outright ignore, the judiciary's limited capacity. Opponents of such protections routinely write as if "government by judiciary" were a real and worrisome possibility. Meanwhile, there has been very little work exploring why the judiciary has such limited capacity or how we should expect this limitation to affect its constitutional decisions. Certainly, popular discourse on the Supreme Court and constitutional law reflects virtually no appreciation for these issues.[3]

This is the first book-length work on constitutional law to take judicial capacity seriously. Its thesis is threefold. First, the constraints on judicial capacity are a product of both the structural organization of the judiciary and certain widely shared but little discussed professional norms of American judges. Of special importance is the Supreme Court's commitment to reviewing virtually every lower-court decision that invalidates a federal law, which greatly reduces the volume of litigation the Court can handle in domains affecting the constitutionality of federal legislation.

Second, in many important constitutional domains, the constraints of judicial capacity create an almost irresistible pressure on the Supreme Court to adopt clear but clumsy categorical *rules,* whose application prospective litigants and lower-court judges can readily predict in advance. Conversely, those constraints create strong pressure on the Court to avoid vague *standards,* which allow for more nuance but also generate greater uncertainty, increasing the volume of litigation and the frequency of conflict among lower-court decisions.

One example of such a categorical rule is the Supreme Court's modern interpretation of Congress's Article I commerce power, a major battleground of American federalism. Under that interpretation, Congress is permitted to regulate economic activities, like production and distribution, but not noneconomic activities, like violent crime, even when those noneconomic activities substantially affect the national economy. To apply (or predict the application of) this rule, lower courts and prospective litigants need not know anything about the problem Congress sought to address, the underlying purpose of the commerce power, or the practical effects of the challenged legislation. They need merely to determine whether the activities regulated by that legislation are economic or noneconomic.

Third, in many important constitutional domains, the constraints of judicial capacity also create very strong pressure on the Supreme Court to defer to the constitutional decisions of other government actors. Such deference reduces the expected value of bringing suit by increasing the odds that the government will prevail. This, in turn, reduces the volume of litigation. Why would plaintiffs incur the costs of bringing a lawsuit if they know they are probably going to lose?

An example of such deference is the rational-basis test, which the Supreme Court has adopted variations of in many different constitutional domains. Where this test applies, the Court will uphold a challenged government action so long as there is any conceivable rational basis for finding it constitutional. Needless to say, this is an extremely low bar.

Often the constraints of judicial capacity compel the Supreme Court *both* to adopt clear rules *and* to defer to other government actors. As a result, American constitutional law is shot through with strong doctrines of deference and clumsy categorical rules that are difficult to explain except as responses to the constraints of judicial capacity.

These strategies for allocating the Supreme Court's limited capacity are a form of *rationing*. The Court's capacity to decide constitutional questions is a scare resource. In many important domains, it cannot decide all, or even most, constitutional questions. The Court must therefore employ some mechanism for determining which questions it will decide. In theory, that mechanism could be a lottery, a market, or a queue—all time-tested methods for allocating scarce resources of other kinds. But for good and obvious reasons, the Court has been unwilling to choose the cases it decides by lot. It has also been unwilling to sell its services to the highest bidder or simply to decide constitutional cases in the order they are filed. Instead, in many of the most important constitutional domains, the Court has carefully allocated its limited capacity through a combination of clear, categorical rules and strong judicial deference. Thus does the Supreme Court ration the Constitution.

At this point I need to define terms. By judicial capacity, I mean the total volume of cases the court system is capable of handling. I do not mean the capacity of the judiciary to produce reliably good decisions, which I shall call *judicial competence*. Nor do I mean the capacity—or inclination—of the judiciary to produce social change against the tide of dominant political forces, which I shall call *judicial independence*.

Both judicial competence and judicial independence are the subjects of substantial literatures. Indeed, in one form or another, they have dominated the agenda of constitutional theory for more than half a century. For decades, scholars have debated whether courts represent a reliable "forum of principle" or an imperious aristocracy; whether courts possess the fact-finding tools and expertise to make reliable decisions on empirically difficult constitutional questions; whether courts are meaningfully independent of the political process; and, if they are, whether they are capable of producing meaningful social change in the teeth of political opposition. It is hardly surprising that these questions have garnered substantial attention. They are obviously important.

The principal aim of this book is to show that judicial capacity is comparably important. This claim rests on three premises. First, the limits of judicial capacity help to explain the shape and evolution of many important constitutional doctrines. Why have the conservative Roberts and Rehnquist Courts not sharply limited federal power or endorsed broad constitutional protections for private property against government regulation? Why did the liberal Warren Court not use the Equal Protection Clause to remedy economic inequality, between the races or otherwise? Why have justices across the political spectrum not been tempted to invalidate congressional delegations of regulatory power to disfavored administrative agencies? In each of these contexts, the Supreme Court has adopted a broadly deferential posture toward the political process. On the rare occasions when it engages in serious review, its decisions take the form of relatively hard-edged categorical rules that clearly insulate the vast majority of government action from serious scrutiny. Many of these rules are difficult to explain except as efforts to shield the courts against an overwhelming volume of litigation that the Supreme Court would feel compelled to review.

Second, judicial capacity's influence on doctrine is a crucial determinant of judicial competence, one that constitutional scholars have almost completely overlooked. In particular, when the Supreme Court attempts to second-guess Congress, the President, or state governmental actors, capacity constraints often force it to do so in the form of clumsy categorical rules. This dynamic, in turn, produces constitutional doctrines that are at best crude proxies for the underlying purposes they are meant to serve. Recall the economic / noneconomic activity distinction from the Court's modern commerce-power decisions. This rule sends a clear signal to lower courts and prospective litigants, but it does a poor job of accomplishing the Court's stated purpose of distinguishing the "truly national" (which includes many noneconomic activities) from the "truly local" (which includes many economic ones). The pressure that capacity constraints place on the Court to employ such functionally unsound rules provides an important, though not necessarily decisive, reason to distrust the Court, quite apart from more familiar arguments about judges' lack of expertise, access to relevant information, and democratic accountability.

Third, the constraints on judicial capacity impose important limits on the Supreme Court's ability to challenge dominant political forces. These limits, too, have been largely overlooked. Simply put, capacity constraints frequently force the Court to adopt a posture of deference toward Congress, state legislatures, and other governmental actors. To do otherwise would invite more litigation than the Court could handle. If the government always wins, by contrast, there is little reason for would-be reformers to bring suit. But of course, it is difficult to challenge dominant political forces while adhering to a broadly deferential approach. This is not to say that the Supreme Court will never swim against the tide of public opinion. It clearly has in the past and will certainly do so again. But the limits of judicial capacity sharply constrain the scope and the duration of its ability to challenge dominant political forces.

In short, judicial capacity is essential to understanding the development of American constitutional law and the role of the Supreme Court in American society. It is also essential to the practical work of legal reformers and the lawyers who represent them. Both of these groups need to know when they can and cannot expect the Court to act and how the constraints of judicial capacity will affect the options available to the Court when it does. Too often these topics are discussed without any regard to the institutional realities and limits under which the Supreme Court labors. They are almost never discussed with an adequate appreciation for the submerged hydraulic influence of judicial capacity.

The book unfolds as follows. Part I explains the source and character of the constraints on judicial capacity and develops a positive—that is, a descriptive and predictive—theory of the influence of judicial capacity on the constitutional decisions of the Supreme Court. This theory serves as the basis for a judicial capacity model of Supreme Court decision-making, which attempts to explain the influence of judicial capacity on the broad contours of American constitutional law and to predict the future course of their development.

The judicial capacity model makes three novel contributions: First, it emphasizes the role of certain deeply rooted professional norms in constraining judicial capacity—in particular, the Supreme Court's felt obligation to review any lower-court decision invalidating a federal statute. The sacrifice, or even the relaxing of these norms, would greatly expand judicial capacity. But few have argued for that sort of change and, as a matter of prediction, it seems quite unlikely.

Second, the model explains why the constraints of judicial capacity have far greater bite in some constitutional domains than in others. It also identifies the domains in which this is the case—those in which the potential volume of litigation is unusually high and those in which the Supreme Court feels compelled to grant review in an unusually large fraction of cases. Where both of these criteria are satisfied, the predictive and explanatory power of judicial capacity is at its zenith.

Third, the model identifies categorical rules and judicial deference to other governmental actors as the two principal tools used by the Supreme Court to manage its limited capacity in domains where those limits operate most powerfully. Categorical rules reduce uncertainty, encouraging settlement and uniformity in lower-court decisions and thus reducing the number of cases the Supreme Court feels compelled to decide. Deference to other governmental actors reduces the expected benefits of constitutional litigation—why sue if the government always wins?—with the same result.

In addition to laying out a theory of judicial capacity and the judicial capacity model, Part I develops a framework for testing that model against the Supreme Court's past decisions. This framework centers on three well-established models of judicial decision-making—legalist, attitudinal, and strategic—which serve as a baseline for comparison throughout the book. The most important test of the judicial capacity model is whether it can explain aspects of Supreme Court decision-making that these models cannot. If it can, that counts as powerful evidence in its favor.

The proof is in the pudding—in this case, the constitutional decisions of the U.S. Supreme Court. Part II examines the predictions of the judicial capacity model across a wide range of important constitutional domains. In effect, these domains serve as case studies, spanning each of the principal structural features of the U.S. Constitution: federalism, separation of powers, and individual rights. Examples include the federal commerce power, the nondelegation doctrine, and regulatory takings. Each of the domains discussed in this Part involves either an unusually high volume of potential litigation or unusually high stakes—in the sense that the Court feels strongly compelled to grant review in an unusually large fraction of cases. Most involve both. As such, the judicial capacity model predicts that the Supreme Court will feel strongly constrained to employ some combination of strong deference to other governmental actors and hard-edged categorical rules.

With very rare exception, that is the pattern that the Court's decisions have followed in each of these domains. Both aspects of the pattern—the Court's consistently broad deference and its unwillingness to invalidate government action except in the form of hard-edged, categorical rules— are often difficult to explain except by reference to judicial capacity. Even where other models are equally capable of explaining the Court's decisions, the judicial capacity model helps to reinforce those explanations, making them deeper and more fully satisfying. In this way, the pattern of the Supreme Court's decisions provides substantial evidentiary support for the judicial capacity model, while the model sheds substantial light on the constitutional law created by those decisions.

Part III draws out three normative—that is, evaluative or prescriptive— implications for constitutional theorists, legal reformers, and practicing lawyers. First, ought implies can. Any lawyer, academic, or social activist who wishes to invoke the aid of the courts in a project of social reform must consider whether their goals can be accomplished within the constraints of judicial capacity. For the most ambitious goals, the answer will often be "no" or "not completely." Even where the answer is not categorically negative, it will often be helpful—or even imperative—to tailor proposed reforms to the limits of judicial capacity. For instance, new limits on congressional power to regulate commerce may need to be formulated as fairly narrow categorical rules to have any realistic prospect for success.

Second, be careful what you wish for. In any given case, expanded protection of constitutional rights or enforcement of constitutional limits on government power might seem highly, even obviously, desirable in the abstract. After all, state and federal legislatures, administrative agencies, and executive officials make plenty of mistakes. But in many of the most important constitutional domains, the limits of judicial capacity will sharply constrain the Court's options for protecting rights or enforcing constitutional limits. In particular, the limits of judicial capacity will often require those rights and limits to be cast in the form of crude, categorical rules, which protect both more and less than necessary. As a result, expanded judicial protection may do more harm than good.

Third, for better or worse, the Supreme Court is David, not Goliath. The limits of judicial capacity substantially limit its power to constrain democratic majorities. Constitutional decisions that block the will of national majorities for any substantial length of time across any substantial breadth of issues will usually generate substantial litigation. In many of the most important constitutional domains, the potential volume of litigation will be too great for the Court to handle, pushing the Court back to its default posture of broad deference, perhaps qualified by narrow, categorical limits at the margin.

This limitation on the Supreme Court's power to challenge popular majorities does not and should not immunize the Court from democratic criticism. It is clearly possible for the Court to overstep its proper bounds, and to improperly thwart majoritarian governance, in particular cases. The risk of this happening is greater in some constitutional domains than others, but the risk is real, and some individual decisions can be hugely significant. Think of *Hammer v. Dagenhart,* which blocked any federal regulation of child labor for a generation, or *Roe v. Wade,* which invalidated the abortion laws in most states for going on fifty years, or *NFIB v. Sebelius,* which denied Medicaid coverage to millions of Americans living just above the poverty line.[4]

The list could go on, but we should not lose sight of the forest for the trees. The Supreme Court is a consequential but ultimately tiny, almost marginal, institution, strongly constrained by its limited capacity. It stands no chance of becoming "the apex of government," in Justice Scalia's memorable phrase. Defenders of American democracy should focus their efforts elsewhere.[5]

I

Understanding Judicial Capacity

CHAPTER ONE

Structural and Normative Underpinnings

This chapter develops a theory of judicial capacity, rooted in the hierarchical structure of the American judiciary and in certain widely shared but little discussed professional norms—what I will call "normative commitments"—of American judges. The most important work on judicial capacity traces the limited capacity of the courts to the pyramid-like structure of the federal judicial system, with the ninety-four district courts as its broad base, the thirteen courts of appeals as its somewhat narrower middle section, and the "one Supreme Court" mandated by Article III as its apex. The theory is that having just one court at the apex of the system, just one court that possesses authority to make nationally binding decisions of federal law, creates a kind of bottleneck. The capacity of the system as a whole is constrained by the capacity of the single court that sits at its top.[1]

This structural explanation is an important part of the story, but it is not the whole story. Nothing in the hierarchical structure of the judiciary requires the Supreme Court to approach its work in any particular way. Specifically, nothing in the hierarchical structure of the judiciary requires the Court to spend as much time as it does on the cases that it decides. If the justices were so inclined, they could decide cases by coin flip instead of by briefing and oral argument. Coin flips are fast. The Court could do an effectively unlimited number of them per year. If the justices approached their decisions in this way, they would totally eliminate the bottleneck at the top of the American judiciary. Alternatively, the Court might delegate final decisional authority to individual justices or even their law clerks. Neither would eliminate the Supreme Court bottleneck as would decision by coin flip, but either would expand the Court's decisional capacity fairly dramatically.

None of these is a remotely plausible scenario. But the mere fact that they are possible without abandoning the hierarchical structure of the judicial system shows that this structure alone cannot explain the limited capacity of the judiciary. Any full explanation of the limits on judicial capacity needs to account for the widely shared judicial norms that make it unthinkable for the Court to decide cases by coin flip or in other ways that might radically expand its capacity relative to what the structural theorists have assumed that capacity to be. That norms play a role in constraining judicial capacity may seem fairly obvious. But they have received little attention in the literature and, as we shall see in Chapter 2, their precise content is crucial to understanding just how the limits of judicial capacity affect the substance of constitutional law.[2]

What are those norms? The first and most basic is a commitment to maintaining minimum professional standards of judging. At the Supreme Court level, this involves an elaborate briefing process, oral argument, internal deliberation, and public justification of the Court's decisions—all of which are expensive and time-consuming. Adherence to this norm alone probably caps the capacity of the Supreme Court at somewhere between 150 and 200 full-dress decisions per term, roughly what the Court decided at its peak in the early twentieth century.[3]

Of course, the Court's jurisdiction is almost entirely discretionary. It might therefore respond to any increase in demand simply by refusing to hear more cases. But other widely shared judicial norms make this approach unlikely. The most important of these is a commitment to maintaining a reasonable degree of uniformity in the interpretation and application of federal law—or, stated in reverse, a commitment to eliminating significant disuniformity in this domain. In any hierarchical judicial system, the decisions of the lower courts will produce divergent and discordant legal interpretations. Generally, the Supreme Court strives to mitigate this problem by granting certiorari and issuing nationally binding decisions in areas of significant disuniformity among the lower courts. Significance here encompasses both the extent of the disuniformity (how many lower courts disagree about how much) and its practical impact. In some legal domains, the Court is unwilling to countenance even the possibility of disuniformity raised by a single unreviewed lower-court decision. For instance, the Court appears to feel strongly compelled to review nearly every invalidation of a federal statute. By contrast, the Court is much more willing to tolerate disuniformity in lower-court invalidations of state and local laws, the interpretation (as opposed to invalidation) of federal statutes, the exclusion of unconstitutionally obtained evidence, and so on.[4]

To perform this function, the Court needs both to cull such cases from the great mass of petitions for certiorari it receives and then to decide them. If the total volume of litigation overwhelms the Supreme Court's capacity to do either, its ability to preserve the uniformity of federal law will be seriously undermined. Thus, for the Court to maintain its commitment to uniformity, while also maintaining a commitment to minimum professional standards, the volume of federal litigation must remain limited. More precisely, the number of cases the Court must decide to eliminate significant disuniformity must not exceed its capacity of 150 to 200 full-dress decisions per term.

This may not seem that difficult, given that the modern Supreme Court routinely decides fewer than 100 cases per term. The appearance is deceiving. If the Supreme Court made any serious attempt to limit the federal commerce power; to extend the Equal Protection Clause beyond race, gender, and sexual-orientation discrimination; or to limit congressional delegations of regulatory power to administrative agencies, the resulting volume of litigation would be enormous. And this is just a short list of examples. The list could go on at some length—and does in subsequent chapters. To be clear, the Court certainly could decide more cases than it does now. And perhaps it should. The important point is that it could not decide much more than 150 cases per year without sacrificing its commitment to minimum professional standards.[5]

The Supreme Court's New Deal experience is illustrative. This was the only time in the modern era that the Court seriously attempted to rein in the constitutional power of Congress. In so doing, the Court substantially increased the expected benefits of litigation challenging federal legislation, with spectacular results. In the summer of 1935 alone, more than 100 district judges held Acts of Congress unconstitutional, issuing more than 1,600 injunctions against New Deal legislation. The fact that the Court has generally shaped constitutional law to avoid overwhelming its capacity in this way—and is thus presently able to operate comfortably below its maximum capacity—should not be construed as evidence that its capacity is unlimited or overabundant.[6]

Put differently, it is not the ratio of the Supreme Court's current caseload (70 to 80 cases) to its maximum capacity (150 to 200 cases) that matters. It is the ratio of the Court's maximum capacity to the potential volume of litigation the Court would invite—and feel compelled to decide itself—if it ignored its capacity limits. In the constitutional domains that are the focus of this book, that volume is hundreds or thousands of cases, far more than the Court could handle without abandoning its commitments to minimum professional standards and the uniformity of federal law.

A final norm bears mentioning. That is the widely shared judicial commitment to timely and efficient access to the legal system. Unlike minimum professional standards and the uniformity of federal law, this norm has little to do with the Supreme Court bottleneck effect. In fact, it applies with the greatest force to the work of lower courts, especially the federal district courts. As the volume of litigation increases, the ability of the lower courts to process cases in a timely and efficient fashion, while maintaining a commitment to minimum professional standards, is diminished. Assuming that, at some point, the Supreme Court will find the impact intolerable, this norm will operate as a constraint on judicial capacity.[7]

We are now in a position to reassess not only where the limits of judicial capacity come from but also, in a deeper sense, what those limits actually are. To the extent that theorists have considered this question at all, they have generally assumed these limits to be basically analogous to limits on the physical capacity of a vessel or a bottle—hard structural constraints. But this analogy to physical capacity is misleading. What we are really talking about when we talk about the limits of judicial capacity is the unwillingness of Supreme Court justices to sacrifice certain normative commitments, whose sacrifice would expand the capacity of courts.[8]

In other words, the limits of judicial capacity are not a fact of nature, in the sense of limited time and material resources. At least they are not only a fact of nature in this sense. Nor are they simply or irrevocably hardwired into the structure of the judiciary. They are also the product of a collective, and contingent, choice on the part of American judges—but a choice that is unlikely to change significantly any time soon, because the norms it is based upon are so widely shared and deeply embedded in American legal culture. For present purposes, I bracket the possibility that some or all of these norms have structural determinants—such as public and political pressure that might result if judges abandoned them. That is probably part of the story, but for the purposes of my argument here, it is the fact of the norms, rather than their origins, that is crucial.

These norms are not monolithic. Different justices will be committed to them with different degrees of firmness. They will also have different ideas about what constitute minimum professional standards or intolerable disuniformity or intolerable delays in the timeliness or efficiency of access to the court system. But as an empirical matter, I believe these disagreements exist within a fairly narrow band. Put differently, I believe there would be very substantial resistance among Supreme Court justices to wholesale abandonment of these norms—or even to significant relaxation of them. To offer just two examples, it is essentially unthinkable that any justice—today or at any other point in modern history—would decide cases by coin flip or regularly vote against review of lower-court decisions invalidating federal statutes, given the risk of disuniformity that such decisions create in the enforceability of laws with nationwide scope. So long as this remains the case, so long as there is a strong baseline level of commitment to these norms of judicial decision-making, the Supreme Court will be constrained to avoid deciding cases in any way that sharply increases the volume of litigation flowing into the federal courts.

What about judicial budgets, which are minuscule in comparison to those of many institutions whose work courts are charged with reviewing?

Is this an important constraint on judicial capacity? Yes and no. It is certainly difficult to imagine an institution as small as the federal judiciary comprehensively policing an institution as large as the political process. A larger budget could pay the salaries of more judges and support staff, which would enable the lower courts to decide more cases involving a broader range of government action. But budgetary and staffing constraints are neither sufficient nor necessary to explain the limits of judicial capacity.[9]

They are insufficient because, even at present budgetary levels, the courts could decide vastly more cases if Supreme Court justices were willing to sacrifice the broadly held norms discussed above. They are unnecessary because even a much larger budget would do little to eliminate the bottleneck at the top of the judicial pyramid. Indeed, expanding the number of Supreme Court justices might actually reduce the Court's capacity by making deliberations more cumbersome. And expanding the number of lower-court judges would increase disuniformity in their interpretations of federal law, increasing pressure on the Court's docket. For all of these reasons, I bracket budgetary issues in my subsequent analysis.[10]

CHAPTER TWO

The Judicial Capacity Model

T his chapter builds on the theory of judicial capacity laid out in
Chapter 1 to construct a judicial capacity model of Supreme Court
decision-making. This model predicts that, in certain important constitutional domains, the limits of judicial capacity create strong pressure on
the Supreme Court to adopt hard-edged categorical rules, defer to the political process, or both. The reason is straightforward. In these special
domains, a departure from deferential or rule-based decisions would invite more litigation than the Court could handle without sacrificing minimum professional standards. The decisions of the Supreme Court are
of special interest because it is the limited capacity of that court, in con-
junction with widely shared judicial norms, that sharply constrains the
capacity of the federal judiciary as a whole. The Court's constitutional
decisions are of special interest because, as we shall see, they are the decisions most directly and predictably affected by the constraints of judicial capacity.

The first and most obvious thing we can say on this subject is that the
Court will be constrained to decide cases in a way that keeps the total
volume of litigation below some threshold level, beyond which the basic
normative commitments discussed in Chapter 1 would be threatened. In
this formulation, "total volume of litigation" is a shorthand. The real issue

of interest is demand on the capacity of the judiciary, which is determined not just by the number of the cases but also by their complexity and their tendency to produce disuniformity. The bottom line is that the Supreme Court cannot spend more capacity than it has. It cannot invite more litigation than the court system as a whole can handle consistent with the bedrock normative commitments of most justices. It must, to coin a phrase, ration the Constitution.

Here and throughout, I frequently speak of "the Court" as a unitary institution. This is obviously a shorthand. In actuality, the Court is composed of nine justices, who cast their votes independently and often clash over both the results of particular cases and broader jurisprudential questions. For my purposes, however, treating the Court as a unitary institution poses relatively few dangers because the norms that limit judicial capacity are so broadly held. I do not mean that these norms will necessarily—or even often—push the members of the Court toward consensus, only that whatever group constitutes a majority in a given case is likely to feel constrained by them.

Of course, this alone tells us relatively little. Just as a wartime government might allocate scarce supplies of sugar or flour in a wide variety of ways, the Court might employ a wide variety of tools or approaches to keep its expenditures of capacity below the ceiling imposed by these normative commitments. What, if anything, do the limits of judicial capacity tell us about which of these tools the Court will employ in any given constitutional domain?

The Judicial Capacity Budget

An analogy from the humble domain of home economics may be helpful. Imagine a family of four with an annual budget of $100,000. There are some things that such a family flat-out cannot afford. It cannot buy a $300,000 Ferrari, even on credit. It cannot buy a $5 million house—it could not get a mortgage or make the payments if it did. Still, such a family can draw up its budget in an almost infinite number of ways. The family could buy a new Lexus SUV. It would have to cut back in lot of other areas, and this is probably not the choice most families would make, but it could be done. The family could take three extravagant Caribbean vacations a year. It might need to live in a one-bedroom apartment to do so, but it could be done. Certainly, the limits of the family budget will be relevant to these decisions, in the sense that those limits dictate the nature of the trade-offs each decision requires. But the budget would not constrain the family's decisions in the hard sense of placing any of them firmly off limits. Whether the family buys the Lexus or takes the vacations will depend not only, or even principally, on its budgetary constraints but instead on the value it places on these things relative to other potential uses of its limited funds.

In the same way, the Supreme Court might take a wide variety of approaches to budgeting the judiciary's limited capacity. Just as a family might splurge on a new car or an expensive vacation, the Court might choose to invite more litigation in some areas, by making substantive law more friendly to plaintiffs or employing vague standards that produce greater uncertainty, making settlement more difficult and divergent lower-court decisions more likely. Of course, the Court is unlikely to pursue an increase in uncertainty or a reduction in settlement as an end in itself. Rather, these are the factors that make vague standards expensive in terms of judicial capacity. What makes them attractive—the judicial equivalents of a Caribbean vacation—is the power they afford to tailor application of legal norms more closely to their underlying purposes. Alternatively, the Court might choose to loosen pleading standards or to liberalize Article III standing requirements, and thereby invite a broader range of litigants to bring claims that would not otherwise be brought or that would otherwise be thrown out at the preliminary stages of litigation. These options are all on the table, so long as the Court is willing to make compensating trade-offs that keep the total volume of litigation below the threshold imposed by judicial capacity.[1]

These trade-offs, too, could take any number of forms. The Court might make substantive law in some other area less friendly to plaintiffs, thus reducing the expected value of litigation. The Court's recent expansion of qualified immunity and other obstacles to judicial review of constitutional claims against state and local officials are plausible examples of this strategy. Or the Court might employ more categorical rules in the hope of reducing disuniformity in the lower courts and encouraging settlement by potential litigants. Such rules reduce disuniformity among lower courts by reducing mistakes and making deviation easier to police. They encourage settlement by reducing uncertainty and more closely aligning adverse parties' assessments of the risk-adjusted value of litigation. Alternatively, the Court might make various procedural rules more stringent to reduce the volume and complexity of litigation across the board. The Court's recent decisions tightening pleading standards under Rule 8 of the Federal Rules of Civil Procedure arguably fit this bill. The range of permutations is practically infinite.[2]

Of course, many of the factors affecting the total volume of litigation are outside the direct control of the judiciary. Within broad constitutional limits, Congress controls the jurisdiction of the federal courts and thereby the kinds of disputes those courts are permitted or required to hear. Congress also has the power to make the procedural rules governing federal litigation more or less stringent. Perhaps most important, it has the power to create new substantive rights (and to eliminate old ones), thereby creating or eliminating whole classes of litigation. Other factors that the judiciary has little control over but that have the potential to substantially affect its workload include the cost of legal services and the availability of free legal services to those who cannot afford to pay. Social and economic changes, too, can have a large impact.[3]

None of this, however, changes the basic reality: Whatever the balance of external factors, the Supreme Court must so manipulate the levers in its control as to keep the volume of litigation below the ceiling imposed by its bedrock normative commitments. In doing so, it enjoys a wide range of choice.

At first blush, this freedom of choice appears to undercut substantially the predictive power—and the actual significance—of judicial capacity. Given the wide range of options available to the Court, all that the limits of judicial capacity tell us is that we can reliably expect it to choose among the set of options that fall below its capacity threshold. But the really interesting question is which options from this large set the Court is likely to choose. In most contexts, that question is not going to be answered or answerable by the limits of judicial capacity. If the Court wants to recognize an implied right of action under Title IX of the Education Amendments of 1972, it can do so. If it wants to employ a mushy balancing test to define the free speech rights of public employees, it can do so. If the Court makes enough choices of this sort, compensating trade-offs will be required. But in this, too, the Court will have many options. The Court's choice, like our hypothetical family's, will be driven by considerations other than capacity, which will function at most as a background constraint. I will call contexts in which this is true "normal legal domains."[4]

Not all legal domains, however, are normal in this sense. Indeed, the most important constitutional domains are not. This insight is the cornerstone of the judicial capacity model.

Again, the family budget analogy helps to illustrate the point. In managing the limited capacity of the judiciary, the Supreme Court may have many options, but many is not the same as all. There are judicial analogues to a $300,000 Ferrari or a $5 million house—certain classes of decisions that would not only require compensating trade-offs but that, by themselves, would invite litigation beyond the overall capacity of the Supreme Court (or at least come so close as to be practical nonstarters). Domains of this sort fall into two frequently overlapping categories, which I shall refer to as "high-volume" and "high-stakes." In these domains, the nature and volume of litigation that the Supreme Court would invite by ignoring the constraints of judicial capacity is such that no procedural recalibration or shifting of resources from other areas could stem the tide.

As a consequence, to maintain its commitment to minimum professional standards and the uniformity of federal law, the Court effectively has two choices. First, it can make substantive law less friendly to plaintiffs and thereby reduce the expected value of bringing a lawsuit. In the context of constitutional law, this means deferring more extensively to the political process—that is, refusing to second-guess the constitutional judgments of other government actors. Such deference is a commonplace of constitutional law but varies greatly from one context to another.

Second, the Court can employ clear categorical *rules* for deciding cases, which reduces uncertainty and thereby encourages greater voluntary compliance and settlement outside of court. If parties can predict how courts will decide cases in advance, there is less reason to go to the trouble and expense of litigating them. Settlement is cheaper and easier and yields a roughly similar result. Clear rules also promote uniformity among lower-court decisions, reducing the need for Supreme Court review to achieve this end. In effect, categorical rules enable courts to resolve large numbers of cases—all of those covered by the rule—*en masse*. The trouble with rules is that they sacrifice nuance for clarity. This makes them crude tools for achieving most legal goals.[5]

The opposite of a rule is a *standard:* a legal norm that permits consideration of all or most facts that are relevant to its underlying purpose. Standards often embrace distinctions of degree and case-by-case judicial "balancing" of competing considerations. This makes them relatively nuanced tools for achieving most legal goals. The trouble with standards is that they sacrifice clarity for nuance, rendering their application difficult to predict in advance. If parties cannot anticipate how the law will be applied, they are less likely to voluntarily comply and more likely to take their chances in court. When they do, standards also increase the frequency of conflict among lower-court decisions. The result is more litigation that the Supreme Court feels compelled to review.

Where both deference and categorical rules are consistent with the limits of judicial capacity, the Court is free to choose between them on grounds unrelated to capacity. Often, however, the Court will feel compelled to employ both in combination. This is the judicial capacity model in a nutshell: In high-volume and high-stakes domains, the Court will be strongly constrained to employ some combination of deference and categorical rules.

Put more formally, the model's independent or explanatory variables (or causal conditions) are stakes and volume. Its dependent variables (or outcomes) are deference and doctrinal form (categorical rules versus vague standards). The model's core prediction is that, above a certain threshold, and especially in combination, high stakes and high volume will strongly constrain the Court to employ some combination of strong deference and categorical rules. Crucially, the inverse is not necessarily true. In normal domains—that is, domains in which both volume and stakes are below the relevant thresholds—the Court may or may not find deference and categorical rules attractive for reasons other than judicial capacity. In this sense, the model is asymmetric. It holds that high-volume and high-stakes are *sufficient,* not that they are *necessary,* to constrain the Court to employ some combination of strong deference and categorical rules. As such, the model makes no prediction one way or the other about how the Court will behave in domains where it is not strongly constrained by the limits of judicial capacity.[6]

High-Volume Legal Domains

In high-volume domains, the potential volume of litigation that the Supreme Court would invite by ignoring constraints of judicial capacity are so great that no procedural recalibration or shifting of resources from other areas could possibly stem the tide. The potential volume of litigation, in turn, is largely determined by three principal factors: (1) the quantity of existing and future government action that the constitutional provision in question could plausibly be read to invalidate; (2) the magnitude of the benefits that such invalidation would generate for prospective plaintiffs; and (3) the number of prospective plaintiffs either collectively or individually capable of mustering the resources to litigate. A high-volume domain is one in which all three of these factors are large enough that departing from deference and categorical rules would *in that domain alone* invite more litigation than the Supreme Court could handle consistent with its foundational normative commitments.[7]

Some examples will be helpful. Regulatory takings and Equal Protection are two good ones. Regulatory takings are regulations that reduce the value of private property in such a way or to such an extent as to constitute the "taking" of that property for public use, which the Fifth Amendment prohibits "without just compensation." Equal Protection prohibits the government from treating different citizens or groups of citizens differently without a persuasive reason. Uncompensated regulatory takings and violations of Equal Protection are prohibited at both the federal and state / local levels under the Fifth and Fourteenth Amendments, respectively. The Takings Clause is incorporated against the states through the Due Process Clause of the Fourteenth Amendment. The Equal Protection Clause applies to the federal government via "reverse incorporation" under the Fifth Amendment.[8]

These are not domains in which the Court feels compelled to grant review of just any decision striking down government action. They often do not involve federal law. In fact, they often involve challenges to executive action, rather than legislation, and especially to executive action at the state and local levels, which is often quite limited in scope. All of these factors generally raise the Supreme Court's tolerance of disuniformity and reduce the fraction of lower-court decisions it feels compelled to review.[9]

Yet despite this fact, both regulatory takings and Equal Protection have the potential to invite more litigation than the Court could handle, consistent with even a basic commitment to uniformity. They also have the potential to invite more litigation than the lower courts could handle consistent with a basic commitment to timely and efficient access to the legal system. A robust reading of either the Equal Protection Clause of the Fourteenth Amendment or the Takings Clause of the Fifth Amendment, articulated in the form of a vague standard, would call into question a very large fraction of the U.S. Code. It would also call into question a very large fraction of state and local laws and a great number of administrative agency and other executive actions at all levels. This includes environmental, labor, workplace safety, consumer protection, securities, banking, and myriad other regulations at the federal level and similar regulations at the state and local levels, along with land use, zoning, licensing, and traffic regulations of every description, as well as the executive actions by which these various regulations are carried out. Every one of these laws and executive actions treats different groups of persons differently, with very material consequences. Every one also negatively affects the value of some personal or real property, in many cases quite substantially. As such, if the Court departed from deference and categorical rules in either of these domains, the benefits of invalidation would be great enough that some party or parties would bring suit to challenge a vast number of government actions.[10]

This is not to suggest that all these laws and executive actions would be rendered constitutionally invalid. For purposes of judicial capacity, what matters is not how many government actions are actually struck down but how many are called into question to the point of generating serious litigation. In the case of Equal Protection and regulatory takings, the volume of such litigation would be far more than the federal court system, and in particular the Supreme Court, could handle, consistent with widely shared commitments to minimum professional standards, the uniformity of federal laws, and timely and efficient access to the legal system.

For this reason, we can predict with a reasonable degree of confidence that judicial capacity will significantly constrain the way in which the Court decides equal protection and regulatory takings cases. In particular, we can predict that the Court will feel constrained either to employ clear-cut categorical rules, which reduce uncertainty for potential litigants and thus reduce the volume of litigation, or to abandon anything resembling the full potential enforcement of either of these provisions. Quite possibly it will feel compelled to do both. It may not have to back off completely from any serious review, but it will have to back off a lot and in a way that draws a fairly categorical line, clearly insulating most government action from judicial scrutiny.

As Chapters 9 and 10 will elaborate, the pattern of the Court's decisions in these areas is consistent with these predictions. Under the Equal Protection Clause, virtually all government classifications are subject to minimal rational-basis review. The few exceptions are narrow, clear-cut, and subject to strict scrutiny, a form of rigorous review that the Court carefully cabins to this handful of exceptional cases. Similarly, under the Takings Clause, the vast majority of regulations are subject to the highly deferential test of *Penn Central Transportation Co. v. City of New York.* The two narrow exceptions—"permanent physical invasion" and "complete elimination of a property's value"—are subject to clear-cut rules of per se invalidity. There are occasional deviations from this pattern, typically short-lived, but the general tendency in both domains is consistent with the judicial capacity model.[11]

Other plausible examples of capacity-constrained decisions in high-volume domains include the Supreme Court's post–New Deal substantive due process doctrine, carefully limited to a few discrete "fundamental liberties," and the Court's long-standing adherence—with only minor exceptions—to a rigid, conceptually unsatisfying state-action doctrine. A more expansive or less categorical version of either doctrine would greatly expand the range of government action (and inaction) subject to constitutional challenge. Should the Court ever take this step, "the federal courts will be overwhelmed by cases challenging on constitutional grounds local zoning and rent control ordinances, state and local licensure laws, and a vast array of federal, state, and local regulatory measures." Unsurprisingly, the Court has shown no interest in heading down this path, despite substantial agitation by conservatives and libertarians for more rigorous due-process review of economic regulation and by civil rights proponents for a more flexible state action doctrine.[12]

One apparent counterexample deserves mention. That is the constitutional rights revolution of the 1950s and 1960s, which generated an enormous volume of new litigation. This important historical episode might seem to contradict the judicial capacity model's prediction that the Court will generally be compelled to defer other government actors in high-volume domains. Conspicuously, however, none of the new constitutional rights established during this period threatened anywhere near as large a swath of government activity as would a broad interpretation of equal protection or regulatory takings. In fact, most affected the single, circumscribed sphere of criminal prosecutions. That is not to say that these rights were incapable of generating substantial litigation. They clearly did. But they are best understood as falling within normal domains—the judicial equivalents of Caribbean vacations or Lexus SUVs, rather than Ferraris or $5 million houses. For the same reasons, the Court's retreat from many of these rights in subsequent decades should probably not be understood as compelled by the limits of judicial capacity. Capacity may have been one factor behind this retreat, but it was hardly the only one, as evidenced by the willingness of most liberal justices to stay the course.[13]

High-Stakes Legal Domains

The second class of cases in which the judicial capacity model predicts that capacity will have real predictive force I call "high-stakes" domains. As with high-volume domains, the reason we can expect capacity to have real predictive force in high-stakes domains is that they are analogous to a Ferrari or a $5 million house. They represent situations where no amount of procedural recalibration or shifting of resources from other areas could compensate for the volume of litigation the Court risks inviting. The defining feature of high-stakes domains is that the Supreme Court is much less willing to tolerate disuniformity among the decisions of lower courts. In many of the domains that fit this description, the Court is willing to tolerate virtually no disuniformity. In particular, it feels compelled to grant review in almost any case in which the lower court invalidates a federal law.[14]

From this, it follows fairly straightforwardly that, even at much lower total volumes of litigation, the pressure on the Court is going to build very quickly. Some hypothetical numbers may be helpful for purposes of illustration. Suppose that, in a normal legal domain, the Court feels compelled to grant review of 1 in 75 serious petitions. In recent years the Court's overall grant rate has hovered just below 1 percent, but this includes many nonserious petitions. In a typical high-stakes domain, by contrast, the Court might feel compelled to grant 1 petition in 10. The difference in the rates of review becomes even more significant when we consider that, in normal domains, the number of petitions for certiorari filed is presumably already reduced by the low odds of success. In high-stakes domains, therefore, even a decision that invites much less aggregate litigation is going to very quickly produce a significant demand on the Supreme Court, triggering the bottleneck effect discussed in Chapter 1.[15]

Again, the bottleneck effect is not solely a function of the hierarchical structure of the judiciary. It is a combination of that structure and the widely shared bedrock norms that the Court is unwilling to sacrifice. For this reason, in high-stakes domains we can predict that the Court will be constrained much as it is in high-volume domains. It will be forced to rely on hard-edged categorical rules, which reduce disuniformity among lower courts and encourage settlement, and more stringent tests of liability, which discourage litigation by lowering its expected payoff. A pure high-stakes domain is one in which the Court is constrained in these ways simply because it feels compelled to grant review in such a large fraction of cases, notwithstanding a low potential volume of litigation. It is difficult to come up with examples of pure high-stakes domains.

Hybrid Legal Domains

Much more important than pure high-stakes domains are hybrid domains. These domains involve both high volume and high stakes. For that reason, judicial capacity is likely to constrain the Court's decision-making in these domains more sharply than in any other context.

The quintessential example of a hybrid domain is the Commerce Clause, which authorizes Congress to regulate commerce "among the several states." The Commerce Clause qualifies as high-volume because the potential volume of litigation that a plaintiff-friendly test of liability or a vague standard would invite is enormous. The reason is simple: The fraction of federal legislation grounded in the commerce power is enormous, encompassing most federal criminal, consumer protection, environmental, energy, antidiscrimination, banking, securities, labor, food and drug, and workplace safety regulations, to name just a few. Moreover, many deep-pocketed parties would stand to benefit from the invalidation of any given commerce-power statute. Thus, there would be no shortage of plaintiffs if the Court ignored the constraints of judicial capacity in this domain. Every law that could be challenged would be challenged.[16]

The Commerce Clause also qualifies as a high-stakes domain because any statute invalidated under it will be a federal statute, meaning the Court will feel strong pressure to grant review. So here, too, we should expect the Court to feel strongly constrained by judicial capacity. Here too we have a $300,000 Ferrari or a $5 million house that the Court simply cannot afford to buy—does not have enough capacity to buy—no matter how much it is willing to raise pleading standards or reallocate resources from other legal domains.

The pattern of the Court's modern Commerce Clause decisions is the predictions of the judicial capacity model. In a nutshell, the Court has been broadly deferential to Congress, while imposing a few narrow limitations on congressional authority at the margins, in the form of clear, categorical rules. Several of these decisions will be discussed in more detail in Chapter 4.

Summary

To review, in normal domains, the most we can say about judicial capacity is that it will operate as a kind of background constraint. The Court will need to be generally conscious of capacity to keep the total volume of litigation below the threshold necessary to preserve the bedrock norms of American judges. But it will have a wide range of choice in meeting this objective. The exception to this general rule occurs in high-volume domains and high-stakes domains, where we can fairly confidently predict that judicial capacity will create strong pressure on the Court to embrace hard-edged categorical rules, defer to the political process, or both. The predictive power of capacity is even stronger in hybrid domains, which involve both a high potential volume of litigation and also high stakes of the sort that would compel the Court to grant review in an unusually high percentage of cases coming up from the lower courts.

Of course, the categories of "high-volume," "high-stakes," and "hybrid" domains are in some sense artificial. What ultimately matters is the number of potential cases in which the Supreme Court would feel compelled to grant review. This number is inevitably and always a function of both stakes and volume. In a domain where the Court only feels compelled to grant review in 0.01 percent of cases, even a potential volume of tens of thousands of cases will not pose much of a threat to the Court's limited capacity. Similarly, in a domain where the potential volume of cases is only 50 per term, even a Court that feels compelled to grant review in 20 percent of such cases will not feel much constrained by the limits of judicial capacity.

Nevertheless, in many important domains, the judicial capacity model predicts that the Court will feel strongly constrained. In some of those domains, volume plays a much greater role than stakes. In others, stakes are more important. In most, both volume and stakes play a large role. The categories of high-volume, high-stakes, and hybrid domains are simply a convenient way of capturing this fact. When referring to these domains collectively, I shall call them "capacity-constrained domains."

CHAPTER THREE

Refining the Model

In capacity-constrained constitutional domains, the model predicts that the limits of judicial capacity will strongly constrain the Supreme Court to defer to the political process, employ hard-edged categorical rules, or both. Now that we have this core claim of the judicial capacity model before us, we are in a position to specify the contours of the model more precisely. To that end, this chapter offers five caveats that clarify the limits of the model's assumptions and predictions. These caveats paint a fuller picture of how judicial capacity shapes Supreme Court decision-making and should help to dispel potential sources of confusion.

First, judicial capacity is clearly not the only influence or constraint that shapes Supreme Court decision-making, even in high-volume and high-stakes domains. Rather, the Court's limited capacity is an important constraint that shapes the context and confines in which other influences operate. Of particular importance, the judicial capacity model does not deny the dominant political-science view that ideology plays a large role in Supreme Court decision-making. It merely suggests that, in many important constitutional domains, the limits of judicial capacity substantially constrain the options available to the justices to pursue their capacity-independent agendas.[1]

Free Enterprise Fund v. PCAOB is a good example. This 2010 decision involved a novel restriction on the President's authority to remove members of the Public Company Accounting Oversight Board—a watchdog agency established in 2002 after the Enron and WorldCom scandals. To insulate the Board from corrupting political influence, Congress provided that its members could only be removed for good cause. Furthermore, Congress vested the power to remove members of the Board not in the President, as is customary, but in the Securities Exchange Commission, whose members are themselves protected against removal by the President, except for good cause. A five-justice majority of the Supreme Court found this "stacking" of good-cause removal restrictions unconstitutional.[2]

Quite possibly, those five justices reached this decision because of their conservative ideological commitment to unitary presidential control of the federal administrative state. Ideology, however, does not explain the form their decision took. Specifically, it does not explain their endorsement of a categorical rule prohibiting multilayer good-cause removal restrictions, rather than a more functional standard. Nor does it explain their decision to ignore one-layer good-cause removal restrictions and essentially all other forms of congressional interference with presidential administration unrelated to removal—aspects of the decision that commanded agreement from all nine justices. These are hugely consequential elements of the decision—and of constitutional law more generally—that political-science models overlook, largely because they are difficult to count. The judicial capacity model, by contrast, is keenly attuned to these softer, qualitative aspects of Supreme Court decisions and goes a long way toward explaining them.[3]

This picture of judicial decision-making as a mixture of ideological and jurisprudential considerations is a staple of the new institutionalist literature in political science. It is also consistent with recent empirical work blending new institutionalism with attitudinal and strategic traditions and a more general trend in political science toward recognizing the importance of factors beyond political ideology in Supreme Court decision-making.[4]

Second, the judicial capacity model does not assume that the Supreme Court will always recognize perfectly what kind of decisions would invite an overwhelming volume of litigation. Justices generally have a strong intuitive understanding of what kinds of decisions invite large volumes of litigation. But justices obviously can and do make mistakes. Across the run of cases, however, the system places hydraulic pressure on the Court toward more stringent standards of liability and hard-edged rules because litigants respond when the justices make mistakes. More specifically, the volume of litigation increases, which pushes the Court, when it veers off course or begins to veer off course, to back off its mistaken predictions.

A slightly different but related question is how well and how clearly we can expect justices to understand the limits of judicial capacity (as opposed to the volume of litigation their decisions are likely to generate). Here, too, the model does not assume anything like judicial omniscience. At any given point in time, justices may have only a vague sense of what the limits of judicial capacity are. But to return to the family budget analogy from Chapter 1, they know they cannot buy a Ferrari or a $5 million house. And in the relatively rare event that the justices seriously overestimate judicial capacity or underestimate the capacity effects of their decisions, the iterative nature of the litigation process gives them an opportunity to return any purchases that look profligate in retrospect. For this reason, the model does not purport to predict how the Court will decide every individual case. Rather, it predicts the broad pattern the Court's decisions will follow in capacity-constrained domains.

Third, the model does not assume that the influence of judicial capacity on Supreme Court decision-making is necessarily conscious. Rather, that influence affects the boundaries of the thinkable. Consider, again, the example of *Free Enterprise Fund v. PCAOB*. A decision requiring serious review of all interference with presidential control over administrative agencies would have produced (a) an overwhelming volume of litigation that (b) the Court would have felt compelled to review.[5]

Whether the justices consciously, semiconsciously, or subconsciously conceive of these issues in terms of judicial capacity, the judicial capacity model posits that they would consider such results unthinkable (in part because they have been so defined by previous generations of justices, responding to the limits of judicial capacity). If justices do consider such results unthinkable, we should expect them to pursue their preferred policy outcomes through doctrinal forms designed to avoid this sort of capacity overload. As Part II will demonstrate, this prediction helps to explain puzzles in the Court's past decisions that no other plausible alternative can. It also complements and enriches the explanatory power of other well-known models of judicial decision-making.

Fourth, although this book focuses exclusively on the Supreme Court's constitutional decisions, the limits of judicial capacity operate generally. In particular, the two types of domains I have identified regarding which capacity is likely to exert an especially strong influence—high-stakes and high-volume—are not in principle confined to constitutional cases. In practice, however, they almost always will be. This is not to say that only constitutional litigation can place significant strain on judicial capacity. There are all kinds of nonconstitutional litigation that severely tax the judiciary. The federal drug laws are an obvious example. The civil action for victims of gender-motivated crimes of violence, created by the Violence Against Women Act and invalidated by the Supreme Court in *United States v. Morrison,* might have been another one, had it survived.[6]

Nevertheless, nonconstitutional demands on judicial capacity will usually fall into the first category discussed in Chapter 1—what I have called "normal domains." To return to the family budget analogy, they are trips to the Caribbean, not Ferraris or $5 million houses. Capacity might be one thing we can expect the Court to consider in these domains. But the limits of judicial capacity are not going to constrain the Court here with anything like the severity they do in capacity-constrained constitutional domains. The major reason for this is that the Court is much more willing to tolerate disuniformity in statutory domains than it is in constitutional domains. Of course, this observation is a general one. There may be exceptions. If there are, nearly everything I have said about the way judicial capacity affects the Court's decisions in high-volume and high-stakes constitutional domains would apply to nonconstitutional domains that meet these descriptions. That is all I shall have to say about this subject.[7]

Fifth, the model does not assume that the judicial norms that underlie judicial capacity are in any sense monolithic or perfectly static over time. Both the content of these norms and the degree of intensity with which they are held obviously fall along a spectrum. These norms have also obviously evolved in important respects over time, sometimes in response to changing demands on judicial capacity. If the Court wants to take on more litigation in one area (or is compelled to do so by circumstance or legislation), it has to make some change to compensate. It can accomplish this through substantive decisions that reduce the expected value of litigation in other areas. Or it can do so through procedural and case-management decisions that reflect a change in the assessment of what basic professional norms require. Such changes have been quite pronounced at the Court of Appeals level, where the rate of summary disposition increased and the time allowed for oral argument decreased dramatically during the appellate caseload explosion of the 1960s and 1970s. Many of these changes persist to this day.[8]

Despite this, the judicial capacity model has a great deal of explanatory power in the high-volume and high-stakes domains that are the focus of this book. The reason is that they all involve Ferraris and $5 million houses. Norms might change to raise the family budget from $100,000 to $150,000 or even $200,000. (We might think of relaxing professional norms as the judicial equivalent of currying favor with a wealthy but unsavory relative.) But at least in the near future, norms seem unlikely to change enough for the Court to afford a Ferrari or a $5 million house— that is, to engage in searching review, in the form of vague standards, in high-volume or high-stakes domains—even if it is willing to scrimp in other areas.

Put differently, there is nothing inevitable about the Court's commitment to minimum professional standards and reasonable uniformity. What is inevitable and unavoidable is the trade-off between those norms and the Court's limited capacity. Theoretically, this trade-off could be managed in many different ways. The Brazilian Supreme Federal Court, for example, appears to be far less deferential and to rely on fewer categorical rules than the U.S. Supreme Court. To do so, however, it necessarily tolerates significant disuniformity in the decisions of lower courts and even among its own decisions. It also delegates far greater decision-making authority to administrative staff. In the United States, by contrast, the Supreme Court's commitment to minimum professional standards and uniformity is sufficiently deep, long-standing, and invariant across the political spectrum that the judicial capacity model should have robust predictive power for some time to come.[9]

The extent to which the model applies looking backward is a more difficult question. The role of the Supreme Court and the structure of the federal judiciary have changed dramatically over the course of American history, as have the role and scope of the federal government as a whole. In light of these changes, it is certainly possible that the limits of judicial capacity operated differently in earlier periods of American history than they do today. But the existence of high-volume and high-stakes legal domains is hardly a new development. Nor are the Court's commitments to minimum professional standards and preserving the uniformity of federal law. The judicial capacity model should have real explanatory power for any period in which these conditions obtain, as they have at least since the New Deal and probably since the rise of the federal administrative state at the turn of the twentieth century.[10]

Of course, even in this period, judicial capacity has hardly remained static. The number of federal trial and appellate judges grew sevenfold from 1901 to 2001. Federal magistrate judges were created in 1968, expanding the capacity of federal trial courts. And the last significant vestiges of the Supreme Court's mandatory appellate jurisdiction were eliminated in 1988. None of these changes, however, fundamentally altered the bottleneck effect that drives the model.[11]

For all of these reasons, the argument of this book extends only to the modern era, which I define as extending from President Franklin Roosevelt's first term forward. During that time, the federalism, separation of powers, and individual rights domains I discuss clearly qualify as capacity-constrained domains, as Part II will demonstrate. Before FDR's first term, the federal government was significantly smaller. Just as important, different norms governed Supreme Court decision-making, mostly due to the Court's much larger mandatory jurisdiction prior to the Judiciary Act of 1925. For the reasons just explained, these differences complicate the predictions of the judicial capacity model, requiring a deeper investigation of these earlier periods than I can undertake in this book.[12]

CHAPTER FOUR

Testing the Model

The judicial capacity model is an explanatory and predictive model. It must therefore stand or fall based on its power to explain the relevant empirical data—in this case, the pattern of U.S. Supreme Court decisions. Logically, that power turns on two questions: First, is the pattern of the Supreme Court's decisions in capacity-constrained domains consistent with the model's predictions? Second, can the judicial capacity model explain important aspects of that pattern that other models of judicial decision-making cannot? To these two questions, we can add a third, not directly relevant to explanatory power but highly relevant to the model's overall contribution: Can the judicial capacity model improve our understanding of Supreme Court decision-making even where other models are equally consistent with the pattern of the Court's decisions?

The logic behind these questions is straightforward. If the pattern of the Court's decisions is consistent with the judicial capacity model but inconsistent with—or simply unexplained by—the most plausible alternative models, then that lends strong support to the judicial capacity model. If some subset of the empirical evidence is consistent with multiple plausible explanations, including the judicial capacity model, that reveals a previously unrecognized need to analyze and investigate the relative causal significance of those explanations and any interactions among them. This need is all the more pressing if one of the explanations is novel and calls into question more established accounts, as the judicial capacity model is and does. Together, these three questions constitute a framework for systematically testing the judicial capacity model against the pattern of Supreme Court decisions discussed in Part II.[1]

To set the stage for that testing, this chapter restates the predictions of the model, with a special eye to testing their consistency with the pattern of Supreme Court decisions. It then introduces the most plausible competing models of Supreme Court decision-making and compares predictions of these models with those of the judicial capacity model. The goal is to clarify what counts as evidence supporting the judicial capacity model. The chapter concludes by working through the logical implications if some subset of the evidence is equally consistent with the predictions of the judicial capacity model and those of one or more competing models. For a more technical explanation of the analytical approach described in this chapter, interested readers are directed to the Methods Appendix.

Consistency

In capacity-constrained domains, the judicial capacity model predicts that the Supreme Court will be strongly constrained to employ some combination of strong deference and categorical rules. If most or all of the Court's decisions in these domains employ deference, categorical rules, or both, then the pattern of the Court's models is consistent with the model's predictions. Because both deference and doctrinal form are matters of degree, however, it is necessary to ask how much deference and reliance on categorical rules the model predicts.

This question cannot be answered numerically, because the relevant variables are not readily quantifiable. Nor is there a single answer that applies uniformly across all capacity-constrained domains. Rather, in the relevant constitutional domains, the judicial capacity model predicts the Court will be *strongly* constrained to employ some combination of deference and categorical rules such that *the government will almost always win,* or *the application of the Court's test will almost always be readily predictable by judges and litigants,* or both. This prediction is obviously not perfectly precise and its content will vary to some extent by context. Nevertheless, it is quite demanding and easily falsifiable. If the prediction holds for the capacity-constrained constitutional domains analyzed in Part II, that is very preliminary evidence that judicial capacity constrains Supreme Court decision-making in those domains.

Plausible Alternative Explanations

The consistency of the Supreme Court's decisions with the judicial capacity model is only preliminary evidence because the Court's decisions might be equally consistent with the predictions of other models of judicial decision-making. If that is the case, the Court's heavy reliance on deference and categorical rules in capacity-constrained domains might be the result, not of limited judicial capacity, but of other factors altogether, such as legal doctrine, judicial ideology, or fear of political backlash. To demonstrate that judicial capacity actually constrains the Court, it is necessary to rule out plausible alternative explanations supplied by other models. More precisely, it is necessary to ask whether the judicial capacity model can explain important aspects of the Supreme Court's constitutional decisions that other models cannot. If the answer is yes, there is good reason to believe that judicial capacity has real constraining force. It may not be the only explanation for the Court's reliance on deference and categorical rules, but if it can explain significant features of the Court's decisions that other models cannot, that is powerful evidence in favor of the judicial capacity model.

There are hundreds, if not thousands, of subtly different models of judicial decision-making in the existing literature, but the most influential fall into three reasonably well-defined categories: legalist, attitudinal, and strategic. Treated here as ideal types, each of these models makes different predictions that can be compared with the predictions of the judicial capacity model.

Legalist Models

Legalist models, largely informal and mostly propounded by academic lawyers, seek to explain Supreme Court decisions in terms of traditional legal materials, such as constitutional text, history, and precedent. Legalist models can also be defined in the negative, as theories "in which careerism and ideology play no role"—or, more realistically, play only a minor and subordinate role. Broadly speaking, legalist models predict that the Supreme Court will defer to other institutional decision-makers and cast its decisions in the form of clear categorical rules when the traditional legal materials enumerated above dictate that it do so. These materials, of course, vary from one constitutional domain to the next. Comparing the explanatory power of the judicial capacity model to that of legalist models therefore requires a careful and context-specific analysis of the traditional legal materials across a range of constitutional domains. If the pattern of the Court's decisions is inconsistent with the traditional legal materials, or simply cannot be accounted for by those materials, that is evidence in favor of the judicial capacity model.[2]

In addition to domain-specific legal materials like text and precedent, some versions of the legalist model encompass general, politically impartial commitments of the sort associated with the legal process school. Among these are principled commitments to the rule of law and judicial restraint. The former is generally presented as an end in itself; the latter is usually grounded in concerns about the judiciary's relative lack of democratic legitimacy or institutional competence. These two commitments are especially important, for present purposes, because they appear to predict the same results as the judicial capacity model. As Justice Antonin Scalia famously put it, the rule of law is a "law of rules." Thus, justices motivated by a commitment to the rule of law should be strongly partial to decisions cast in the form of hard-edged categorical rules. Similarly, judicial restraint by definition entails judicial deference to other institutional actors. Thus, justices motivated by a commitment to judicial restraint should be strongly partial to judicial deference.[3]

Despite these genuine parallels, no major legalist work predicts that judicial competence or rule-of-law values will systematically constrain the

Supreme Court to defer to other institutional decision-makers or to embrace categorical rules, and it is difficult to conceive of a plausible set of legalist assumptions that would support such a prediction. Nor does any major legalist work predict that the Court will be willing to depart from broad deference only in the form of categorical rules and vice versa. Rather, most legalist models simply posit that these normative commitments are among the broad list of legal constraints that, in some unspecified combination, drive the decisions of most justices most of the time.[4]

The judicial capacity model, by contrast, does predict that judicial capacity will systematically constrain the Supreme Court to employ some combination of strong deference and categorical rules, at least in capacity-constrained domains. To the extent that the pattern of the Court's decisions exhibits these features, that counts as evidence in its favor of the judicial capacity model, which unlike the legalist model, can explain them. This is not to suggest that judicial restraint and rule-of-law considerations play no causal role in Supreme Court decision-making, only that the judicial capacity model is capable of explaining aspects of the Court's past decisions that these considerations cannot. Because this point applies in the same way to every capacity-constrained domain considered in Part II, my subsequent discussion of the legalist model shall be limited to the traditional legal materials specific to each of those domains. I shall, however, return to the subject of judicial restraint in Chapters 12 and 13.

Attitudinal Models

Attitudinal models of judicial decision-making are, in general, far more rigorously specified than legalist models and have, over the course of several decades, been subject to extensive quantitative testing. Simply put, these models predict that Supreme Court justices "will cast their votes on the basis of their personal political ideologies." Distinguishing political ideology from principled jurisprudential commitment is a somewhat tricky question. Broadly speaking, however, attitudinal models predict that conservative justices (and thus conservative majorities) will vote in favor of conservative outcomes and that liberal justices (and majorities) will vote in favor of liberal outcomes. In their strongest form, these models argue that justices "always vote their unconstrained attitudes."

The logical implication is that justices will vote to uphold any legislative or executive act that they would have favored as a legislator or executive official and invalidate any act they would have opposed in those capacities.[5]

The attitudinal model clearly captures something important about Supreme Court decision-making. Scores of quantitative studies spanning nearly half a century show that ideology is an important driver of judicial votes by Supreme Court justices. This might seem to leave little room for judicial capacity or other nonideological influences, but the appearance is deceiving for at least two reasons. First, the cases decided by the Supreme Court are a tiny and decidedly nonrandom sample. Even if the justices vote ideologically in this most difficult subset of cases, they may well agree across ideological lines in many or most of the great mass of cases that never make it to the Supreme Court. Indeed, if they did not, it would perennially be open season on whatever government actions were— or seemed likely to be—opposed by a majority of justices as a matter of policy. This has never been the case.[6]

Second, the attitudinal model's narrow focus on judicial votes leaves it with virtually nothing to say about the choice between rules and standards or the content of Supreme Court decisions more generally. In addition to important questions of doctrinal form, this means that the attitudinal model fails to account for important areas of overlap reflected in justices' opinions but not their votes. In commerce-power cases, for example, the attitudinal model accurately predicts that conservative justices are far more likely than liberal justices to vote down liberal federal statutes. But it completely overlooks the highly deferential reading of the commerce power embraced even by most conservative justices—one sufficient to sustain many statutes that those justices would likely vote down as legislators.[7]

In sum, attitudinal models are quite good at explaining judicial votes of Supreme Court justices in decided cases, but they cannot explain why justices on either end of the political spectrum would pass up so many opportunities to increase the stringency of their favorite constitutional doctrines. Nor can they explain the justices' failure to opportunistically deploy other constitutional doctrines to invalidate government actions that they oppose on policy grounds. Nor can they explain why the Court would nearly always feel compelled to cast its decisions in the form of hard-edged categorical rules when invalidating government action in capacity-constrained domains. To the extent that the pattern of the Court's decisions exhibits these features, that counts as evidence in favor of the judicial capacity model, which can explain them.

Strategic Models

Strategic models incorporate many of the insights of attitudinal models and supplement them with principles of game theory, sometimes referred to as positive political theory or PPT. Their basic insight is that justices do not pursue their ideological goals in a vacuum but instead take into account the likely reactions of their fellow justices and other institutional actors whose outputs the Supreme Court is charged with interpreting and reviewing. As with attitudinal models, the literature applying and testing strategic models of judicial decision-making is enormous and varied. To oversimplify greatly, its main prediction is that justices will frequently moderate their decisions to hold together majority coalitions and to avoid triggering political retaliation that would render their decisions futile or worse.[8]

This insight helps to explain why justices would sometimes vote differently than they would as legislators. Strategic models are therefore somewhat better able to explain strong judicial deference than are attitudinal models—but only somewhat. They can explain why extreme liberal and conservative justices do not reach out to invalidate (or write opinions that would have the effect of invalidating) every government action they would oppose as legislators. Doing so would jeopardize their ability to sustain a majority behind their opinions. Strategic models can also explain why the Court might sometimes refrain from invalidating government actions that contravene the policy views of the median or pivotal justice. In extremely rare cases, such restraint may be necessary to avoid triggering a constitutional amendment that would render the Court's decision futile or worse. In slightly more cases, restraint may be necessary to avoid costly political retaliation—in the form of congressional jurisdiction stripping or budget cutting or presidential noncompliance with judicial orders, and so on. But the risk of such retaliation is generally quite low and is likely to be understood as such by most justices most of the time.[9]

Strategic models are therefore only capable of explaining judicial deference to government action that contradicts the policy preferences of the median justice in contexts where costly political retaliation is a real and worrisome possibility. They cannot explain judicial deference to government action of this sort in the far more common contexts where serious political retaliation is exceedingly unlikely. They also cannot explain the persistence of judicial deference in the face of significant ideological shifts in control of the Court or the political branches. Nor can they explain why the Court would be willing to invalidate government action in capacity-constrained domains but only in the form of hard-edged categorical rules. To the extent that the pattern of the Court's decisions exhibits these features, that counts as evidence in favor of the judicial capacity model, which can explain them.[10]

Another variation on the strategic model, developed in a more recent body of literature, merits brief mention. This version of the model focuses on the hierarchical relationship of the Supreme Court with lower courts, rather than the horizontal relationship between the Supreme Court and the other branches of government. Unlike earlier strategic and attitudinal accounts, this "hierarchical model" is primarily concerned with questions of doctrinal form, as opposed to judicial votes or case outcomes. To over-simplify again, its main insight is that categorical rules can function as a tool for Supreme Court justices to discourage and monitor noncompliance with their decisions. The idea is that the lower federal courts will feel more constrained by Supreme Court rulings cast in the form of hard-edged rules and that deviation from such rules will be easier to detect than would be the case if the Court cast its decisions in the form of vague standards.[11]

This attention to doctrinal form represents real progress over the narrow focus on judicial votes that dominated the earlier political-science literature, but it comes at a cost. Instead of making concrete predictions, the hierarchical model identifies a variety of complex considerations of degree that are likely to influence the doctrinal position of the Court's decisions on the rule-standard spectrum. These include the ideological distribution of the justices, the perceived ideological distance between the Court and the lower federal courts, and the perceived costs of employing a categorical rule that is over- and under-inclusive relative to its underlying purpose. Because all of these factors are likely to vary from case to case and over time, "it is unlikely that one approach will consistently be superior." In other words, the only prediction that the hierarchical model supports is that the choice of doctrinal form will be unpredictable. That model therefore cannot explain why the Supreme Court would exhibit a stable and predictable preference for rules when invalidating government action in high-stakes, high-volume, and hybrid domains. If the pattern of the Court's decisions demonstrates such a preference, that counts as evidence in favor of the judicial capacity model, which can explain it.[12]

Other Models

In addition to legalist, attitudinal, and strategic models, the literature on judicial behavior encompasses various other models too diverse and eclectic to consider in any systematic way here, though I will address some of them in passing as the occasion demands. Some of these models are formal and supported by quantitative analysis; others are informal and supported by qualitative analysis. A number travel under the banner of "new institutionalism," but unlike legalist, attitudinal, and strategic models, this loosely organized school holds few core assumptions in common and makes few common predictions that could be compared to those of the judicial capacity model. Other loose families of models include the "new judicial politics of legal doctrine" and "regime theories" of various stripes.[13]

Many of these other models enrich our understanding of judicial decision-making, but none that I am aware of directly contradicts the judicial capacity model or attempts to test or account for the role of judicial capacity in Supreme Court decision-making. Nor, to the best of my knowledge, are any of these other models capable of explaining the pattern of the Supreme Court's decisions in capacity-constrained domains as fully as the judicial capacity model. For the remainder of this book, I will therefore put these other models to one side and focus on legalist, attitudinal, and strategic models as the most plausible competitors. If the judicial capacity model is capable of explaining the pattern of the Court's decisions in any given domain more fully than these alternatives, that is powerful evidence of judicial capacity's constraining power in that domain. If this explanatory power extends to all of the domains explored in Part II, that is powerful evidence that the judicial capacity model generalizes to all capacity-constrained domains.

Overlapping Predictions

Even if the judicial capacity model more fully explains some features of the Supreme Court's decisions than do legalist, attitudinal, and strategic models, other features of the Court's decisions in any given constitutional domain may be equally consistent with the predictions of one or more of these alternative models. More concretely, in some contexts the legalist, attitudinal, and strategic models might predict the same results—strong deference and categorical rules—as the judicial capacity model. Where this is the case, the judicial capacity model is fully sufficient to explain the pattern of the Court's decisions, but it is not necessary. The same goes for the other models. This is the thorny problem of observational equivalence.[14]

Observational equivalence is an "endemic" problem in the study of judicial decision-making and must be handled with care and sensitivity. For present purposes, it requires the careful weighing of four logical possibilities. First, in contexts where the predictions of the judicial capacity model and alternative models overlap, some factor or factors other than judicial capacity—for example, legal precedent or ideology—might be doing all of the causal work and judicial capacity none of it. This is always possible. The judicial capacity model could be wrong in attributing any logic at all to the Court's decisions. Or it could be wrong in assigning judicial capacity a meaningful causal role. But so long as the underlying assumptions of the model are plausible, internally consistent, and help to explain features of the Court's decisions that no other model can, neither of these is the most plausible conclusion.[15]

A second possibility is that judicial capacity is doing all of the causal work and the factors behind other models are playing no causal role. This, too, is possible but not the most plausible conclusion. The assumptions of the legalist, attitudinal, and strategic models are all plausible and internally consistent, and each of those models seems to explain at least some important features of judicial decision-making. So long as these models are consistent with the Court's embrace of deference and categorical rules and provide a plausible explanation for these features of the Court's decisions in capacity-constrained domains, we should be hesitant to disregard them without good reason.

This leaves two remaining and nonexclusive possibilities. First, in some contexts, multiple overlapping forces, including judicial capacity, might push the Supreme Court toward deference or categorical rules. Call this *joint causation*. Second, one or more competing explanations for the Court's decisions might be wholly or partially *endogenous* to—that is, a function of—limited judicial capacity (or vice versa). In either case, the judicial capacity model would contribute substantially to our understanding of Supreme Court decision-making.

Let us take the possibility of joint causation first. If judicial capacity and other causal forces overlap completely, then the elimination of judicial capacity constraints would have no effect at all on the pattern of the Supreme Court's decisions. The same conclusion follows if one or more such forces operates with *greater* constraining force than judicial capacity (in the sense of constraining the Court to be more deferential and rule-bound than would the limits of judicial capacity standing alone). In either case, judicial capacity would be doing no independent causal work. By contrast, if the causal forces in question overlap only partially, or if judicial capacity operates with greater constraining force than the others, then judicial capacity would do independent causal work. More specifically, the elimination of capacity constraints would give the Court greater, but not unlimited, freedom to depart from a deferential, rule-bound approach in the relevant constitutional domains. Of course, where the predictions of competing models are observationally equivalent, the evidence is, by definition, insufficient to support any confident choice among these alternatives.

Even if that were all that could be said, the judicial capacity model would make an important contribution to the study of Supreme Court decision-making by identifying judicial capacity as a plausible competitor to the dominant models of judicial decision-making. Put differently, observational equivalence is a two-way street. If the pattern of the Court's decisions is equally consistent with the predictions of multiple models, the judicial capacity model cannot claim victory over its competitors, but neither can its competitors claim victory over it. Instead, we are left with a pressing need to disentangle these various causal explanations, especially judicial capacity, which has received far less attention than the others. Simply recognizing this need would be a meaningful advance.

But we can say more than this. A joint or overlapping cause that does no independent work in the presence of other such causes becomes very significant when those causes erode or disappear. As Richard Pildes has shown, this is a very real possibility with some other potential explanations for judicial deference, including the political process for federal judicial appointments. If those explanations are losing their force or are likely to do so in the near future, it is of pressing importance to determine whether other constraints, such as judicial capacity, remain in place. The same goes for other causal factors, such as judicial ideology or principled legal commitments to judicial restraint and the rule of law, which seem more likely to wax and wane over time than do the limits of judicial capacity. I shall have more to say about this in Chapters 12 and 13.[16]

This still leaves what is perhaps the most intriguing possible explanation for observational equivalence. The predictions of the judicial capacity model might overlap with those of other models because the causal forces underlying those models are endogenous to limited judicial capacity, or vice versa. For example, as noted above, the Court's strong deference to the political process might be partly explained by a principled legalist commitment to judicial restraint, premised on limited judicial competence. On close examination, however, such an explanation turns out to be closely bound up with the limits of judicial capacity. That is because capacity constraints often limit the Court to the unsatisfactory options of crude categorical rules and strong deference to the political process. If the Supreme Court had unlimited capacity, it could formulate its decisions far more sensitively and would have less reason to defer to the political process for reasons of institutional competence. The same goes for fears of political recalcitrance or retaliation, which are often invoked to explain judicial deference. One reason such fears might have bite is that sustained recalcitrance would bury the courts, and the Supreme Court in particular, under an avalanche of litigation. If the Court had unlimited capacity, it would not have to worry about this potential downside of aggressive judicial review. I shall return to these questions in Chapters 12 and 13.

Again, where the predictions of competing models are observationally equivalent, the evidence cannot settle these questions. That is the definition of observational equivalence. Rather, they must be analyzed theoretically or the models in question must be refined to make further progress. But just by raising these questions for consideration, the judicial capacity model makes a significant contribution. This is in addition to any features of the Supreme Court's decisions that the judicial capacity model is uniquely capable of explaining—or explains better than its major competitors. As Part II of this book demonstrates, those features are many and important. It is principally on the basis of this claim that the judicial capacity model must stand or fall.

II

The Judicial Capacity Model Applied

T his Part examines how the predictions of the judicial capacity
model fare in several of the most important constitutional domains to which the model applies. In domains spanning federalism (Chapters 5 and 6), separation of powers (Chapters 7 and 8), and
individual rights (Chapters 9 and 10), the model's predictions are not only
consistent with the pattern of Supreme Court decisions but also help to
explain features of those decisions that none of its major competitors can.
Even where other models are equally consistent with the pattern of the
Court's decisions, the judicial capacity model identifies important new
questions for analysis and investigation.

The constitutional domains analyzed in this Part include a substantial preponderance of the capacity-constrained domains to which the
model applies. These domains were chosen because they span each of the
three main dimensions of U.S. constitutional law and because it is infeasible to discuss all clear examples of such domains in a single book. Apart
from the acute judicial capacity problems they raise, the domains discussed here have little in common. Not only do they implicate different
structural issues, they involve a great diversity of policy questions and
ideological stakes. This diversity strongly suggests that the explanatory
power of the judicial capacity model is not limited to the specific domains

explored in this Part but generalizes to the full universe of capacity-constrained domains.[1]

Furthermore, although it is infeasible to demonstrate at length here, the capacity-constrained domains not considered in this Part—such as substantive Due Process, the Privileges or Immunities Clause, and the taxation power—all conform substantially to the predictions of the model. In each case, the great bulk of government action is subject to categorically deferential rational-basis review, if it is subject to any judicial review at all. Those few cases in which government action is subject to meaningful judicial review are narrowly and categorically defined, and most are subject to stringent judicial scrutiny approximating a per se rule of invalidity. I am aware of no clear example of a capacity-constrained domain that does not substantially conform to the predictions of the judicial capacity model. This further strengthens the argument that the model generalizes to all capacity-constrained domains. No normal domains are included in this Part because the model makes no predictions about such domains, making them analytically irrelevant.[2]

Each chapter in this Part consists of three sections. An opening section describes the pattern of the Supreme Court's decisions in the constitutional domain in question. A middle section demonstrates the inability of other models to explain important features of that pattern—what I call "the doctrinal puzzle." A final section demonstrates the judicial capacity model's ability to explain what the other models cannot and, as relevant, its ability to identify new and important questions for further analysis and investigation. Together, these sections provide powerful evidence of the model's explanatory power for each constitutional domain discussed. The accumulation of such evidence across the wide range of constitutional domains explored in this Part demonstrates the breadth of the model's application. The result is a robust and wide-ranging body of evidence supporting the judicial capacity model, which in turn sheds significant new light on many of the most important domains of U.S. constitutional law.

The parallel structure of the chapters in this Part is logically compelled by the analytical approach laid out in Chapter 4. For each capacity-constrained constitutional domain, that approach requires a careful and systematic comparison of the pattern of the Supreme Court's decisions with the predictions of the judicial capacity model and other leading models of Supreme Court decision-making. Because the judicial capacity model makes similar predictions across all capacity-constrained constitutional domains, a certain amount of repetition proved unavoidable. I have tried to keep this to a minimum without arbitrarily varying my approach simply for variation's sake or forcing readers to refer back to earlier chapters with undue frequency. A side benefit of this approach is that the chapters in this Part are substantially independent of one another. Each can be read individually or out of sequence without substantial loss of comprehension.

Federalism

The constitutional law of federalism revolves around a small handful of congressional powers that, in combination, have underwritten a vast expansion of the federal government over the past century. Of these powers, the two most important by far are the commerce and spending powers, both granted to Congress by Article I, Section 8. The main constitutional questions surrounding both of these powers are whether the Supreme Court should enforce constitutional limits on federal power to preserve a meaningful role for state governments, and if so, what those limits should be. The Court's attempts to answer these questions are the focus of the two case studies explored in this section. Together, these case studies demonstrate the power of the judicial capacity model to illuminate the constitutional law of federalism and vice versa.[1]

The basic story is familiar. For much of the nineteenth century, the federal government played a relatively modest, even marginal, role in the life of the nation. This is not to say that the United States was a libertarian Eden. State and local governments played an active and enormously consequential role in regulating economic affairs and social life more generally. But the great bulk of governmental power was concentrated at these lower levels. Indeed, for much of the nineteenth century, the most important federal function was mail delivery, and the most important federal agency was the Post Office.[2]

This state of affairs changed rapidly and dramatically with the industrial, transportation, and communication revolutions of the mid to late nineteenth century. The proximate result of these revolutions was a far more integrated and industrialized national economy. This new economy, in turn, created a powerful demand for federal action to address the many social and economic problems that followed in its wake. Two World Wars and the Great Depression greatly accelerated these developments. The Supreme Court mounted a brief, pitched resistance to this expansion of federal power in the early 1930s, but the Court quickly ceded the field almost completely. By the mid-twentieth century, vast federal regulatory and spending programs, ranging from the Sherman Antitrust and Fair Labor Standards Acts to Social Security and the interstate highway system, had radically and permanently transformed the balance of power between the federal government and the states.[3]

Today, most observers look back on this transformation as well-nigh inevitable. Very few think the Supreme Court could have done much to prevent it—or even to seriously slow it down. Nevertheless, calls for more stringent judicial enforcement of constitutional limits on federal power remain a staple of the constitutional literature. Supreme Court decisions like *NFIB v. Sebelius,* which partially invalidated the Affordable Care Act, have raised hopes—and fears—that the Court might be poised to take up these calls in a meaningful way.[4]

Both supporters and opponents, however, have largely ignored the antecedent question of whether the Supreme Court has the capacity to restrain federal power in the ways advocated for. Even scholars more sensitive to institutional limits have overlooked a crucial question: How does the judiciary's limited capacity influence the substance and doctrinal form of the constitutional law of federalism? The judicial capacity model fills these gaps in the literature. In turn, the constitutional law of federalism provides powerful evidence supporting the judicial capacity model.

CHAPTER FIVE

The Commerce Power

No constitutional provision has contributed more to the growth of federal power than the Commerce Clause, which grants Congress the power "to regulate commerce . . . among the several states." Coupled with the Necessary and Proper Clause, which grants Congress the power to "make all Laws which shall be necessary and proper for carrying into Execution the foregoing powers," the Commerce Clause provides the constitutional authority for federal regulation of a stunningly broad array of subjects. Examples range from environmental protection to workplace safety to consumer finance to banking and securities to child pornography to narcotics trafficking. It is largely thanks to the commerce power that "there is now virtually no significant aspect of life that is not in some way regulated by the federal government."[1]

The commerce power was controversial from the beginning, largely because it was seen as the likeliest avenue for federal regulation of the domestic slave trade. For most of the nineteenth century, however, the demand for federal regulation was low. As a result, Congress exercised the commerce power only sparingly. As every first-year law student knows, this changed beginning in the late nineteenth century, when Congress enacted the Interstate Commerce and Sherman Antitrust Acts. The pace of federal commerce regulation picked up markedly during the first decades of the twentieth century, and veritably exploded during and after Franklin Roosevelt's New Deal.[2]

Initially this expansion of federal power met only sporadic resistance. During the period from 1890 to 1919, the Supreme Court invalidated a handful of important commerce-power statutes but upheld many others. Judicial resistance greatly intensified during the New Deal when a conservative majority of the Court aggressively blocked the Roosevelt administration's attempt to turn the commerce power into a comprehensive, all-purpose tool for social and economic regulation. This resistance provoked a ferocious political backlash, culminating in Roosevelt's thinly veiled Court-packing plan of 1937. All this is familiar ground. Less familiar is the tidal wave of constitutional litigation triggered by the Court's effort to limit the commerce power. As McNollgast explains, "the number of cases threatened to overwhelm the judicial system, and the Supreme Court in particular."[3]

In the face of these formidable threats, and spurred by several new Roosevelt appointees, the Court beat a quick and comprehensive retreat from further constitutional scrutiny of commerce-power legislation. For nearly sixty years, the Court did not invalidate a single commerce-power statute. Only within the past two decades has the Court felt bold enough to impose two narrow, categorical limits on the commerce power, the first and only limits it has attempted to enforce since 1936.[4]

The Supreme Court's broad deference to federal commerce-power legislation has been crucial to the development of the modern regulatory state. Yet none of the leading models of Supreme Court decision-making can readily explain it. Since the New Deal, the Court has had both legal and ideological reasons to impose meaningful limits on the commerce power and few strategic reasons not to do so. No justice to serve on the Supreme Court during this period, even the most liberal, has openly disputed that the federal government is one of enumerated and thus limited powers. Many conservative justices profess to be deeply committed to this principle. Yet nearly all of these justices have signed opinions that, as a practical matter, treat the commerce power as unlimited. If the Court recognizes these limits in principle, why does it so rarely enforce them in practice?

Some of the Court's deferential approach is surely attributable to the legal and ideological preference of liberal justices for broad federal power.

But conservatives have held a majority of the Court, in some form or fashion, for nearly fifty years. Limiting the commerce power would have provided those justices with a powerful tool for eliminating all manner of federal regulations opposed by conservatives. Even liberal justices should have opportunistic reason to invalidate the occasional commerce-power statute that promotes conservative policy objectives, such as mandatory arbitration, limited tort liability, or harsh criminal penalties for nonviolent offenders.[5]

Finally, none of the leading models can readily explain why every constitutional limit the Court has imposed on the commerce power in the modern era—including those imposed during the New Deal showdown—has taken the form of a crude categorical rule. There is no compelling textual or functional argument for any of these rules. In fact, quite the contrary: all of them are plainly crafted by judges and fail to sensibly divide power between the federal government and the states by anyone's lights. Nor can judicial ideology explain the Court's consistent preference for rules over standards. Doctrinal form is just that—form, not substance. The strategic model's only prediction about doctrinal form is that it is unpredictable.

Unlike the leading models of Supreme Court decision-making, the judicial capacity model can explain the Court's strongly deferential and rule-bound approach to the commerce power. In a nutshell, the commerce power is both a high-volume and a high-stakes domain. As such, any serious effort to limit that power would call into question a vast amount of federal legislation and bury the Court in litigation it would feel strongly compelled to review. The Court therefore only enforces limits on the commerce power when it can do so in the form of relatively narrow categorical rules, which clearly insulate most congressional action from constitutional challenge and encourage settlement as to those actions they invalidate.

The Pattern of Supreme Court Decisions

The modern history of the commerce power has two dominant themes: strong judicial deference to Congress and categorical constitutional limits, mostly quite narrow ones, on federal power. To fully appreciate the pattern of Supreme Court decisions from which these themes emerge, it is helpful to start at the beginning.

Early History

The Supreme Court first had occasion to interpret the commerce power in the case of *Gibbons v. Ogden,* an 1824 dispute over steamboat transportation between New York and New Jersey. The crucial issue was whether navigation—the transportation of persons—qualified as commerce as that term was used in the Commerce Clause. In an opinion that remains the starting point for modern commerce-power jurisprudence, Chief Justice John Marshall held that the answer was clearly yes. In so doing, he adopted an extremely broad definition of commerce. "Commerce, undoubtedly, is traffic," he wrote. "But it is something more: it is intercourse," which is to say "interaction."[6]

In addition, Marshall held that Congress's power to regulate commerce "among the several states" extends not only to commerce that crosses state lines but to all commerce "which concerns more States than one." Coupled with the Necessary and Proper Clause, contemporaneously interpreted in *McCulloch v. Maryland,* this holding also gave Congress the power to adopt all laws "useful," "convenient," or "beneficial" to the regulation of commerce concerning more states than one. Moreover, as *McCulloch* made clear, it was the province of Congress, not the courts, to judge the degree of a law's usefulness and convenience to the exercise of the legislature's enumerated powers. At the same time, both *Gibbons* and *McCulloch* affirmed that the powers of Congress were limited and that the Necessary and Proper Clause could not be used as a pretext for exceeding the constitutional boundaries of those powers.[7]

The New Deal Constitutional Showdown

The tension between these principles and Marshall's broad construction of the Commerce Clause and Necessary and Proper Clauses was well recognized at the time. But for most of the nineteenth century, demand for national regulation was sufficiently limited that this tension remained largely theoretical. That changed when Congress began to flex its regulatory muscles in the 1880s and 1890s, gingerly at first but with increasing boldness as the twentieth century progressed. As Larry Lessig has elegantly explained, this left the Supreme Court with a choice. It could adhere to the letter of its Marshall-era precedents, even in the face of radical economic transformation that greatly increased their potential breadth, or it could impose new, judicially crafted limits on the commerce power to preserve the principle of limited federal power that those precedents purported to respect. Ultimately, the Court chose the latter course, at first tentatively and then forcefully, as Roosevelt's election and New Deal program made clear just how dramatic an upheaval of American federalism was in the offing.[8]

The Supreme Court's doomed resistance to this upheaval culminated in *Carter v. Carter Coal,* a 1936 decision invalidating the Bituminous Coal Conservation Act of 1935 as beyond Congress's commerce power. The Court employed three doctrinal moves to find the Act invalid. First, it held that the Act's regulations of labor relations and working conditions in coal mines regulated manufacturing, which was categorically distinct from commerce and therefore beyond federal regulatory authority. Second, the Court held that Congress's regulatory power reached only activities with direct effects on commerce, not those with merely indirect effects—a distinction the Court drew in logical, rather than practical, terms. In essence, the Court counted the causal links connecting coal mining to interstate commerce. It refused to consider the practical magnitude of the effects or the practical need for national regulation in any particular context. Third, the Court omitted any discussion or consideration of Congress's authority under the Necessary and Proper Clause to regulate matters that were not themselves commerce but were nevertheless useful, convenient, or beneficial to the regulation of commerce.[9]

All of these techniques featured in the Supreme Court's earlier commerce-power decisions and all have the character of categorical rules, designed to clearly and cleanly distinguish between permissible and impermissible exercises of congressional authority. Of course, not all categorical rules succeed in this objective, and there is good reason to doubt that those employed in *Carter Coal* would have remained clear and predictable under the pressures of sustained litigation—or that they even remained so at the time *Carter Coal* was decided. The important point is that the limits the Court sought to impose on the commerce power during the New Deal showdown—the first time that such limits would threaten a truly significant quantity of federal legislation—all took this doctrinal form. Indeed, a majority of the Court insisted that the only alternative to categorical limits on the Commerce Clause was a slippery slope to absolute federal power.[10]

Justice Benjamin Cardozo disagreed. In a widely admired dissent from *Carter Coal*'s commerce-power holding, Cardozo advocated a more standard-like approach, one recognizing that "the law is not indifferent to considerations of degree." More specifically, he urged the Court to apply the direct/indirect effects test with "suppleness of adaptation and flexibility of meaning," rather than the formal, logical approach of the majority. Above all, Cardozo insisted that the validity of federal commerce-power legislation could be sensibly evaluated only in light of the "particular conditions" of the case and the breadth of the need for federal action suggested by those conditions. At the same time, Cardozo emphasized his support for judicially enforced limits on federal power.[11]

Six Decades of Deference

Less than a year later, in the face of Roosevelt's Court-packing plan and the onslaught of litigation generated by its prior decisions, the Supreme Court began its retreat from serious scrutiny of federal commerce-power legislation. The first step in that retreat was *NLRB v. Jones & Laughlin Steel Company*, which Cardozo joined, but the highly contextual, fact-sensitive standard he advocated for evaluating commerce-power challenges would never be embraced by the Court in any future case. Instead, *Jones & Laughlin* ushered in a regime of essentially categorical deference. Echoing Cardozo, the majority opinion of Chief Justice Hughes acknowledged that "the distinction between what is national and what is local . . . is necessarily one of degree." But Hughes quickly added that "it is primarily for Congress to consider and decide the fact of the danger and meet it."[12]

This deference to congressional judgments would become the dominant theme of the Court's commerce-power jurisprudence in the post–New Deal era, as the Court's subsequent decisions in *United States v. Darby* and *Wickard v. Filburn* confirmed in short order. After *Wickard,* its author, Justice Robert Jackson, wrote privately, "If we were to be brutally frank, . . . what we would say is that in any case where Congress thinks there is an effect on interstate commerce, the Court will accept that judgment." Whatever modest equivocations the Court felt compelled to include in its opinions, Jackson's message came through loud and clear. For the next sixty years, both lower courts and litigants widely regarded the federal commerce power as having no judicially enforceable limits.[13]

The Court formalized this categorical rule of deference in the rational-basis test announced in *Katzenbach v. McClung,* which upheld Title II of the Civil Rights Act of 1964 as a valid exercise of the commerce power. Simply put, where legislators "have a rational basis for finding a chosen regulatory scheme necessary to the protection of commerce," the Court held, "our investigation is at an end." Suffice it to say, this test is very easily satisfied. In fact, no federal legislation has ever been invalidated under it.[14]

The Return of Categorical Limits

Such deference was the hallmark of the Supreme Court's commerce-power decisions from 1937 until 1995. In that year, a case called *United States v. Lopez* heralded a return of categorical limits, albeit much more modest ones than the Court had attempted to impose before 1937. *Lopez* invalidated the Gun-Free School Zones Act as beyond Congress's commerce power, principally on the ground that the Act's prohibition on possession of firearms in school zones was a regulation of noneconomic, rather than economic, activity. Three years later, *United States v. Morrison* reaffirmed *Lopez* but went one step further, clarifying that the rule for noneconomic regulation is one of virtually per se invalidity. That is to say, federal regulations of noneconomic activities will virtually always be held invalid, without regard to their impact on interstate commerce or the quality of the legislative record. At the same time, the Court made clear that federal regulations of economic activity remain subject to highly deferential review.[15]

For present purposes, the economic / noneconomic distinction established in these decisions has two especially important features. First, like the limits imposed in *Carter Coal,* that distinction takes the form of a categorical rule. If an activity is economic, Congress almost certainly has the authority to regulate it, subject only to highly deferential rational-basis review. If an activity is noneconomic, it lies categorically outside the federal commerce power. No considerations of degree or nuanced evaluations of the case-specific need for national action are required, only a categorical judgment about the nature of the activity regulated.

Second, the economic / noneconomic distinction imposes a far-narrower limit on federal power than those imposed in *Carter Coal.* There is simply very little federal legislation that regulates noneconomic activities. The narrowness of this limit was reinforced by the Court's 2005 decision in *Gonzales v. Raich,* which defined economic activity with a breadth that seems clearly designed to place nearly all federal regulation on the economic side of the line. As a double security, *Raich* also extended the categorically deferential rational-basis test to noneconomic activity regulated as part of a larger regulatory scheme. This leaves all but a minute fraction of federal commerce-power legislation subject to rational-basis review, whose deferential character *Raich* conspicuously underscores.[16]

The activity / inactivity distinction embraced by a majority of the Supreme Court in *NFIB v. Sebelius* possesses the same two noteworthy features. In this 2012 decision, a five-justice majority upheld the Affordable Care Act's individual mandate—which requires all nonexempt persons to purchase health insurance—as a valid exercise of Congress's taxation power. The Court's five conservative members, however, simultaneously voted to hold that the individual mandate exceeded the scope of Congress's commerce power. The ground for this aspect of the Court's decision was that the individual mandate constituted a regulation of economic inactivity—the failure to purchase health insurance—rather than economic activity. This holding had no practical effect on the individual mandate; one source of constitutional authority is all any legislation requires. But it altered the meaning of the commerce power for future cases.[17]

In explaining the Court's commerce-power holding, Chief Justice Roberts was explicit that his reading of the Commerce Clause—broadly shared by the four other conservative justices—threatened only a single federal statute. And, like *Lopez* and *Morrison,* it did so on the basis of a categorical distinction—in this case, between activity and inactivity. As with the economic/noneconomic distinction, no considerations of degree or elaborate evaluations of the case-specific need for national action are required, only a categorical judgment about the nature of the object of federal regulation: Is it an activity or inactivity? All nine justices, moreover, appeared to agree that Congress could pass the perfect economic equivalent of the individual mandate under the taxation power, so long as it invoked that power explicitly. This makes the limit imposed by *NFIB* seem very narrow indeed.[18]

The Doctrinal Puzzle

The pattern of the Supreme Court's modern commerce-power decisions presents two distinct puzzles: First, why have the Court's post-1937 decisions deferred so strongly to Congress? Second, why has the Court oscillated between categorical limits on the commerce power and categorical deference to Congress in the form of the rational-basis test, rather than embracing the sort of supple, case-specific standard advocated by Justice Cardozo's *Carter Coal* dissent? No leading model of Supreme Court decision-making can readily answer these questions.

Post-1937 Deference

Since 1937, the Supreme Court has subjected the vast majority of federal commerce-power legislation to highly deferential rational-basis review. This strong and persistent deference to Congress is puzzling because the Court has both legal and ideological motives for limiting the commerce power and few strategic motives for maintaining such a restrained posture. Put in reverse, the legalist and attitudinal models both predict that the Court should have imposed more limits on the commerce power than it has. The strategic model predicts that the Court will back off efforts to limit the commerce power that threaten serious political backlash, of the sort triggered by the Court's aggressive efforts to roll back the New Deal.

But this prediction cannot readily explain why the Court deferred so abjectly to Congress for the next sixty years and, even today, has imposed only two exceedingly narrow categorical limits on federal commerce authority.

Let us begin with the Supreme Court's legal motives for limiting the commerce power. Despite the Court's long record of deference to Congress, no Supreme Court justice who served during this period—not even those appointed by Franklin Roosevelt in the aftermath of the New Deal constitutional showdown—has openly professed to believe that the commerce power grants the federal government unlimited regulatory authority. Many of the conservatives who served during this period, in fact, regard limited federal power as a first principle—perhaps *the* first principle—of American constitutionalism. Even liberal justices have frequently praised the virtues of federalism and generally seem to recognize that many issues are better left to state and local authorities. Yet nearly all of these justices have signed opinions that read the commerce power as effectively unlimited. Some of this might be attributed to the precedential force of New Deal decisions like *Jones & Laughlin* and *Wickard v. Filburn,* but such decisions left the Court plenty of room to impose meaningful limits on the commerce power, had a majority of the Court been so inclined. It was only the Supreme Court's willingness to stand idly by as the lower courts turned these decisions into a rule of categorical deference that ultimately cemented this reading of them. Even if these precedents were a serious obstacle, the Court is not formally bound by its own decisions and not infrequently overrules itself. Its failure to do so in this instance requires explanation that the legalist model cannot supply.[19]

From a cruder political standpoint, the commerce power is the principal foundation for the modern regulatory state, bête noire of American conservatism since at least the New Deal. If Supreme Court justices vote like legislators, as the attitudinal model posits, strict constitutional limits on the commerce power ought to be a highly attractive means for judicial conservatives to invalidate federal regulatory legislation they oppose on policy grounds. Even liberal justices, who tend to strongly support the regulatory state, ought to be tempted to opportunistically invalidate harsh federal drug laws, federal preemption of state tort law, and the many other exercises of the federal commerce power that promote conservative policy goals.[20]

Yet, in the past eighty years, the Court has only twice invalidated federal commerce-power legislation, and those two decisions are carefully written to insulate the vast majority of such legislation from meaningful judicial scrutiny. The same goes for *NFIB v. Sebelius,* which nominally imposed a narrow new limit on the commerce power, while upholding the Affordable Care Act's insurance-purchase mandate as a valid exercise of the federal taxation power. If Supreme Court decisions are driven primarily by ideology, as the attitudinal model contends, this long record of restraint is difficult to understand.[21]

The strategic model is somewhat more helpful, but only somewhat. Fear of political reprisal might well explain why the Supreme Court retreated from its aggressive attempts to limit the federal commerce power in the face of Roosevelt's 1937 Court-packing plan. But even if that is the case—a much controverted issue on which I take no position here—the strategic model cannot readily explain why the Court continued to defer so strongly and so long to federal commerce legislation after the immediate threat of Roosevelt's Court-packing plan had passed. The memory of this political backlash and the institutional threat it posed to the Court might plausibly have deterred another all-out assault on the regulatory state. But it does not explain why the Court's liberals and conservatives have both refrained from opportunistically invalidating commerce-power legislation that they oppose on ideological grounds. Nor does it explain why the Court's conservatives have never been seriously tempted to impose meaningful across-the-board limits that would curb, but not overturn, the modern regulatory state. (*Lopez, Morrison,* and *NFIB* are far too narrow to count.) The failure of Congress to mount any successful retaliation even to deeply unpopular decisions like *Citizens United v. FEC,* the flag-burning cases, and the school prayer cases suggests that the Court's conservatives could have taken this step without serious risk, especially during one of the numerous periods of unified Republican control or divided partisan control of the federal government. The strategic model, therefore, cannot persuasively explain their failure to do so.[22]

Preference for Categorical Rules over Standards

During the modern era, the Supreme Court has oscillated between the categorical deference of the rational-basis test and categorical limits on the commerce power, consistently refusing to embrace the sort of vague, fact-sensitive standard that Justice Cardozo advocated in his *Carter Coal* dissent. Both the aggressive limits the Court attempted to impose on the commerce power during the New Deal constitutional showdown and the far more narrow limits the Court has imposed on the commerce power over the past twenty years have all been categorical in nature. The Court's deference to Congress under the rational-basis test has been similarly categorical; no commerce-power legislation has ever been invalidated under that test.

No leading model of Supreme Court decision-making can readily explain this unwavering preference for categorical rules. Neither the attitudinal nor the strategic model makes any strong predictions about the doctrinal form of Supreme Court decisions. If anything, the hierarchical branch of the strategic model predicts that the doctrinal form should vary over time with a complex array of frequently shifting variables, including the ideological diversity of the lower federal courts and the ideological distance between those courts and the Supreme Court. That is not, of course, what we see in the Court's modern commerce-power decisions.

The legalist model presents a somewhat trickier case. It predicts that doctrinal form will reflect legal factors like constitutional text, structure, and judicial precedent. In the case of the commerce power, however, both constitutional text and structure seem to favor Justice Cardozo's context-sensitive standard, rather than the categorical approach taken by the Court. Judicial precedent is a bit murkier but certainly did not compel—and thus cannot explain—the Court's categorical approach. To see why that approach is puzzling from a legalist perspective, it is necessary to consider constitutional text, structure, and judicial precedent in some detail.

Let us begin with the constitutional text. The Commerce Clause authorizes Congress to regulate "commerce . . . among the several states." *Lopez* and *Morrison* limit the commerce power to economic activity, which at first blush seems to be a fair, if somewhat broad, synonym for commerce. Conversely, it seems uncontroversial that noneconomic activity is *not* commerce. *United States v. Morrison* encourages this reading, frequently using the terms "noncommercial" and "noneconomic" interchangeably. Similarly, it seems plausible to say that "commerce" is a form of activity, and that whatever its precise bounds, it does not encompass economic *in*activity. In *NFIB*, Chief Justice Roberts makes this point explicitly. The same is true of *Carter Coal*'s manufacturing/commerce distinction. While perhaps more debatable, it is at least plausible that commerce is limited to trade and therefore distinct from manufacturing.[23]

The problem with this textual defense of the Court's categorical limits is that Congress's regulatory power over guns, violent crime, and health insurance is not defined by the commerce power alone. It also includes the Necessary and Proper Clause, and nothing in the text of the latter limits Congress's power to either "commerce" or "activity." Rather, as authoritatively construed by *McCulloch v. Maryland,* the Necessary and Proper Clause grants Congress the power to pass all laws "appropriate," "useful," or "convenient" to the exercise of its commerce power. Justice Scalia made this point nicely in his *Gonzales v. Raich* concurrence.[24]

It may be true, as Chief Justice Roberts argues in *NFIB,* that the Necessary and Proper Clause implicitly incorporates the principle that Congress's powers are enumerated and therefore limited. But this just brings us back to where we started: How did the Court arrive at these particular limits? The text of the Necessary and Proper Clause is no help. Indeed, as read by *McCulloch,* that text closely mirrors the context-specific standard advocated by Justice Cardozo, under which Congress's power to regulate noncommercial activities like manufacturing would turn on the degree of need for such regulation.[25]

What about constitutional structure? *Lopez, Morrison,* and *NFIB* cite two structural justifications for limiting federal power: (1) distinguishing "between what is truly national and what is truly local"; and (2) "protect[ing] the liberty of the individual from arbitrary power." Certainly, these are not the only purposes one might attribute to the American federal system. But even with respect to these explicitly stated justifications, the economic/noneconomic, activity/inactivity, and manufacturing/commerce distinctions fare remarkably poorly. Put simply, not all economic activities require national regulation, and plenty of noneconomic activities (and economic inactivities and manufacturing operations) do require such regulation. Nor does federal regulation of the former present any greater threat to individual liberty than the latter. Principled legal views vary on the optimal scope of federal power. But whatever one's view on this question, the categorical limits the Court has imposed are extremely crude screens for separating permissible from impermissible exercises of federal authority.[26]

Notably, none of the justices who joined the *Lopez, Morrison, NFIB,* or *Carter Coal* majorities made any meaningful attempt to explain why the federal government is systematically better situated to regulate economic activity or, conversely, why the states are systematically better situated to regulate noneconomic activity or economic inactivity or manufacturing. Nor has any justice attempted to explain why federal regulations of noneconomic activity and economic inactivity pose a systematically greater threat to individual liberty than do regulations of economic activity. Instead, the justices endorsing these limits simply assert that the only alternative is unlimited federal power.[27]

That is, in fact, the principal alternative to such limits embraced by the Court—and by the dissenting justices in *Lopez, Morrison,* and *NFIB*—over the past eighty years, but it is not the only one. At any point during this period, the Court could have embraced the sort of context-sensitive standard advocated by Justice Cardozo. That approach would require the Court to ask, case by case, whether federal regulation is really appropriate, useful, or convenient, or whether state and local governments can handle the problem in question on their own. This seems more consistent with both constitutional text and constitutional structure than any of the Court's categorical limits (which are artificial and structurally obtuse) or the Court's categorical deference (which fails to take seriously either the textual enumeration of federal powers or the benefits of federalism). The mystery, then, is why the Court has never adopted—or even seriously considered—Cardozo's approach.

Does judicial precedent provide the answer? Eventually the Court's categorically deferential post-1937 approach to the commerce power became firmly entrenched in legal doctrine. But judicial precedent does not explain how or why this entrenchment occurred. Things could have been otherwise, and constitutional text and structure suggest that they should have been. Why weren't they? Judicial precedent also does not explain the Court's unwillingness—over the course of eighty years—to reconsider its categorically deferential approach in favor of the context-sensitive standard advocated by Justice Cardozo. *Lopez, Morrison, NFIB,* and *Jones & Laughlin* all demonstrate that the Court has been willing to reconsider well-established precedents under some circumstances. Given the strong textual and structural arguments in favor of Justice Cardozo's approach, judicial precedent cannot readily explain the Court's refusal ever to seriously consider it.

The Judicial Capacity Model Applied

The Supreme Court has both the motive and the opportunity to vigorously limit the commerce power, but it has consistently refused to do so for the past eighty years. The Court has also consistently cast its commerce-power decisions in the form of crude categorical rules, with little textual or structural foundation. The judicial capacity model helps to explain both of these otherwise puzzling features of the Court's modern commerce-power decisions.

The commerce power is both a high-stakes and a high-volume domain. It underwrites an enormous quantity of legislation, and all of that legislation is federal legislation—meaning that almost any time a lower court invalidates a commerce-power statute, the Supreme Court will feel compelled to grant review. This includes the vast majority of federal criminal laws, as well as the vast majority of federal regulation on subjects ranging from environmental protection to food and drug safety to consumer protection to antitrust to banking and securities to national energy markets to aviation safety. Each of these laws, in turn, contains innumerable discrete regulations of individual behavior that might be subject to constitutional challenge, depending on the Supreme Court's interpretation of the commerce power.[28]

Of course, it is not only the quantity of threatened legislation that determines the volume of potential litigation. It is also the magnitude of the benefits that such invalidation would generate for prospective plaintiffs and the number of prospective plaintiffs either collectively or individually capable of mustering the resources to litigate. Because the array of commerce-power legislation is dizzyingly broad, so is the array of prospective challengers who would stand to benefit from its invalidation. In almost every area regulated under the commerce power, however, prospective plaintiffs fall into one of two groups—(1) regulated businesses or industries, which spend millions or billions of dollars on regulatory compliance; or (2) criminal defendants, who face substantial prison terms and are represented by government-funded counsel. White-collar criminal defendants, in some sense, straddle the two categories. They have much to lose and plenty of money to spend advancing any legally plausible defense. If this were not enough, a substantial pro bono bar, consisting of both nonprofit public-interest organizations and sophisticated members of the private bar, stands ready to assist overburdened public defenders with high-profile constitutional litigation on behalf of indigent criminal defendants. For any given commerce-power regulation, some individual, business, or group of businesses will almost always have both the incentive and the resources to bring whatever constitutional challenges the Court's commerce-power doctrine makes plausible. Accordingly, the commerce power qualifies as a high-volume and high-stakes domain. The judicial capacity model therefore predicts that the Court will feel strong pressure to interpret that power broadly, employ hard-edged categorical rules, or both.[29]

This, in fact, is just what we see when we examine the Supreme Court's modern commerce-power decisions. Apart from its aggressive attempt to roll back the New Deal, the Court has only twice in its modern history struck down federal commerce-power legislation as unconstitutional. On one other occasion, in *NFIB v. Sebelius,* the Court found the Affordable Care Act's insurance-purchase mandate invalid as an exercise of the commerce power, while upholding it as an exercise of the taxation power. In all of these cases, the limits the Court imposed on the commerce power took the form of narrow categorical rules that leave the vast majority of commerce-power legislation subject to rational-basis review, which no commerce statute has ever failed. The Court's refusal to act aggressively in this high-stakes and high-volume domain is entirely consistent with the model's predictions.

Obviously, judicial capacity is not the only factor that affects the Court's decisions. The ideology of the justices, the level of concern they harbor

about federal overreach, and their understanding of constitutional federalism also matter greatly. But the ways in which these factors influence
the Court's constitutional decisions are strongly constrained by judicial
capacity. Take *United States v. Lopez* as an example. The judicial capacity
model does not explain the Court's decision to invalidate the Gun-Free
School Zones Act or the Court's renewed interest in limiting federal power
under the Commerce Clause. But it does explain the Court's choice to
pursue these objectives through a categorical distinction between economic and noneconomic activity.

From the standpoint of judicial capacity, this rule has two advantages.
First, it appears to threaten only a tiny number of federal laws. Since *Raich*
was decided in 2005, no federal Court of Appeals has invalidated any
commerce-power legislation for regulating noneconomic activity. Second,
the economic / noneconomic distinction is crafted in clear and categorical terms, which reduces uncertainty for potential litigants and thus
reduces the volume of litigation. This is not to say that this distinction
will never cause confusion or debate; no categorical rule is that clear. But
especially under the broad definition of economic activity adopted in
Raich, the constitutional inquiry mandated by *Lopez* and *Morrison* is
comparatively cut and dried. The same goes for *NFIB*'s categorical rule
against federal regulation of economic inactivity, which threatened only
one existing federal statute and came gift-wrapped with instructions enabling Congress to achieve the same practical result under the taxation
power. Unlike other models of Supreme Court decision-making, the
judicial capacity model explains why the Court would find these categorical limits attractive.[30]

It also helps to explain the Supreme Court's reluctance to adopt Justice Cardozo's context-sensitive approach to the commerce power. That
approach would have required the Court to assess the constitutionality
of commerce-power legislation by evaluating the practical need for national regulation on a case-by-case basis. From a textual, structural, and
even an ideological standpoint, this test has much to recommend it. As
explained above, it tracks the text of the Necessary and Proper Clause
and takes seriously the need for congressional flexibility reflected in that
provision. Moreover, it does so without denigrating the Constitution's
structural commitment to limited federal power, which justices across the

political spectrum regard, in varying degrees, as both practically desirable and important to the constitutional design. There is, however, one big problem. If applied with any real stringency, Cardozo's nebulous test would call into question a vast quantity of federal legislation, generating a large volume of litigation, nearly all of which the Court would feel compelled to grant review. In effect, the Court would be declaring itself open to reevaluating, on a case-by-case basis, the practical need justifying every federal commerce-power statute. This is just the sort of approach that the judicial capacity model predicts the Court will be compelled to avoid in capacity-constrained domains like the commerce power.[31]

Finally, the judicial capacity model explains why the Court has not been tempted to revive *Carter Coal*'s stringent categorical limits on the commerce power. Despite their rule-like form, those limits are so stringent that their application would generate an enormous volume of litigation. In particular, to categorically prohibit federal regulation of manufacturing, the Court would have to invalidate hundreds of federal laws. Even in 1937, the Court's attempt to enforce this prohibition produced an overwhelming volume of litigation. Today the range of commerce-power laws that such a prohibition would threaten is vastly larger.[32]

Reviving the manufacturing/commerce distinction would also require the Court to draw a line between commerce and manufacturing, which are often closely intertwined, across a large run of cases. This is something the Court struggled mightily with even before its 1937 retreat from serious commerce-power scrutiny. This struggle, too, would likely be greater today than it was then, leading to greater uncertainty, despite the ostensibly categorical nature of the manufacturing/commerce distinction. This, in turn, would lead to more litigation. Part of what makes the *Lopez* and *NFIB*'s narrow categorical limits sustainable is that they come into play—and thus under stress—in so few cases. That obviously would not be true of a revived commerce/manufacturing distinction. The judicial capacity model therefore helps to explain why so few justices—really, only Justice Thomas—have been tempted to turn the clock back to 1936.[33]

Even if the categorical nature of the commerce/manufacturing distinction could keep litigation within manageable bounds, it would produce results that many justices would find unpalatable. Among other things, that rule would probably require invalidation of large sections of the

Controlled Substances Act, the Clean Air and Water Acts, federal anti-trust law, federal labor law, federal employment discrimination law, and so on. There is good reason to think that such extreme results would give pause to many justices. Such results might also create a real risk of po-litical backlash, providing a strategic reason for the Court to leave *Carter Coal* safely entombed. In the capacity-constrained domain of the com-merce power, however, the Court cannot adopt vague standards without inviting an unsustainable volume of litigation. Thus, the Court is forced to choose between the unpalatable results of a *Carter Coal*–like prohibi-tion and the large-scale sacrifice of limited federal power entailed by the nibble-around-the-edges approach of *Lopez, Morrison,* and *NFIB*. Given this choice, it is unsurprising that the Court has selected the latter course. This is a good illustration of the way in which the judicial capacity model interacts with the justices' ideological preferences and strategic calculations.[34]

In sum, the judicial capacity model explains features of the Supreme Court's commerce-power decisions that no other model can. Although the Court has both legal and ideological motives to limit the commerce power, the limits of judicial capacity prevent it from doing so except in the form of a narrow categorical rule of the sort imposed in *Lopez, Mor-rison,* and *NFIB*. The Court also has legal and perhaps strategic motives to cast its interpretation of the commerce power in the form of a context-specific standard, but it has never done so. The judicial capacity model explains why. In these ways, the model illuminates a crucially important area of constitutional law. In turn, the pattern of the Court's commerce-power decisions provides powerful evidence in its favor.

CHAPTER SIX

The Spending Power

O nly one federal power rivals the significance of the commerce power. That is the spending power, the Article I power of Congress to spend federal revenues in pursuit of the "General Welfare." Coupled with the Necessary and Proper Clause, this power includes the ancillary power to place conditions on the eligibility of individuals and states to receive federal funds, generally known as the "conditional spending power." Since the mid-twentieth century, federal spending authorized by these powers has accounted for roughly one-fifth of the national economy. Each year, the federal government spends trillions of dollars on matters ranging from health care to education to social security to housing to environmental protection to military procurement.

This spending may well shape behavior as extensively as all federal regulations combined.[1] The reason is simple. Whether federal funds are disbursed directly to individuals or through the intermediary of state governments, they invariably come with strings attached. To qualify for certain federal agricultural subsidies, farmers must allow their fields to lie fallow. To qualify for others, they must grow specific crops. To qualify for federal highway funds, states must not permit the sale of alcohol to persons below the age of twenty-one. To qualify for federal education funds, states must follow the principles of federal antidiscrimination law. And so on and so forth. Such carrots influence behavior at least as surely as the sticks—the penalties—that punish violations of regulations adopted under the Commerce Clause and other federal regulatory powers. Indeed, from an economic standpoint, carrots and sticks are, in most respects, functionally equivalent.[2]

From the beginning, the federalism implications of the spending power provoked debate and concern. James Madison and other proponents of limited federal power quickly recognized that the power to spend is the power to call the tune for all recipients of federal largesse, notably including state governments. Put differently, an unlimited federal spending power amounted to unlimited federal power, full stop. Yet despite early and intense controversy over the proper limits on that power, particularly on the subject of federal infrastructure spending or "internal improvements," the Supreme Court has only twice in its history invalidated federal spending legislation. One of those decisions, *United States v. Butler,* was effectively overruled within a year. The other, *NFIB v. Sebelius,* is still good law and poses more complicated questions. At the end of the day, however, it is only one decision—one whose holding is so peculiarly tailored to the Affordable Care Act that it seems likely to prove "a ticket good for one day only."[3]

The Supreme Court's nearly wholesale deference to federal spending legislation has been crucial to the development of the modern welfare state, as well as the vast complex of federal–state joint ventures generally known as "cooperative federalism." Yet none of the leading models of Supreme Court decision-making can readily explain it. Since the New Deal, the Court has had both legal and ideological reasons to impose meaningful limits on the spending power and few strategic reasons not to do so. Many conservative justices are, or have been, strongly committed to limited federal power as a matter of constitutional principle, and the federal spending power poses at least as great a threat to that commitment as any other source of constitutional authority. Limiting the federal spending power would also be a highly convenient mechanism for invalidating any number of economically redistributive programs that conservatives generally oppose on ideological grounds. Given the number of conservatives on the Supreme Court over the past fifty years, it is puzzling that one or both of these motives should not have tempted the Court to impose meaningful constitutional limits.[4]

Unlike the leading models of Supreme Court decision-making, the judicial capacity model can explain the Court's restrained approach to the spending power. In a nutshell, the spending power is both a high-stakes and a high-volume domain. It underwrites an enormous quantity of legislation, and that legislation is all federal, meaning that the Supreme Court feels strongly compelled to grant review any time a lower court strikes it down. Moreover, the constitutional questions raised by the spending power are inherently murky matters of degree, with the potential to cast a cloud of uncertainty over a very large swath of federal legislation. For these reasons, the judicial capacity model predicts that the Court will feel strongly compelled to defer to federal spending legislation.

The Pattern of Supreme Court Decisions

The spending power has its roots in Article I, Section 8, clause 1, which grants Congress the "Power to lay and collect Taxes, Duties, Imposts and Excises, to pay the Debts and provide for the common Defence and general Welfare of the United States." Although this text does not expressly authorize Congress to spend the funds raised through the taxes it imposes, that power has from the beginning been understood as implicit in the clause. Also from the beginning, the federal spending power has been the subject of constitutional controversy. This controversy, like so many others in the early republic, was best crystallized in a dispute between Alexander Hamilton and James Madison. The nub of the issue was whether the spending power was an independent grant of constitutional authority or whether it was limited to the purposes specified by the other enumerated powers granted to Congress by Article I, Section 8. Predictably, Hamilton took the former position and James Madison the latter one.[5]

The Supreme Court first squarely addressed this controversy in 1936 in the case of *United States v. Butler*. Decided at the height of the Court's resistance to the New Deal, *Butler* involved a challenge to the provisions of the Agricultural Adjustment Act of 1933, which taxed farmers who exceeded federally imposed crop quotas for the purpose of subsidizing those who allowed their land to lie fallow. *Butler* ultimately struck down these provisions on the ground that they represented not an ordinary federal subsidy but an attempt to circumvent the limits on Congress's commerce power established in other Supreme Court decisions of the era. Nevertheless, the Court firmly sided with Hamilton, recognizing the spending power as an independent source of congressional authority to promote the general welfare in ways beyond the specific purposes enumerated in Congress's other Article I powers. Prior to *NFIB*, *Butler* was the only time the Supreme Court ever invalidated an exercise of the congressional spending power, and it is best understood as an anomaly required to protect the Court's narrow commerce-power decisions of the early 1930s.[6]

Two 1937 decisions reaffirmed the Court's commitment to the broad Hamiltonian view, while effectively overruling *Butler*'s anti-circumvention reading of the spending power. Together, *Helvering v. Davis* and *Steward Machine Co. v. Davis* upheld the Social Security Act of 1935, thus inaugurating nearly eight decades of uninterrupted judicial deference to Congress's spending power. During this period, the principal spending-power issue the Court faced was Congress's ability to impose conditions on grants to state governments (as opposed to individual citizens) for purposes of encouraging—or forcing—states to adopt federally favored policies. The reason for this shift was simple. Following the Court's post–New Deal retreat from serious scrutiny of the federal commerce power, there was little reason for Congress to resort to the spending power as a mechanism for circumventing limits on its commerce-power authority to regulate individual citizens.[7]

The Court's most important spending-power decision of this era was *South Dakota v. Dole*, decided in 1987. *Dole* rejected a challenge to the National Minimum Drinking Age Act of 1984, which withheld 5 percent of federal highway funds from states that did not adopt a legal drinking age of at least twenty-one. The Court emphasized that federal spending legislation must satisfy five requirements, only three of which are necessary to elaborate here. First, such legislation must promote the general welfare. Second, the conditions imposed on federal grants must be reasonably related to the purpose of the federal program of which those funds are a part. This is often referred to in the academic literature as the "germaneness requirement." Third, "the financial inducement offered by Congress" must not be "so coercive as to pass the point at which 'pressure turns into compulsion.'" I shall refer to this as the "anti-coercion principle." In theory, any one of these three requirements might have served as a meaningful constitutional limit on the federal spending power. But the consensus view of commentators, supported by twenty-five years of decisions following *Dole,* was that the decision represented a blank check to Congress.[8]

This changed, or appeared to, with the Court's recent decision that the Affordable Care Act's Medicaid expansion was unconstitutionally coercive of state governments that wished not to participate. Both the *NFIB* decision and the Affordable Care Act are quite complex. But to understand the spending-power aspect of *NFIB,* it is necessary only to appreciate one key point: the Act requires states to participate in a substantial expansion of Medicaid, the principal federal program providing health care to the poor, in order to remain eligible to receive any federal Medicaid funds. "A State that opts out of the Affordable Care Act's expansion in health care coverage thus stands to lose not merely 'a relatively small percentage' of its existing Medicaid funding, but *all* of it."[9]

In holding this portion of the Act unconstitutional, Chief Justice Roberts's controlling opinion, joined by Justices Breyer and Kagan, relied on three principal factors: (1) the dramatic size of the Act's Medicaid expansion, almost 40 percent of the preexisting federal Medicaid budget; (2) states' long-term reliance on federal funds they had been receiving under the preexisting Medicaid program; and (3) the enormous size of the grants the Act threatened to withdraw from nonparticipating states. The basic logic of the decision is that Congress cannot use the leverage afforded by its conditional spending power to coerce states into actions that Congress could not command them to take directly.[10]

The four joint dissenters, whose votes were necessary to make a majority, advocated a simpler and apparently broader test: Do the states have any practical option to refuse compliance with the challenged condition on their eligibility to receive federal funds? If not, the joint dissenters would hold the condition unconstitutionally coercive.[11]

Standing alone, both of these tests would qualify as fairly vague and not especially deferential standards. But the tests do not stand alone. Both the Roberts opinion and the joint dissent are careful to signal that the standards they embrace will almost never be violated. They convey this message in several ways. First, both opinions emphasize Medicaid's uniqueness. In particular, they emphasize the enormous size of federal Medicaid grants in comparison to the grants provided under any other federal program. Second, both opinions sign on to precedents embracing a broad conditional spending power. The Roberts opinion goes so far as to endorse use of the spending power to "encourage a State to regulate in a particular way, and influence a State's policy choices" in ways Congress could not require directly. Third, despite the breadth of its coercion analysis, the joint dissent appears to recognize the gravity of the issue and endorses an extremely deferential standard of review under the anticoercion principle. Only when coercion is "unmistakably clear" would the dissenters invalidate conditional spending legislation. Fourth, Chief Justice Roberts's opinion strongly implies that the conditions embodied in Medicaid itself, despite its enormous size and the states' apparent inability to refuse participation, are perfectly constitutional. If this is the case, it is difficult to imagine any federal spending legislation besides the Affordable Care Act that would be unconstitutional under Roberts's controlling approach.[12]

The Doctrinal Puzzle

Under both legalist and attitudinal models of judicial decision-making, the Supreme Court's strong deference to congressional spending legislation is puzzling. As noted above, federal spending is a hugely consequential mechanism for the exertion of federal power, one that eclipses nearly every other federal power in scope and significance, with the sole exception of the commerce power. For conservative justices committed to constitutional limits on federal power, an unchecked federal spending power ought to be a standing affront. From a cruder political standpoint, the spending power is the principal foundation for the modern social welfare state, a principal target of American conservatism since at least the New Deal. If

Supreme Court justices vote like legislators, as the attitudinal model posits, strict constitutional limits on the spending power ought to be a highly attractive means for judicial conservatives to invalidate redistributive legislation they oppose on policy grounds. Even liberal justices, who tend to strongly support the welfare state, ought to be tempted to opportunistically invalidate spending legislation that pressures states, for example, to cooperate with federal drug enforcement or to adopt rigid standardized testing in public schools. Yet in the past eighty years the Court has only once invalidated federal spending legislation. If Supreme Court decisions are driven primarily by ideology, as the attitudinal model contends, this restraint is difficult to understand.[13]

Such restraint is also difficult to understand if the justices are motivated by legal factors. Of course, it is possible to argue that the Constitution does not place any limits on federal spending authority. But that has never been the Supreme Court's position. With their insistence that federal spending (a) promote the general welfare, (b) be reasonably related to conditions on eligibility for federal funds, and (c) not be used to force states to comply with federal mandates, decisions like *Dole* and even *Steward Machine Co.* offer plenty of doctrinal ammunition for justices motivated to impose meaningful limits on the federal spending power. If the Court is willing to recognize these limits in theory, why does it refuse to enforce them in practice?[14]

It is possible, of course, to argue that the spending power presents difficult line-drawing problems: distinguishing the general welfare from the particular; defining how close a connection is required between federal spending and the conditions on its use; locating the point at which "persuasion turns into compulsion." These are all tricky issues. But the Court is willing to draw constitutional lines in other contexts. For example, the Court has repeatedly fashioned categorical rules to limit the federal commerce power, and it has incorporated vague standards of reasonableness into various strands of Fourth Amendment doctrine. With so many ideological temptations to impose limits on federal spending, it is genuinely puzzling why the Court would not take one of these approaches in the context of the spending power.[15]

The strategic model is somewhat more helpful, but only somewhat. Fear of political reprisal might explain why the Supreme Court has not adopted the extreme position, advocated by at least one libertarian scholar, of banning all federal aid to states. For most of the twentieth and early twenty-first centuries, the Court could plausibly have assumed, or at least feared, that such an all-out assault on cooperative federalism would provoke a serious backlash of some sort. But this does not explain why the Court's liberals and conservatives have both refrained from opportunistically invalidating the occasional spending-power statute. Nor does it explain why the Court's conservatives have never been seriously tempted to impose more modest but still meaningful across-the-board limits. As noted in Chapter 5, the failure of Congress to mount a successful retaliation to any of the Court's deeply unpopular post–New Deal decisions suggests that the Court's conservatives could have taken this step without serious risk. The strategic model cannot explain their failure to do so.[16]

The Judicial Capacity Model Applied

The judicial capacity model helps to explain the Court's consistent refusal to vigorously limit the federal spending power. The spending power, like the commerce power, is both a high-stakes and a high-volume domain. It underwrites an enormous quantity of legislation, and all of that legislation is federal—meaning that the Supreme Court will feel compelled to grant review virtually any time a lower court invalidates a spending-power statute. As of 2006, there were 814 different federal programs distributing funds to the states, subject to many thousands of conditions on the use of and eligibility for the receipt of federal funds. In 2010 the federal government distributed $608 billion to state and local governments, making federal aid to the states the third-largest budget item after Social Security and defense spending. Most federal expenditures are authorized under the Spending Clause, rather than an enumerated power, including such political and historically significant legislation as Social Security itself, the American Recovery and Reinvestment Act of 2009, the No Child Left Behind Act of 2001, and the Personal Responsibility and Work Opportunity Reconciliation Act of 1996.[17]

Of course, it is not only the quantity of threatened legislation that determines the volume of potential litigation. It is also the magnitude of the benefits that such invalidation would generate for prospective plaintiffs and the number of prospective plaintiffs either collectively or individually capable of mustering the resources to litigate. Here the main prospective plaintiffs are state and local governments, for whom hundreds of billions of dollars and freedom from onerous federal conditions are at stake. If this were not enough, the interests of private businesses burdened by federal regulations will often align with those of states, increasing the pool of resources available to challenge any federal program that stands a plausible chance of being invalidated as unconstitutional. For any given program, some individual state or states will almost always object to some of the conditions Congress places on its disbursement of funds. For all of these reasons, the spending power qualifies as a high-volume and high-stakes domain. The judicial capacity model therefore predicts that the Court will feel strong pressure to interpret that power broadly, employ hard-edged categorical rules, or both.[18]

This, in fact, is what we see when we examine the Court's historical treatment of the Spending Clause. Including the Court's partial invalidation of the Medicaid expansion in *NFIB,* the Court has only twice in its history struck down federal spending legislation as unconstitutional. Apart from these decisions, the Court has formulated its Spending Clause doctrine in terms approaching a rule of categorical deference. To be sure, the Court never said explicitly that the spending power was without judicially enforceable limits. But what matters for judicial capacity purposes is the expectations of litigants. As the academic commentary makes clear, the operative pre-*NFIB* understanding was that the spending power was a blank check. This was partly the product of the virtually unanimous lower-court rejection of spending power challenges and partly the product of the Court's refusal to reverse any of these decisions. Even *NFIB* is most plausibly read to invalidate only a single, outlying federal statute. This is just the sort of strong deference that the judicial capacity model predicts in capacity-constrained domains.[19]

This history is broadly similar to the modern history of the commerce power recounted in Chapter 5. Even in capacity-constrained domains, that history suggests that a motivated Supreme Court has room to impose and sustain limits on federal power, *so long as those limits clearly insulate the vast majority of federal legislation from constitutional attack.*

One might expect the Court to have adopted a similar course in the context of the spending power. However, none of the potential limits on that power that have been suggested by courts and commentators meets the italicized criterion. Most are vague and standard-like. If applied rigorously, they would call into question a large and uncertain fraction of spending-power legislation. The others are so stringent that, despite their categorical nature, they would threaten to overwhelm the Court with challenges to a very broad array of federal legislation.

For illustrative purposes, I will discuss four such limits. The first is the requirement that federal spending and conditions attached to it promote "the general welfare." The Court has paid lip service to this requirement throughout the modern era, but has all along made clear that it has no intention of questioning Congress's judgments on the subject. Some commentators have urged that the Court put more teeth into the general welfare requirement. But as the Court has repeatedly recognized, general welfare is such a malleable concept that any attempt to enforce it seems destined to cast a pall of uncertainty over a very large fraction of federal spending legislation. With uncertainty comes litigation.[20]

A slightly more promising limitation on the spending power is the germaneness requirement recognized in *Dole*. As the *Dole* Court formulated this requirement, it mandates that the conditions imposed on federal grants to state governments be reasonably related to the broader purpose those grants are intended to serve. As the Court has applied it, however, this requirement has simply amounted to another form of rational-basis review. It is easy to see why. Any attempt by the Court to make rigorous judgments of degree about the level of connection between particular conditions and particular federal purposes is likely to call into question a great deal of federal spending legislation.[21]

Justice Sandra Day O'Connor's dissent in *Dole* proposed an apparently more rule-like version of the germaneness test, which has been further developed by Lynn Baker. Their test would permit Congress to impose conditions only on the way that federal funds are spent, not as a means of "encouraging" unrelated policy choices. While apparently clear-cut and categorical in principle, this standard seems likely to be subject to substantial uncertainty and manipulation in practice. Quite apart from any uncertainty, it would also threaten a large fraction of federal spending legislation, much of which imposes conditions that go beyond "designating authorized uses or specifying accounting methods." In both of these respects, Justice O'Connor's and Baker's proposals are a far cry from *Lopez, Morrison,* and *NFIB* with their categorical insulation of all economic regulation from serious Commerce Clause scrutiny.[22]

A third potential limit on the spending power is the anti-coercion principle mentioned in *Dole* and applied to invalidate the Medicaid expansion in *NFIB*. While the Court can get away with applying a tightly circumscribed version of this principle in a single case, a test requiring the Court to distinguish between financial encouragement and coercion in any substantial fraction of federal spending programs would plunge a great deal of legislation into uncertainty and invite a correspondingly large volume of litigation.[23]

In this respect, *NFIB* illustrates an important point about the judicial capacity model. As explained in Chapter 3, that model does not, and could not, purport to predict the outcomes in every individual case. Rather, it claims to predict general patterns in the Supreme Court's constitutional decision making. In capacity-constrained domains, the limits of judicial capacity create strong pressure on the Court to defer to the political process, or adopt hard-edged categorical rules, or both. But the Court clearly retains some room in individual cases to depart from these approaches.

The reason the Supreme Court retains this flexibility is that one decision does not, on its own, produce an avalanche of litigation. It takes time for the constitutional litigation bar and other stakeholders to digest and understand a ruling. Indeed, the full import of a ruling remains uncertain until it is fleshed out in subsequent decisions of the lower courts and eventually the Supreme Court. Unless and until the Court makes clear in future cases that it is willing to apply *NFIB*'s anti-coercion principle rigorously, the litigation resulting from that decision is likely to remain within manageable bounds. Until that time, a constitutional litigation bar that is familiar with—has in some sense internalized—the Court's unwillingness to invite an avalanche of litigation is unlikely to mobilize to create one.

Finally, at least one academic commentator, Ilya Somin, has advocated for categorically banning federal subsidies to state governments. From the standpoint of judicial capacity, this rule does have the benefit of clarity.

But even Somin himself recognizes it as impracticable. He attributes this impracticability to strong political support for Spending Clause legislation and hopes that this obstacle may be overcome in the long run. But even if the Court possessed the political will to impose such a rule, it would threaten such a large mass of federal legislation as to almost certainly bury the Court under an avalanche of litigation. This is true despite the categorical character of Somin's proposed rule. Any rule that threatens such a massive quantity of popular legislation is certain to provoke substantial resistance, and thus litigation, no matter how clear its application to individual cases.[24]

The point of reciting all these judicial capacity problems is to demonstrate the difficulty of imposing a narrow categorical limit on the federal spending power analogous to the limits imposed on the commerce power in *Lopez, Morrison,* and *NFIB.* This difficulty helps to explain the Court's historically deferential approach to the spending power. It also makes sense of the Court's failure to impose any meaningful limits on the spending power between *U.S. v. Butler* and *NFIB,* despite the justices' strong legal and ideological motivations—and strategic flexibility—for doing so.

In sum, the judicial capacity model explains features of the Supreme Court's spending-power decisions that no other model can. Although the Court has both legal and ideological motives to limit the spending power, the limits of judicial capacity prevent it from doing so except in the form of a clear categorical rule that is simply unavailable in this context. The Court's only remaining option is to adopt an approach of nearly wholesale deference. In this way, the judicial capacity model illuminates a crucially important and generally understudied area of constitutional law. In turn, the pattern of the Court's spending-power decisions provides powerful evidence in favor of the judicial capacity model.

Separation of Powers

The constitutional law of separation of powers is vast and multifaceted, but the most important modern issues in this area nearly all involve presidential power and the administrative state. Thus, while this Section is titled "Separation of Powers," it might as easily be called "Executive Power." Spanning two important constitutional domains, the case studies explored in this section demonstrate the power of the judicial capacity model to illuminate the constitutional law of separation of powers, and vice versa.

The executive branch of the United States is colossal. Including the armed services, it employs over four million persons—more than 1 percent of the U.S. population. Excluding the armed services, its full-time permanent employees number roughly two million, spanning hundreds of agencies, boards, and commissions. Collectively, this bureaucracy generates thousands of new regulations annually and is responsible for administering tens, if not hundreds, of thousands more. It also adjudicates over a million cases, of bewildering variety, and initiates uncountable thousands of enforcement actions. Including military outlays, the projected budget of the executive branch for fiscal year 2018 is nearly $4.1 trillion. Excluding military outlays, it is roughly $3.5 trillion. This figure exceeds the gross domestic product of all but two other countries in the world.[1]

The federal judiciary, by contrast, is Lilliputian. Including the Federal Judicial Center and the Administrative Office of the United States Courts, it totals barely 33,000 employees. Its projected budget for fiscal year 2018 is just $8 billion—less than the gross domestic product of Sioux City, Iowa. Increasingly, scholars have recognized that such a tiny institution could never hope to seriously restrain one as large as the executive branch. Indeed, it is now something of a commonplace that most constitutional law governing executive power is made outside the courts. Nevertheless, from the nondelegation doctrine to the removal power to presidential war powers, calls for more stringent judicial review continue unabated.[2]

Recent Supreme Court decisions have kindled hope—and dismay—that these calls may fall on increasingly receptive ears. Both supporters and opponents, however, have largely ignored the antecedent question of whether the Court is actually capable of restraining executive power—or congressional interference with it—in the ways advocated for. Even scholars more sensitive to institutional limits have overlooked a crucial question: How does the judiciary's limited capacity influence the substance and doctrinal form of judge-made law governing executive power? The judicial capacity model fills these gaps in the literature. In turn, the constitutional law of separation of powers provides further evidence supporting the judicial capacity model.[3]

CHAPTER SEVEN

The Nondelegation Doctrine

The widespread delegation of rule-making power to administrative agencies is a central pillar of the modern administrative state. Binding administrative regulations adopted pursuant to such delegations far outnumber laws passed through the ordinary legislative process. It is virtually impossible to imagine today's federal government without them. Yet the delegation of such rule-making authority has always rested on uncertain constitutional foundations. For nearly two centuries, the Supreme Court has proclaimed that the Constitution limits Congress's ability to delegate its legislative power to the executive branch. Over that same period, and especially since the New Deal, Congress has delegated enormous power to federal agencies in the course of erecting the modern regulatory state. Legal scholars have long urged the Court to intervene and limit this unbridled delegation. The Court has generally refused this invitation, having invoked the "nondelegation doctrine" to invalidate federal legislation just twice in its history. As Cass Sunstein memorably put it, that doctrine has had one good year and more than two hundred bad ones.[1]

This restraint has been crucial to the development of the federal bureaucracy, but none of the leading models of Supreme Court decision-making can readily explain it. Since the New Deal, the Court has had both legal and ideological reasons to put meaningful teeth in the nondelegation doctrine and few strategic reasons not to impose at least some limits. The judicial capacity model, by contrast, can explain the Court's restrained approach. In a nutshell, the nondelegation doctrine is peculiarly unsuited to clear categorical rules, and the uncertainty created by a vague standard would invite an avalanche of litigation. Unable to enforce the nondelegation doctrine without overwhelming its capacity, the Court has felt strongly compelled to defer to the political process.

The Pattern of Supreme Court Decisions

The nondelegation doctrine has its roots in Article I, Section 1 of the Constitution, which vests "all legislative powers" in Congress. By vesting Congress with *all* legislative power, the Constitution arguably bars Congress from delegating its legislative power to the executive branch. Article II, however, vests "*the* executive power" in the President, and executing the laws inevitably involves some discretion. In a world of limited resources, enforcement priorities must be set and communicated to thousands of ground-level officials, spread over an enormous geographic territory. The decisions of those officials, in turn, must be reviewed and, in some cases, reversed to ensure equitable and coherent enforcement of the law. Emerging issues must be identified, evaluated, and triaged; interagency conflicts must be negotiated; and so on. Moreover, the exercise of such discretion on a large scale virtually necessitates the establishment of general rules to govern the functions of subordinate officials and to provide notice to regulated parties.[2]

At what point does such rule-making cross the line from executive to legislative power? The answer is hazy at best. The core purpose of the nondelegation doctrine, however, is to preserve the distinction between legislative power, vested in Congress, and executive power, vested in the President.[3]

The Supreme Court has recognized the nondelegation doctrine as a constitutional principle since at least the late nineteenth century, if not earlier. In its early decisions, the Court broadly declared that Congress may not delegate legislative power, full-stop. For example, in *Field v. Clark,* the Court announced: "That Congress cannot delegate legislative power to the President is a principle universally recognized as vital to the integrity and maintenance of the system of government ordained by the Constitution." Despite this bold talk, the Court upheld every congressional delegation it encountered. For instance, the Court allowed Congress to lay out general guidelines, while delegating the responsibility to "fill up the details."[4]

The Court attempted to synthesize its nondelegation precedent in *J.W. Hampton, Jr. & Co. v. United States.* This famous case involved a challenge to the Tariff Act of 1922, which delegated to the President the power to adjust tariffs if rates failed to "equalize . . . differences in costs of production." In upholding the Act, the Court announced what is now the litmus test for acceptable congressional delegation: Congress may delegate legislative authority, as long as it provides an "intelligible principle" to guide the exercise of the delegated authority. At least ostensibly, the requirement of an intelligible principle distinguishes legislation from execution of the law. The former involves the exercise of unguided rule-making authority, the latter the carrying into effect of an intelligible principle.[5]

As already noted, the Supreme Court has only twice in its history invoked the nondelegation doctrine to strike down legislation. Both instances occurred in 1935 at the height of the Court's resistance to the New Deal, and both involved the same law. First, in *Panama Refining Co. v. Ryan,* the Court invalidated a provision in the National Industrial Recovery Act (NIRA), which authorized the President to prohibit the shipment of oil produced in excess of quotas. Again, in *A.L.A. Schechter Poultry Corp. v. United States,* the Court struck down another provision in the NIRA, which empowered the President to approve "codes of fair competition" for trades and industries. Since almost before the ink was dry, these decisions have been dismissed as politically motivated attempts to undermine the New Deal. While never formally overruled, they have had little effect on subsequent doctrine.[6]

Indeed, since 1936 the Court has upheld every congressional delegation it has reviewed. Interestingly, the Court has continued to trot out the nondelegation doctrine and insist that Congress provide an intelligible principle to guide the execution of delegated authority. But in practice, Congress delegates vast amounts of power to agencies through statutes written in expansive language. For instance, the Court has upheld delegations guided by such nebulous standards as "public convenience, interest, or necessity," "fair and equitable" prices, "just and reasonable" rates, and "excessive" profits. In effect, the Court has transformed the intelligible-principle requirement into a rule of categorical deference— so long as Congress offers *some* guidance, however minimal, the Court will uphold the delegation. As a result, conventional wisdom holds that the nondelegation doctrine is dead, or at least unenforceable.[7]

The Doctrinal Puzzle

Under both legalist and attitudinal models of judicial decision-making, the Supreme Court's abject deference to Congress's delegations of legislative power is puzzling. Applied vigorously, the nondelegation doctrine would be a powerful tool for limiting the federal regulatory state. This potential should make the doctrine an attractive tool for conservative justices, eager to limit federal power and promote economic laissez-faire. Even for liberal justices, who tend to be broadly supportive of the regulatory state, the temptation to opportunistically invalidate conservative regulations should arise with some frequency. Indeed, scholars have repeatedly called on the Court to exhume the nondelegation doctrine for various reasons, and justices have occasionally seemed inclined to do so. Yet for eighty years the Court has stayed its hand and refused to enforce the nondelegation doctrine. If Supreme Court decisions are driven primarily by ideology, as the attitudinal model contends, this restraint is difficult to understand.[8]

It is also difficult to understand if the justices are motivated by legal factors. Of course, it is possible to argue that the Constitution does not, in fact, bar congressional delegation of legislative authority. That is decidedly a minority position. But whatever its merits, denying the validity of the nondelegation doctrine does not explain the Court's historical treatment of the doctrine. Crucially, the Court continues to accept the nondelegation doctrine as a constitutional principle and continues to reiterate the intelligible principle test, albeit in a very deferential form. In fact, the Supreme Court generally upholds congressional delegations in overwhelming fashion. Though observers may be willing to inter the nondelegation doctrine, the Court evidently is not. Given that

the Court is willing to recognize the doctrine, why does the Court refuse to enforce it?[9]

It is possible to argue that the nondelegation doctrine presents a difficult line-drawing problem—distinguishing legislative power from executive power. Indeed, it does. But the Court is willing to draw constitutional lines in other contexts. For example, the Court has repeatedly
fashioned categorical rules to limit the federal commerce power and has
incorporated vague standards of reasonableness into various strands of
4th Amendment doctrine. With so many ideological temptations to invalidate disfavored regulations or to roll back the regulatory state more
generally, it is genuinely puzzling why the Court would not take one of
these approaches in the context of the nondelegation doctrine.[10]

The strategic model fares somewhat better. Fear of political reprisal
might explain why the Supreme Court has not adopted the absolutist nondelegation doctrine of libertarians' dreams. For most of the twentieth
and early twenty-first centuries, the Court could plausibly have assumed,
or at least feared, that an all-out assault on the modern regulatory state
would provoke a serious backlash of some sort. But this does not explain
why the Court's liberals and conservatives have both refrained from deploying the nondelegation doctrine opportunistically to invalidate the
occasional disfavored statute. Nor does it explain why the Court's conservatives have never been seriously tempted to embrace a modest but still
meaningful version of the nondelegation doctrine with the power to curtail, but not overthrow, the federal bureaucracy. As noted in previous
chapters, the inability or unwillingness of Congress to retaliate against
the Court's many deeply unpopular post–New Deal decisions suggests
that the Court's conservatives could have taken this step without serious
risk. The strategic model cannot explain their failure to do so.[11]

The Judicial Capacity Model Applied

If the Supreme Court has both the opportunity and motivation to vigorously enforce the nondelegation doctrine, why has it consistently refused
to do so? The judicial capacity model helps to explain the Court's
restraint.

The nondelegation doctrine is both a high-volume and a high-stakes domain. Congressional delegation of power underpins the entire federal regulatory state. Today, the federal bureaucracy encompasses hundreds of agencies, which employ millions of officials, who execute innumerable tasks. This system is supported by legions of federal statutes, not to mention the fifty-volume Code of Federal Regulations. If the Court decided to vigorously enforce the nondelegation doctrine, it would call into question the entire regulatory state and its attendant laws and regulations. Plenty of well-financed plaintiffs, ranging from the oil and gas industry to manufacturers' associations to pharmaceutical companies to the Chamber of Commerce, would have ample incentive to bring legal challenges. The resulting volume of litigation would be enormous. On top of this, any time a lower court strikes down a congressional delegation of authority, it always invalidates a federal law, meaning that the Court feels strongly compelled to grant review. Thus, a robust reading of the nondelegation doctrine would trigger an avalanche of litigation, almost all of which the Court would feel compelled to review.[12]

For these reasons, the judicial capacity model predicts that judicial capacity will significantly constrain how the Supreme Court interprets the nondelegation doctrine. In particular, the model predicts that the Court will feel strong pressure to employ hard-edged categorical rules, defer to the political process, or both. The nondelegation doctrine, however, is peculiarly unsuited to bright-line rules. Simply put, it is exceedingly difficult to draw a clear distinction between legislative power and executive power. In very broad terms, legislative power involves rule-making, whereas executive power involves implementation and enforcement of rules made elsewhere. But that distinction quickly breaks down. No rule is entirely precise, and thus some judgments must be left to those executing the rule. As a consequence, the implementation and enforcement of rules often take the form of promulgating substantive rules, which is to say, rule-making. In Justice Scalia's words, "a certain degree of discretion, and thus of lawmaking, inheres in most executive or judicial action." The upshot is that the Court cannot enforce the nondelegation doctrine through a hard-edged distinction between legislative and executive power. No such distinction exists.[13]

Unable to cleanly distinguish legislative power from executive power, the Court might decide to instead formulate the nondelegation doctrine in terms of a standard. To do so, however, the Court would need to say how much rule-making authority is too much for an agency to exercise. Such an unquantifiable standard would cast a pall of uncertainty over all congressional delegations. With uncertainty comes litigation. Apart from any uncertainty, such a vague standard would also threaten a large fraction of federal statutes, many of which delegate enormous power to agencies in the broadest possible terms. The Court simply could not handle the volume of litigation it would invite (and feel compelled to review) by rigorously enforcing an amorphous nondelegation doctrine. Viewed through the lens of judicial capacity, it is therefore no surprise that the Court has not attempted to police the extent of congressional delegation of power to the executive branch.[14]

Constrained by capacity and unable to fashion hard-edged categorical rules, the Court has just one available avenue to avoid overwhelming its limited capacity: defer to congressional delegations and interpret the nondelegation doctrine narrowly. That is, in fact, precisely what we see when we examine the Court's historical treatment of the nondelegation doctrine. Apart from two decisions in 1935, the Court has never invalidated legislation on nondelegation grounds. In the process, the Court has adopted a broadly deferential posture toward congressional delegation. The difficulty of imposing narrow categorical limits on congressional delegations explains the Court's historically deferential approach to delegations the Court might otherwise be tempted to strike down.[15]

Clinton v. City of New York provides an interesting contrast. In that case, the Supreme Court categorically prohibited the line-item veto. Formally, *Clinton* was litigated under the Presentment Clause. But for all of its discussion of Article I, Section 7, the Supreme Court seemed most acutely concerned with nondelegation principles. By authorizing the President to cancel individual appropriations on his own authority, the Line-Item Veto Act functioned as a delegation of legislative power to the President to cancel individual appropriations on his own authority.[16]

In some sense, *Clinton* was an odd place for the Court to raise nondelegation concerns. As the *Clinton* dissenters pointed out, many delegations of power convey at least as much policy-making authority as the line-item veto. But unlike other delegation cases, *Clinton* afforded the Supreme Court an opportunity to invalidate a congressional delegation of power by invoking a hard-edged categorical rule: Congress cannot delegate the power to amend duly enacted statutes. This rule clearly invalidated just one law, leaving all other congressional delegations free from constitutional doubt. Given a rare chance to enforce the nondelegation doctrine without triggering an avalanche of litigation, the Court took it.[17]

Of course, other factors besides judicial capacity may contribute to the Court's broad deference to congressional delegations of power. At any individual point in time, a majority of justices might be ideologically opposed to the nondelegation doctrine or doubt the doctrine's legal foundations or some combination of the two. This has probably happened in individual cases and may well happen again. But for the reasons elaborated above, neither ideology nor legalist doubts about the nondelegation doctrines constitutional foundations can readily explain the consistent pattern of the Court's decisions since 1935.

The same goes for strategic considerations. As elaborated above, a self-protective reluctance to challenge Congress might explain the Supreme Court's refusal to adopt a radical version of the nondelegation doctrine that would threaten the entire administrative state, but this sort of strategic calculation cannot readily explain the Court's refusal to embrace a moderate version of the doctrine. Moreover, as with the commerce and spending powers, whatever strategic constraints the Court faces in this context might be at least partially traceable to the limits of judicial capacity. One powerful reason to avoid mounting a sustained challenge to the political branches is the large volume of litigation such challenges inevitably produce. In this sense, the Court's strategic aversion to embracing a robust nondelegation might be *endogenous* to the limits of judicial capacity. If that is the case, the judicial capacity model not only helps to explain the Court's behavior; it also enriches our understanding of the strategic constraints on that behavior that lie at the heart of the strategic model.[18]

Finally, some justices may sincerely doubt the Supreme Court's competence to distinguish permissible from impermissible delegations. But this legalist motive, too, may come back to judicial capacity. If the judicial capacity model is correct, it is the constraints of judicial capacity that force the Court to eschew more subtle and sensitive standards in favor of crude and clumsy categorical rules. In other words, the constraints of judicial capacity are themselves an important cause of the Court's limited competence in capacity-constrained domains. This is another case of endogeneity. I shall have more to say on both of these points in Part III.

In sum, the judicial capacity model explains the Supreme Court's categorically deferential approach to congressional delegations of power better than any competing model of Supreme Court decision-making. The pattern of the Court's decisions is fully consistent with the judicial capacity model's predictions. And those predictions explain many features of the Court's decisions that no other model is capable of explaining. Moreover, even in cases where the predictions of the judicial capacity model overlap with the predictions of other models, it helps to identify new possibilities that enrich our understanding of Supreme Court decision-making. In all of these ways, the judicial capacity model improves our understanding of the nondelegation doctrine, which in turn provides strong evidence in its favor.

CHAPTER EIGHT

Presidential Administration

"**P**residential administration" is an umbrella term for the President's constitutional power to set priorities and shape the policy outcomes of the federal administrative process. In a world dominated by administrative governance, there are few more important powers in the presidential toolkit—and few more controversial. Virtually every aspect of federal policy, from environmental regulation to health care to immigration enforcement, is carried out through the machinery of administrative agencies. Especially in the modern era of frequent legislative gridlock, the President's ability to control and direct this cumbersome machinery is crucial to his ability to implement any kind of policy agenda.[1]

Many current and past justices on the Supreme Court subscribe, or have subscribed, to a unitary executive theory of presidential administration. On this view, Article II vests the President with exclusive authority over discretionary decision-making in the executive branch. In reality, Congress exerts enormous influence over the federal bureaucracy. Yet the Court has never made any serious attempt to curb this congressional interference. When the Court has invoked the unitary executive theory, it has done so only to place modest limits on a single, relatively unimportant mechanism of congressional control—good-cause restrictions on the removal of executive officers.[2]

The Court's nearly wholesale deference to congressional interference with presidential administration is puzzling for several reasons. First, a number of (mostly) conservative justices are, or have been, ideologically committed to some version of the unitary executive theory. Second, requiring strong presidential control over the bureaucracy would make Congress less enthusiastic about delegating power, which in turn would slow the growth of the administrative state. This should be appealing to conservative justices. Third, even liberal justices should have opportunistic reason to strike down interference with presidential control during Democratic administrations, especially when Republicans control Congress. Finally, the legal rationale for striking down removal restrictions is fully applicable to other forms of congressional interference; they all impede the President's executive power under the Vesting and Take Care Clauses.[3]

None of the leading models of Supreme Court decision-making can explain these features of the Court's decisions, but the judicial capacity model can. In a nutshell, any serious effort to enforce the unitary executive theory would call into question a vast amount of federal legislation and bury the Court in litigation it would feel strongly compelled to review. The Court therefore only enforces unitary executive principles when it can do so in the form of relatively narrow categorical rules, which clearly insulate most congressional action from constitutional challenge and encourage settlement as to those actions they invalidate.

The Pattern of Supreme Court Decisions

In theory, the nondelegation doctrine governs the extent to which Congress can surrender its power to the executive branch. But after surrendering power, Congress often seeks to retain some measure of control over its exercise. At least nominally, many conservative judges and academics have long insisted that such congressional control is almost always unconstitutional. On this view, if power can be exercised by the President or a federal agency, it must be executive, rather than legislative power, and Article II vests *all* executive power in the President. Article II also imposes on the President—and no one else—a duty to "take care that the laws shall be faithfully executed." Congressional action that impairs the

President's ability to carry out this function or transfers it to others must therefore be unconstitutional. This is known as "the unitary executive theory," and it lies at the heart of some of the most notable executive power disputes in American history.[4]

Despite the commitment of many justices to some version of this theory, the Court has never made any serious attempt to limit pervasive congressional interference with presidential administration. This interference takes myriad forms. The creation of independent agencies, whose top officials are insulated against removal by the President, is an obvious example that receives much attention. But Congress wields many other tools to influence and control federal agencies. Congress can alter an agency's structure or jurisdiction, cut agency personnel, require agencies to give notice before taking action, mandate consultation with other agencies, require congressional review of proposed rules, order performance reviews, threaten special hearings, and cut or impose conditions on funding. In addition, Congress can prod agencies through more informal channels via language in committee reports, instructions during committee hearings, correspondence from congresspersons to committee heads, and oversight hearings. Last and perhaps most significant, the Administrative Procedure Act itself functions as a powerful and sweeping restraint on the President's power to control administrative decision-making. So potent are these tools in combination that the leading political science view of executive-legislative relations is known as the "congressional dominance thesis."[5]

Galled by this widespread congressional interference, unitary executive theorists have long advocated judicial intervention. The Court, however, has refused to meaningfully scrutinize the overwhelming majority of ways in which Congress interferes with presidential administration. The only exception is a small handful of decisions invoking unitary executive principles to limit congressional restrictions on the removal of high-level executive officers. Notably, the text of the Constitution says nothing expressly about the President's power to remove such officials, and the Framers did not discuss this power at the Constitutional Convention. Nevertheless, the Court has inferred from general language in Article II's Vesting and Take Care Clauses that the President must have some power to remove executive officials. On the other hand, while recognizing the President's removal authority, the Court has adopted a broadly deferential stance toward congressional interference with that authority. On the rare occasions when the Court has intervened, it has done so in the form of narrow, categorical rules.[6]

The Supreme Court took its first stab at interpreting the President's removal power in 1926, when it decided *Myers v. United States*. *Myers* involved a challenge to a statute that required the President to secure the advice and consent of the Senate before removing a postmaster first-class. Chief Justice (and former President) Taft penned the lengthy majority opinion that chronicled the judicial, political, and scholarly history of the removal power. Ultimately, *Myers* struck down the restriction on removal of the postmaster. In so doing, *Myers* seemed to grant the President absolute authority to remove the officials he appointed.[7]

The Court quickly backed away from *Myers*. Just nine years later the Court reversed direction in *Humphrey's Executor v. United States*. Decided at the height of the New Deal, *Humphrey's Executor* arose when President Franklin Roosevelt removed the Commissioner of the Federal Trade Commission for political reasons. Congress had provided that the Commissioner was removable only for "inefficiency, neglect of duty, or malfeasance in office." *Myers*'s broad holding appeared to invalidate this removal restriction. Nevertheless, the Court sustained the restriction and announced a new rule: Congress may restrict the removal of officials who perform "quasi-judicial" or "quasi-legislative" functions but not officials who perform "purely executive functions."[8]

In practice, this amorphous standard amounted to a rule of categorical deference. In the fifty years that *Humphrey's Executor* remained good law, the Court did not strike down a single removal restriction under the "functions" distinction. The practical result was to authorize a whole new class of so-called independent agencies insulated from direct presidential control.[9]

The Court issued its next significant removal-power decision more than fifty years later in *Bowsher v. Synar*. In *Bowsher*, the Court rebuffed Congress's attempt to reserve to itself the power to remove the Comptroller General of the United States. In the process, *Bowsher* established a narrow, categorical rule: Congress cannot itself participate in the removal of executive officials, except by impeachment. *Bowsher* marks the only time that the Court has struck down congressional arrogation of removal power to itself.[10]

Two years after *Bowsher,* the Court decided *Morrison v. Olson* and effectively overruled *Humphrey's Executor.* In *Morrison,* the Court considered a challenge to the Ethics in Government Act, which created an independent counsel—removable "only for good cause" by the Attorney General—to prosecute high-level wrongdoing in the executive branch. Under *Humphrey's Executor,* the independent counsel clearly performed an "executive function." And yet the Court upheld the removal restriction. To do so, the Court sidestepped *Humphrey's Executor's* "functions" distinction and announced a new rule to govern the removal power: Congress cannot impose restrictions on removal that "impermissibly burden" the President's authority to supervise the executive branch. In a cursory analysis, the Court found that the Ethics in Government Act passed this test. Following the Court's lead, lower courts have applied *Morrison*'s "impermissible burden" standard as a basically categorical rule of deference.[11]

The Supreme Court did not issue another removal power decision until 2010, when it decided *Free Enterprise Fund v. Public Co. Accounting Oversight Board (PCAOB).* There, the Court considered a challenge to a removal restriction in the Sarbanes-Oxley Act. Passed in the wake of the Enron and WorldCom scandals, the Act created a board to regulate accounting firms and placed this board under the oversight of the Securities and Exchange Commission (SEC). The Act provided that the SEC Commissioner could remove board members only for good cause, and the Commissioner himself could be removed only for good cause. The Court struck down this "stacking" of for-cause restrictions, and for only the third time in its history, invalidated a restriction on the President's removal power. *PCAOB* thus established yet another narrow rule: Congress may not insulate individuals who are exercising significant executive functions with stacked for-cause restrictions.[12]

Justice Breyer issued a strongly worded dissent in *PCAOB,* attacking the majority opinion on several levels. In Breyer's view: (1) invalidation of a second for-cause restriction does not, in fact, increase presidential control; (2) removal restrictions are not a particularly potent form of congressional interference; (3) to whatever extent multiple for-cause restrictions do interfere with presidential control, that interference is justified; and (4) the majority's holding imperils a great swath of tenure protections. Justice Breyer advocated that the Court evaluate the practical effect of removal restrictions on a case-by-case basis, giving Congress a wide measure of deference.[13]

The Doctrinal Puzzle

The Supreme Court's enforcement of the unitary executive theory—or lack thereof—is puzzling for several reasons. First, despite frequent lip service to elements of the unitary executive theory, the Court has generally refused to check rampant congressional interference with presidential administration. Second, when the Court has roused itself to resist such congressional incursions, it has done so in a narrow area of modest importance with no special foundation in the constitutional text—restrictions on removal of executive officials. Third, even within the circumscribed area of the removal power, the Court has established limited, categorical restrictions on the President's removal authority, rather than rolling back all restrictions. None of the leading models of Supreme Court decision-making can explain these features of the Court's decisions.

Congress routinely interferes with presidential administration in myriad ways. A large political science literature demonstrates the power of administrative procedure and agency structure to constrain agency—and thus presidential—policy-making. Among other things, Congress controls the stringency of the procedures governing agency action, institutes study requirements, and shapes the composition of agency decision-makers to reflect the interests of favored constituencies. In these ways, Congress controls the information available to agency decision-makers and gives itself time to act to prevent agency deviations from congressional preferences. Yet the Court has shown no interest in reviewing or limiting these forms of congressional interference—or any others. Of all the myriad ways in which Congress limits the President's control over the bureaucracy, only removal restrictions have received any constitutional scrutiny at all.[14]

Under both legalist and attitudinal models of Supreme Court decision-making, the Court's fixation on this single mechanism of congressional interference is puzzling. The removal power has no special textual significance. That is not to say that the removal power has no plausible constitutional foundation. But the removal power has no *greater* constitutional foundation than a more general freedom to execute the laws free from congressional interference. The Court, however, has refused to scrutinize Congress's other levers of influence over presidential administration. Moreover, from a structural standpoint, other forms of congressional interference pose at least as great—if not a greater—threat to unitary presidential control than do removal restrictions. Thus, if constitutional text, structure, or conservative ideological commitment to the unitary executive theory were motivating the Court, we should expect the Court to be at least as active in policing other forms of congressional interference. The fact that it is not begs explanation.[15]

The point holds even if the justices' motivations are more crudely political. Like removal restrictions, other forms of congressional interference with presidential control make the delegation of power to administrative agencies more palatable to Congress. The more influence Congress exerts over the bureaucracy, the lower its risk in delegating regulatory authority to it. To this extent, these alternate forms of congressional interference facilitate expansion of the administrative state, and with it, federal administrative power. Conservative justices therefore have the same ideological motives to oppose such interference as they do to oppose removal restrictions. Liberal justices have the opposite motives, though as with removal, they have opportunistic reasons to restrain congressional interference during Democratic administrations, especially when Republicans control one or both houses of Congress. The attitudinal model cannot explain why none of the justices have acted on these motives outside the narrow context of removal.[16]

The same goes for the manner in which the Court has policed removal restrictions. To bolster unitary executive control, the Court could simply have restored *Myers*'s categorical prohibition on all removal restrictions. Indeed, in the lead up to *Free Enterprise Fund,* some scholars called on the Court to do just that. More modestly, the Court could have put real teeth into *Morrison*'s prohibition on impermissible interference with the President's supervisory authority. But the Court has not taken this route either. Instead it has adopted narrow rules that prohibit specific and easily identifiable types of removal restrictions. Specifically, it has barred Congress from arrogating removal authority to itself or employing multilevel for-cause restrictions like the one invalidated in *PCAOB*. As it stands, these are the only meaningful restrictions on Congress's power to restrict the President's removal authority. If the Court's aim is unitary presidential control, whether pursued for legal or ideological reasons, why nibble around the edges with such modest rules?[17]

As with the nondelegation doctrine, the strategic model might explain why the Supreme Court has not adopted a maximalist version of the unitary executive theory that would invalidate all independent agencies, tenure protections for civil servants, or the whole of the Administrative Procedure Act. Such an aggressive assault on the modern regulatory state might well have provoked a serious political backlash of some sort. But this does not explain why the Court's liberals and conservatives have both refrained from deploying the unitary executive theory opportunistically to invalidate the occasional disfavored interference with presidential administration. Nor does it explain why the Court's conservatives have never been seriously tempted to embrace a modest but still meaningful version of the unitary executive theory outside the narrow context of the removal power. The Court could almost certainly have taken this step without serious risk of political blowback, especially during one of the numerous periods of unified Republican control or divided partisan control of the federal government. Like the legalist and attitudinal models, the strategic model cannot explain its failure to do so.

The Judicial Capacity Model Applied

The solution to this puzzle lies not in the logic of the unitary executive theory, but in the limits of judicial capacity. Presidential control of the federal bureaucracy, like the nondelegation doctrine, is both a high-stakes and a high-volume domain. The executive branch is gargantuan. It contains hundreds of agencies and commissions and over two million full-time civilian employees. As explained above, Congress influences these agencies and agency officials in multifarious ways. Rigorous enforcement of the unitary executive theory would imperil the existence of independent agencies and would call into question every mechanism of congressional oversight, formal and informal, including the Administrative Procedure Act itself. As with the nondelegation doctrine, powerful and well-financed business and industrial interests would have ample incentives to challenge these mechanisms anytime an administrative decision went against them. The ensuing volume of litigation would be enormous. Moreover, any time a lower court invalidates an instance of congressional influence, it always invalidates a federal law—or at least the official act of a federal entity—meaning that the Court feels strongly compelled to grant review. For these reasons, judicial capacity is likely to sharply constrain the Court's decision-making in this area. Specifically, judicial capacity will create strong pressure on the Court to adopt hard-edged rules, defer to the political process, or both.[18]

That, in fact, is precisely what we see when we examine the Court's historical treatment of presidential control of the federal bureaucracy. The Court has refused to meaningfully limit congressional encroachment on unitary presidential administration. In fact, the Court has only struck down one type of encroachment—restrictions on the removal of executive officials. Even within this narrow area, the Court has only three times struck down removal restrictions. Apart from those decisions, the Court has simply deferred to the political process. The Court's refusal to act aggressively in this high-stakes and high-volume domain is entirely consistent with the judicial capacity model's predictions.[19]

The judicial capacity model also explains why the Court has focused on the President's removal power and why it has invalidated restrictions on it using narrow categorical rules. Unlike most mechanisms of congressional influence, the removal power is discrete; it can be cleanly distinguished from Congress's other powers. As a result, the removal power is relatively susceptible to hard-edged categorical rules that insulate the vast majority of government action from constitutional challenge. The Court's categorical rule against congressional arrogation of removal authority is a prime example. From the standpoint of judicial capacity, this rule has two advantages. First, it appears to threaten only a tiny number of federal laws. Second, it is crafted in clear and categorical terms, which reduces uncertainty for potential litigants and thus reduces the volume of litigation. The same goes for *Free Enterprise Fund*'s categorical rule against stacked for-cause removal provisions. Unlike constitutional text, constitutional structure, or judicial ideology, the amenability of the removal power to such rules explains why the Court has treated it so differently from other forms of congressional interference.[20]

In this respect, *Bowsher* and *Free Enterprise Fund* are closely parallel to *INS v. Chadha*. In Chadha, the Supreme Court imposed a blanket prohibition on legislative vetoes, a common form of statutory provision permitting one or both houses of Congress to override executive-branch decisions after the fact. Although cast as a decision about the procedural requirements for congressional action under Article I, *Chadha*'s most important effect was to eliminate a widely used tool of congressional oversight. The legislative veto undermined unitary presidential control of the bureaucracy by allowing Congress to countermand agency decisions without involving the President. Just as in *Bowsher* and *Free Enterprise Fund*, *Chadha* was able to strike down a mechanism of congressional interference in convincingly rule-like fashion.[21]

To be sure, this holding affected a fairly large number of statutes, more than 200 of which had legislative veto provisions. But it did so in clear and categorical terms that cleanly insulated the great majority of congressional interference with presidential administration from constitutional challenge. Moreover, the clarity of *Chadha*'s rule reduced uncertainty among potential litigants and thus the volume of litigation. Because the Court made clear that it was sticking with *Chadha*'s invalidation of all legislative vetoes, the holding of that case invited little subsequent litigation. What little litigation it did invite could easily be resolved by the Supreme Court through summary affirmance of lower-court decisions applying *Chadha*'s categorical bar on legislative vetoes.[22]

Notably, when the Court has employed mushier standards to protect the President's removal power, they have generally collapsed into highly deferential rational-basis review or been abandoned altogether. For example, *Morrison*'s prohibition on removal restrictions that impermissibly burden the President's supervisory authority has been interpreted by the lower courts as something resembling a rational-basis test. Similarly, *Morrison* discarded *Humphrey's Executor*'s hazy distinction between "quasi-judicial," "quasi-legislative," and "purely executive" functions, which in its entire fifty-year history had never been applied to invalidate a congressional statute. This is consistent with what the judicial capacity model predicts in this high-stakes and high-volume domain, where vague standards invite an unacceptable volume of litigation unless they are effectively toothless.[23]

For similar reasons, the constraints of judicial capacity help to explain the Supreme Court's reluctance to adopt Justice Breyer's approach to the removal power. In *PCAOB,* Justice Breyer advocated evaluating removal restrictions on a case-by-case basis by looking to the practical effect of the restriction. As Breyer himself noted, a hodgepodge of different rules restrict the removal of tens-of-thousands of executive branch officials. If applied with any real stringency, Breyer's nebulous test would call into question all of these restrictions, generating a large volume of litigation, much of which the Court would feel compelled to grant review.[24]

On the other hand, there is reason to doubt that Breyer's test was ever meant to be applied stringently. His lengthy paean to Congress's superior institutional competence and the consequent need for judicial deference is strongly reminiscent of rational-basis review. If Breyer's approach is ever adopted—and it fell only one vote short in *PCAOB*—the judicial capacity model predicts that it will amount in practice to a rule of categorical deference, much like *Morrison* and *Humphrey's Executor* before it.[25]

The judicial capacity model also explains why the Court has not restored *Myers*'s categorical prohibition on all removal restrictions. From the standpoint of judicial capacity, such a rule has the benefit of clarity—it is hard-edged and categorical. But this rule is so stringent that its application would generate an enormous volume of litigation. To categorically prohibit removal restrictions, the Court would have to dismantle independent agencies, including the Federal Reserve. It would also have to closely scrutinize restrictions on the removal of tens-of-thousands of lower-level federal employees, among them administrative law judges, immigration judges, and many other officials charged with performing classically adjudicative functions. (Formally, *Myers* did not extend to restrictions on the removal of inferior officers, but its logic and the logic of the unitary executive theory surely does.) The resulting deluge of litigation would overwhelm the Court's modest capacity. The constraints of judicial capacity therefore make it difficult to imagine the Court reintroducing *Myers*'s prohibition on removal restrictions, however tempted the Court may be to do so. Of course, *Myers* itself was decided before the rise of the modern administrative state, and before the law of standing evolved to permit regulated parties to challenge removal restrictions. Under modern conditions, it is hard to imagine the *Myers* rule lasting as long as it did.[26]

Even if the categorical nature of the *Myers* rule could keep litigation within manageable bounds, it would produce results many justices would find unpalatable. Among other things, that rule would require the Court to strip the Federal Reserve, civil service, and the whole corps of administrative law and immigration judges of removal protection. There is good reason to think that such extreme results would give pause to many justices. Such results might also create a real risk of political backlash, providing a strategic reason for the Court to leave *Myers* where it lies in the dustbin of constitutional history. However, in the high-volume and high-stakes domain of presidential administration, the Court cannot adopt mushy standards without inviting an unsustainable volume of litigation. Thus, the Court is forced to choose between the unpalatable results of a *Myers*-like prohibition and the large-scale sacrifice of the unitary executive entailed by the Court's current, nibble-around the edges approach. Given this choice, it is not surprising that the Court has selected the latter course. This is a good illustration of the way in which the judicial capacity model interacts with the justices' ideological preferences and strategic calculations.[27]

In sum, the judicial capacity model explains the Supreme Court's selective under-enforcement of the unitary executive theory better than any competing model of Supreme Court decision-making. The combination of categorical rules and strong deference exhibited by the Court's decisions is fully consistent with the judicial capacity model's predictions. And those predictions explain many features of the Court's decisions that no other model is capable of explaining. As such, the judicial capacity model improves our understanding of the constitutional law of presidential administration, which in turn provides strong evidence in support of the model.

Individual Rights

The constitutional law of individual rights is broader and more eclectic than either the constitutional law of federalism or the constitutional law of separation of powers. Each of the first eight amendments of the Constitution protects at least one distinct individual right against infringement by the federal government. Many protect more than one such right, and nearly all of these rights play some meaningful role in contemporary constitutional law. The Fourteenth Amendment contains at least three separate protections for individual rights against infringement by state governments: the Due Process Clause, the Equal Protection Clause, and the Privileges or Immunities Clause. The first two of these are arguably the most important sources of individual rights in contemporary constitutional law, while the third has tremendous but as-yet unrealized potential to protect a wide range of individual rights, only some of which are currently protected in other guises.

In most of these domains, the Supreme Court's decisions are not significantly constrained by the limits of judicial capacity. In some, the potential volume of litigation is too low to seriously constrain the Court, mostly because the scope of these provisions is so narrow. The Second Amendment's right to keep and bear arms and the Third Amendment's prohibition on compelled quartering of troops in peacetime are good examples. In others, the potential—and, in fact, the actual—volume of litigation is quite high in absolute terms, but the stakes are sufficiently low that the Court only feels compelled to take a tiny percentage of cases. The various rights protected in the Fourth, Fifth, and Sixth Amendments that make up the constitutional law of criminal procedure are asserted in tens of thousands of lower-court cases per year. But the Court is happy to allow the lower courts to have the last word in the vast majority of these, so the Court's decisions in these domains are not substantially constrained by the limits of judicial capacity. In the terminology of the judicial capacity model, these are normal domains.[1]

Not all individual rights domains are normal, however. The Equal Protection Clause, the Due Process Clause, the Takings Clause of the Fifth Amendment, and the Privileges or Immunities Clause all have the potential to threaten a large quantity of important state and federal legislation, whose invalidation by lower courts the Supreme Court would feel compelled to review. We can put the Privileges or Immunities Clause to one side for present purposes, because it was effectively rendered toothless by *The Slaughterhouse Cases* and has remained so ever since, despite the best efforts of libertarian law professors. The other three clauses all have the potential to call into question the validity of an enormous quantity of legislation at both the state and federal levels. The Equal Protection Clause, which applies to the federal government through so-called reverse incorporation by the Fifth Amendment, prohibits "class legislation." But all legislation treats some classes of persons more favorably than others. The Due Process Clause, found in both the Fifth and the Fourteenth Amendments, prohibits unjustified government interference with individual liberty, but all legislation limits individual liberty. The Takings Clause prohibits the taking of private property for public use without just compensation, but all legislation negatively affects—and thus, arguably, takes—the value of some private property.[2]

The potential breadth of these provisions makes it imperative to clarify their limits. Accordingly, the main constitutional questions in all three of them are whether the Supreme Court should seriously attempt to enforce the individual rights in question, and if so, how to limit the scope of those rights to something less than the complete universe of government action. The Court's attempts to answer these questions are the focus of the two case studies explored in this section, which cover Equal Protection and Takings. I omit further discussion of the Due Process Clause for reasons of space, but the pattern of the Court's modern Due Process decisions is very similar to that of its Equal Protection and Takings decisions. The similarity across these three domains is striking because, in the modern era, liberal justices have tended to favor more stringent Due Process and Equal Protection review, while conservatives have favored a more robust Takings Clause.[3]

In none of these domains, however, has the Court embraced a truly robust approach. Instead, as in each of the capacity-constrained domains examined in earlier chapters, the Supreme Court has consistently adhered to a combination of strong deference and narrow categorical limits that clearly insulate most legislation from serious constitutional challenge. In Equal Protection, this combination goes by the name of tiered scrutiny, a doctrinal framework that subjects a small, clearly defined subset of government classifications to stringent judicial scrutiny, while relegating the rest to minimal rational-basis review. In Takings, the framework has no widely recognized name but consists of a small handful of narrow, per se prohibitions on government action, coupled with the highly deferential *Penn Central* test, which operates in practice much like a form of rational-basis review.

Today most observers take the broad contours of these doctrinal frameworks largely for granted. It is well recognized that all legislation classifies, and few think the Supreme Court could or should engage in serious review of more than a small handful of government classifications. Similarly, it is well recognized that all government regulation affects property values, and few think the Court could or should require the government to compensate property owners for all—or even substantially all—resulting losses. Nevertheless, calls for more stringent—and more standard-like—judicial enforcement of the Equal Protection and Takings Clauses remain a staple of the constitutional literature. In recent years, rational-basis review has attracted particular criticism, from scholars at both ends of the political spectrum. Decisions like *Obergefell v. Hodges* and *Horne v. Dep't of Agriculture* have raised hopes, and fears, that the Court might be poised to step up judicial enforcement of the Equal Protection and Takings Clauses in a meaningful way. A small cottage industry has developed predicting the demise of tiered scrutiny.[4]

As in other capacity-constrained domains, however, both supporters and opponents of more stringent judicial enforcement have largely ignored the antecedent question of whether the Supreme Court has the capacity to undertake or sustain such an approach. Those predicting the end of tiered scrutiny have been similarly inattentive to capacity constraints. Even more institutionally minded scholars have generally failed to consider how the judiciary's limited capacity influences the substance and doctrinal form in these areas. The judicial capacity model fills these gaps in the literature. In turn, the constitutional law of Equal Protection and Takings provides powerful evidence supporting the judicial capacity model.[5]

CHAPTER NINE

Equal Protection

Along with the First Amendment, the Equal Protection Clause of the Fourteenth Amendment is the jewel in the crown of the Constitution's protections for individual rights. *Brown v. Board of Education,* which applied the Equal Protection Clause to invalidate state-mandated racial segregation of public schools, is unquestionably the Supreme Court's most celebrated constitutional decision. Meanwhile, judges, lawyers, and politicians across the political spectrum pledge fealty to "the principle of inherent equality that underlies and infuses our Constitution," which *Brown*'s companion case, *Bolling v. Sharpe,* extended to the federal government through the Due Process Clause of the Fifth Amendment.[1]

Not surprisingly, and despite a superficially broad consensus, liberals and conservatives understand the nature and scope of this principle differently. In recent years this difference has been most evident in affirmative-action and gay-rights cases, with conservatives construing the Equal Protection Clause to prohibit most or all race-based affirmative action but little if any discrimination against gays and lesbians. Liberals, by contrast, have construed the clause to prohibit little if any race-based affirmative action and most or all discrimination against gays and lesbians. Given the heated controversy that these issues have provoked, it is easy to miss what a narrow band this controversy has occurred within. Although the text of the Fifth and Fourteenth Amendments extends to "any person," there is a strong consensus that serious judicial review of governmental discrimination—usually called heightened scrutiny—should be limited to a small handful of discrete rights and disfavored types of discrimination. There is also a strong consensus that, even within these categories, only intentional discrimination—as opposed to government action that has an unintended disparate impact on different social groups—should trigger serious review. Conversely, and also by consensus, all unintentional government discrimination and all discrimination not based on race, gender, or a few other "suspect classifications" is subject to minimal rational-basis review, so long as it does not implicate a short list of fundamental rights.

This combination of narrow categorical limits and strong deference is puzzling for several reasons. First, from a legalist standpoint, the text of the Fifth and Fourteenth Amendments makes no distinction between the types of government discrimination that currently trigger heightened scrutiny and those that trigger only minimal rational-basis review, nor does the long-standing prohibition on class legislation that stands behind both of these provisions. Second, also from a legalist perspective, the various political-process theories that inform heightened scrutiny would all seem to support a substantial expansion of heightened scrutiny, either to laws burdening the poor or to laws favoring concentrated business and industrial interests at the expense of the general public.[2]

Third, both liberal and conservative justices should have a strong ideological motivation to expand serious Equal Protection review. For liberals, such expansion offers the opportunity to extend greater protection to consumers, workers, racial minorities, and the poor. It also offers the opportunity to invalidate social and economic legislation that clearly serves the interests of economic and business elites. For conservatives, expansion offers the opportunity to invalidate social and economic regulation, and perhaps also taxation, that burdens business interests and the wealthy and runs afoul of economic laissez-faire. The prospect of political backlash clearly places some limit on the Court's ability to pursue either of these paths, but it cannot readily explain the Court's near-total forbearance from serious Equal Protection review outside a small handful of fundamental rights and suspect classifications.

None of the leading models of Supreme Court decision-making can explain these features of the Court's decisions. The judicial capacity model can. In a nutshell, a robust reading of the Equal Protection Clause, articulated in the form of a vague standard, would call into question an enormous quantity of federal legislation. It would also call into question innumerable state and local laws and a great number of administrative agency and other executive actions at all levels. The reason is simple and well-recognized by constitutional lawyers: All laws, indeed all government actions, treat some individuals differently from others and, in that literal sense, discriminate—or, to use the jargon of the cases, "classify." To subject all such distinctions to serious review would invite far more litigation than the federal court system, and in particular the Supreme Court, could handle, consistent with the justices' widely shared commitments to minimum professional standards and the uniformity of federal law. The Court therefore seriously scrutinizes government discrimination only when it can do so in the form of relatively narrow categorical rules that clearly insulate most governmental action from constitutional challenge.

The Pattern of Supreme Court Decisions

The Fourteenth Amendment was ratified in 1868, the second in a series of three "reconstruction amendments" adopted in the aftermath of the Civil War with the principal purpose of protecting the rights of formerly enslaved blacks. Among other things, the Amendment established universal birth-right citizenship, overturning the holding of *Dred Scott v. Sandford* that persons "of African descent" could never be U.S. citizens. It also prohibited states from abridging "the privileges or immunities of citizens of the United States"; depriving "any person of life, liberty, or property, without due process of law"; or denying "any person" within their jurisdiction "the equal protection of the laws." Finally, the Amendment granted Congress the power to enforce these provisions "by appropriate legislation."[3]

The original meaning and subsequent interpretation of the Fourteenth Amendment by the Supreme Court are as hotly contested as any subject in American constitutional history. But for present purposes, it is possible to stick to a few largely uncontroversial points. First, while the principal motivation behind the Amendment was clearly to protect formerly enslaved blacks, none of its language is limited to such persons. The Equal Protection Clause, in particular, broadly prohibits states from denying *"any person* the equal protection of the laws." Leading historical accounts trace this prohibition to a deeply rooted "doctrine against 'partial' or 'special' laws"—also called "class legislation"—"which forbade the state to single out any person or group of persons for special benefits or burdens without an adequate 'public purpose' justification." The novelty in the Equal Protection Clause was its extension of this principle to blacks and elevation of the prohibition on class legislation to the status of federal constitutional law.[4]

Second, after a few sporadic initial attempts at enforcing the Equal Protection Clause in favor of blacks, the Supreme Court largely abandoned efforts to police racial discrimination by state governments. Conventional accounts tie this abandonment to the so-called Compromise of 1877, in which mostly southern Democrats agreed to concede the contested presidential election of 1876 in exchange for a surrender on Reconstruction by northern Republicans. The Supreme Court then "followed and cemented the policy shift of Republicans" in *The Civil Rights Cases* of 1883, which held that neither the Equal Protection Clause nor Congress's power to enforce that provision extended to private racial discrimination. Recent revisionist accounts date the abandonment a bit later and paint a somewhat muddier picture, but none disputes that a decisive abandonment took place and began before the turn of the twentieth century.[5]

Third, most of the Supreme Court's early decisions invalidating legislation under the Equal Protection Clause involved economic regulation of businesses, rather than discrimination against blacks or other racial minorities. Indeed, many of the cases today grouped under the headings of "substantive due process" and "liberty of contract," including *Lochner v. New York,* were originally argued as both Equal Protection and Due Process cases on the ground that the challenged regulations constituted "class legislation," singling out some subset of businesses for special burdens or benefits. A number of such cases were also decided, in part or in whole, on Equal Protection grounds. Nevertheless, even the *Lochner* Court, with its supposed laissez-faire pretensions, recognized that all laws treat different classes of persons differently and rejected a large majority of the Equal Protection challenges that came before it.[6]

Fourth, in the aftermath of the New Deal constitutional showdown of 1937, the Supreme Court retreated from almost all meaningful review of legislation under the Equal Protection Clause. This retreat went hand in hand with the Court's retreat from serious review under the Commerce and Due Process Clauses and was announced clearly in the famous case of *United States v. Carolene Products.* Curtly rejecting the plaintiff's due-process and equal-protection challenges to a federal ban on the sale of "filled milk," the Court declared that "regulatory legislation affecting ordinary commercial transactions is not to be pronounced unconstitutional unless . . . it is of such a character as to preclude the assumption that it rests upon some rational basis." This highly deferential test has remained the governing law for the vast majority of Equal Protection challenges up to the present day.[7]

Fifth, starting a few years after *Carolene Products,* the Supreme Court began to develop a short list of narrow and discrete categories of government action that would be subject to much more stringent Equal Protection review. Today, these categories are conventionally boiled down to fundamental rights, such as the right to vote and the due process right of access to the courts, and suspect classifications, such as race and sex. The more stringent review that applies in these contexts is conventionally denominated heightened scrutiny. This standard requires both that the challenged government action serve an especially important state interest and that it be quite closely tailored to that interest. A law that goes much beyond, or falls much short, of what such an interest requires will be held constitutionally invalid. This is a demanding standard, one conventionally assumed to approach a rule of per se invalidity.[8]

Exactly how the doctrine arrived at this point is the subject of considerable debate, but the broad contours are clear enough. Conventional accounts trace the fundamental-rights strand of Equal Protection to *Skinner v. Oklahoma,* which closely scrutinized—and ultimately invalidated—a state mandatory sterilization law that covered chicken thieves but not embezzlers, on the ground that procreation was "one of the basic civil rights of man." The suspect-classifications strand of Equal Protection, for its part, is conventionally traced to *Korematsu v. United States,* which upheld the internment of Japanese Americans during World War II after purporting to subject this race-based policy to "the most rigid scrutiny." Ten years later, *Brown v. Board of Education* made good on *Korematsu*'s false promise and "strict scrutiny" for racial classifications was born. Or so the story goes. Recent revisionist work disputes these pat narratives, suggesting that both strands of Equal Protection—and the heightened scrutiny that is their hallmark—emerged much more tentatively, even haltingly, over a period of decades. Another strand of revisionist work disputes the conventional view that heightened scrutiny is "strict in theory, fatal in fact," with one study reporting that 30 percent of the government actions subjected to strict scrutiny between 1990 and 2003 were ultimately upheld.[9]

For present purposes, it is unnecessary to delve into these debates. The important point is that meaningful Equal Protection review in the modern era has never extended beyond a short list of narrow, discrete rights and suspect classes. In the Warren and Burger Court eras, liberal justices never assembled anything approaching a majority in favor of extending meaningful Equal Protection review to large, diffuse groups such as consumers or workers or the poor. Nor were such important but amorphous interests as health care, food security, housing, tax burden, or welfare benefits ever serious contenders for the list of fundamental rights triggering rigorous Equal Protection review. The Court's invalidation of several gender-based classifications in the early 1970s, ostensibly under rational-basis review, did briefly raise the specter of more rigorous across-the-board scrutiny. But the Court quickly shut down this speculation with decisions like *Craig v. Boren* and *Massachusetts Board of Retirement v. Murgia.* In more recent decades, conservative justices have shown even less appetite for extending meaningful Equal Protection review to mine-run social and economic regulation or progressive taxation or redistributive social welfare programs.[10]

Finally, no substantial number of justices has ever endorsed the Equal Protection equivalent of Justice Cardozo's approach to the Commerce Clause—that is to say, Equal Protection review in the form of an amorphous standard applicable to all manner of government discrimination. This has not been for lack of urging. Leading academics have long advocated for some version of this approach, whether in the guise of a sliding scale, proportionality review, or simply a case-by-case, totality-of-the-circumstances analysis. None put the case better or more succinctly than Justice John Paul Stevens: "There is only one Equal Protection Clause. It requires every State to govern impartially. It does not direct the courts to apply one standard of review in some cases and a different standard in other cases." In this view, Stevens followed a path charted by Justice Thurgood Marshall. Despite their dogged persistence, however, Marshall and Stevens remain essentially alone among modern justices in their sustained advocacy of this approach. Even Marshall arguably failed to adhere to it consistently.[11]

Meanwhile, whether fatal or merely strict, heightened scrutiny has always been confined to discrete categories of rights and classifications, so as to clearly insulate the vast majority of government action—all of which, to repeat, discriminates in the literal sense—from meaningful Equal Protection review. Moreover, even within these discrete categories, heightened scrutiny is limited to intentional government discrimination. Conversely, the many thousands of government actions that disparately but unintentionally impact racial minorities, women, and other suspect classes are subject only to minimal rational-basis review. On these basic matters of black-letter doctrine, there is no significant debate. Lawrence Sager's 1978 summary of the constitutional landscape holds up well: "Only a small part of the universe of plausible claims of unequal and unjust treatment by government is seriously considered by the federal courts; the vast majority of such claims are dismissed out of hand."[12]

The Supreme Court's modern gay-rights cases are fully consistent with this picture. These cases are somewhat unusual in the Court's Equal Protection canon in their studied ambiguity about the applicable level of scrutiny. But despite some scattered references to irrationality in *Lawrence v. Texas* and *Romer v. Colorado,* almost no one thinks the Court was applying traditional rational-basis review in these cases. Nor does anyone think that the de facto heightened scrutiny the Court has applied in cases like *Lawrence* (invalidating a criminal prohibition on same-sex sodomy), *Romer v. Evans* (invalidating a state ban on antidiscrimination protection for sexual orientation), and *Obergefell v. Hodges* (invalidating a state ban on same-sex marriage) is likely to extend beyond discrimination based on sexual orientation and, perhaps, gender identity.[13]

Indeed, the Supreme Court's unwillingness to designate sexual orientation a suspect class seems intended to signal that the universe of suspect classes is closed. The prominent role of fundamental rights—to intimate association and marriage—in *Lawrence* and *Obergefell* also serves to wall these cases off from government discrimination generally. The same goes for the idiosyncratic political-process rationale of *Romer,* which was premised not only on the irrational animus of Colorado toward gays and lesbians but on the unequal political burden created by a state constitutional amendment (as opposed to an ordinary law) singling them out. In other words, these decisions are just the latest examples of the Supreme Court's long-standing practice of limiting meaningful Equal Protection review to a few narrow and discretely circumscribed groups and rights.[14]

The Doctrinal Puzzle

The pattern of the Supreme Court's modern Equal Protection decisions, like its modern commerce-power decisions, presents two distinct puzzles: First, why have the Court's post-1937 Equal Protection decisions exempted nearly all government discrimination from meaningful judicial review? Second, why has the Court limited the meaningful review it does engage in to a small handful of discrete categories, rather than embracing the more flexible case-by-case or sliding-scale approaches advocated by so many commentators (and, occasionally, dissenting justices)? No leading model of Supreme Court decision-making can readily explain either.

Post-1937 Deference

Since 1937 the Supreme Court has subjected the vast majority of government discrimination to highly deferential rational-basis review. This strong and persistent deference is puzzling because the Court has both legal and ideological motives for subjecting a wide range of government action to meaningful Equal Protection scrutiny and few strategic motives for maintaining such a restrained posture. Put in reverse, the legalist and attitudinal models both predict that the Court should have reviewed government discrimination more aggressively than it has. The strategic model predicts that the Court will back off efforts to restrict government discrimination that threaten serious political backlash, of the sort triggered by the Court's aggressive efforts to roll back the New Deal. But this prediction cannot readily explain why the Court has failed to subject the vast majority of government discrimination to anything more than minimal rationality review.

Let us begin with the Supreme Court's legal motives for limiting government discrimination. Despite the Court's long record of deference to most government classifications, no Supreme Court justice in the modern era has openly professed to believe that the Equal Protection Clause—or its federal analogue under the Due Process Clause—protects only "suspect classes" or "fundamental rights." The text of the Clause would certainly not support such a position, and despite some dicta in *The Slaughterhouse Cases,* the pre-1937 Court frequently interpreted the Equal Protection Clause to prohibit class legislation generally, although the jurisprudential categories of that era were different from those of the modern era. Of course, in 2017 the Court's broad deference to most government discrimination is firmly entrenched in decades of case law, which counts as a legalist argument in its favor. But this argument does not explain how the Court's deference came to be so entrenched, and, because precedents can be overruled, it counts as only a partial explanation for why this deference has remained such a stable feature of judicial doctrine for the past eighty years.[15]

To supplement text, history, and doctrine, legalist defenders of the Supreme Court's bifurcated approach to Equal Protection frequently invoke political-process theories of various stripes. Although political-process theory is most commonly identified with John Hart Ely and most commonly deployed to defend Warren Court liberalism, the conservative Equal Protection jurisprudence of the Rehnquist and Roberts Courts is also grounded, implicitly and sometimes explicitly, in a version of political-process theory. The two sides embrace very different understandings of the political process, and hence of political malfunction, but the Court's Equal Protection doctrine has never tracked either very satisfactorily.[16]

Ely and the liberal academics and justices who have built on his work largely view American politics through the prism of "defective pluralism," in which "well-organized groups bargain and compromise with each other in a competitive pluralist political marketplace to secure favorable legislation." While this competitive interest-group bargaining can generally be counted on to serve the public interest, liberals worry that certain groups will be systematically excluded from the bargaining process due to social stigma or other barriers to participation. This results in political malfunction, which Ely and other liberal political-process theorists thought the Court should and, in fact, generally does step into correct.[17]

This theory is normatively appealing and has significant descriptive power, but it cannot explain the Court's failure to provide meaningful protection for perhaps the most powerless out-group of all: the poor. Nor can it explain the Court's restriction of heightened scrutiny to *intentional* discrimination against racial minorities and other suspect classes. If these groups are systematically excluded from the pluralist bargaining process, that process is likely to systematically underrepresent their interests through indifference and inattention at least as often as it does through overt animus.[18]

Modern judicial conservatives, by contrast, tend to view the political process through the prism of public-choice theory. On this view, the political process resembles not a competitive pluralist market but rather a rigged game, in which small, well-organized special interests dominate at the expense of the more diffusely interested and unorganized general public. As Bertrall Ross has argued, this view helps to explain conservative skepticism of affirmative action and other remedial legislation that benefits racial minorities, which conservatives have come to see as special interests, manipulating their organizational advantages to benefit themselves at the expense of the unorganized majority. Affirmative action, however, is only one, relatively small and controversial example of the sort of special-interest legislation that public-choice theory warns against. In fact, public-choice theory suggests that democratic politics is dominated by such legislation, mostly to the benefit of well-organized industrial and business interests. Yet no conservative justice in the modern era has advocated heightened scrutiny of legislation benefiting those interests.[19]

From a cruder political standpoint, liberals and conservatives both have strong ideological motives to enforce the Equal Protection Clause far more vigorously. Because all government action discriminates, a prohibition on unjustified class distinctions is a highly potent—and highly malleable—tool for justices to advance their preferred policy agendas. If Supreme Court justices vote like legislators, as the attitudinal model posits, rigorous Equal Protection review should provide a ready vehicle for judicial conservatives to invalidate just about any regulatory, tax, or spending legislation, state or federal, that these justices oppose on policy grounds. California's Clean Car program treats manufacturers and owners of low-emission vehicles differently from manufacturers and owners of high-emission vehicles. The National Labor Relations Act treats unionized workers differently from nonunionized workers. The federal tax code treats high-income taxpayers differently from low-income taxpayers. The list could go on indefinitely. All of these forms of government regulation are opposed, to a greater or lesser extent, by conservative legislators. All could plausibly be held unjustified if the Court subjected them to meaningful review under the Equal Protection Clause (or its Fifth Amendment analogue). Yet no justice in the modern era has shown a serious appetite for expanding Equal Protection review in this way.[20]

For liberal justices, rigorous Equal Protection review should provide a similarly ready vehicle for extending constitutional protection to the socially and economically disadvantaged. Many government services, from driver's licenses to state-subsidized higher education, treat those who can pay for them differently from those who cannot. The federal tax code treats investors differently from workers and homeowners differently from renters. State funding of public schools treats students in wealthy school districts differently from those in poor districts. Most, if not all, of these policies also have a disproportionate impact on racial minorities, even if the policies are not motivated by overt racial animus. Again, the list could go on indefinitely.[21]

All of these forms of government discrimination are opposed, to a greater or lesser extent, by liberal legislators. All could plausibly be held unjustified if the Court subjected them to meaningful Equal Protection review. Yet even in the heyday of the liberal Warren Court, nothing approaching a majority of the justices showed any appetite for expanding Equal Protection review in this way. Since the retirement of Justices William Brennan and Thurgood Marshall, no justice has shown such an appetite, though it is safe to say that many of the liberals on the modern court would have voted against many of these policies as legislators. From the standpoint of the attitudinal model, this is a genuine puzzle.

As with the commerce power, the strategic model is somewhat more helpful, but only somewhat. Fear of political reprisal might well explain why the modern Supreme Court has never pushed Equal Protection review to the hilt, in either a liberal or a conservative direction. To do so would effectively empower the Court to second-guess all legislative decisions, which would surely provoke significant resistance from both Congress and state legislatures. But the strategic model cannot readily explain why the Court has circumscribed meaningful Equal Protection review to just a handful of discrete rights and suspect classes. More specifically, the strategic model cannot explain why the modern Court's conservatives have never been seriously tempted to exercise meaningful across-the-board review of economic regulations that would curb, but not overturn, the modern regulatory and welfare states. Nor can the strategic model explain why the Court's liberals have never seriously pushed for meaningful protection of consumers, workers, or the poor that would blunt economic inequality and ameliorate the legacy of racial discrimination without upending modern capitalism. Neither of these steps seems likely to have provoked serious retaliation, especially when a sympathetic political party controlled one house of Congress or the presidency. Certainly, the Court has stuck to far less popular stands in recent years, without triggering any effective political resistance. The strategic model, therefore, cannot persuasively explain the Court's failure to take these steps when it had the motive and opportunity to do so.[22]

Preference for Categorical Rules over Standards

During the modern era, the Supreme Court has consistently refused to embrace the sort of vague Equal Protection standard championed by Justice Stevens and a veritable army of academic commentators. Rather, both the fundamental-rights and the suspect-classification branches of Equal Protection doctrine have been, all the way back to their tentative origins, limited to a short list of discrete rights (most notably, the rights to vote and access to court) and suspect classifications (most notably, race and gender). For present purposes, the key point about these areas of heightened Equal Protection review is the clarity and categorical character of their boundaries. Whether the scrutiny applicable within those boundaries is essentially fatal, as conventionally assumed, or merely quite strict, all of them serve to clearly mark off the narrow lines within which that heightened scrutiny applies—and beyond which minimal rational-basis review kicks in. An approach like Justice Stevens's, by contrast, would require courts to consider the justification for government classifications on something like a case-by-case basis, opening an enormous quantity of laws up to plausible Equal Protection challenge.[23]

The Court's deference to legislatures and executive officials under the rational-basis test has been similarly categorical. Vanishingly little government action has been invalidated under that test as applied in Equal Protection cases. The very rare exceptions nearly all involved a rapidly emerging suspect classification (like gender in the 1970s) or a de facto suspect classification (like sexual orientation in recent years). The most notable exception that does not fall into one of these two categories is *City of Cleburne v. Cleburne Living Center,* in which the Court applied a stringent form of rational-basis review to invalidate discrimination against a discrete class—the cognitively disabled—that several concurring members of the Court would have treated as suspect.[24]

No leading model of Supreme Court decision-making can readily explain this nearly unwavering preference for categorical rules. As explained in earlier chapters, neither the attitudinal nor the strategic model makes any strong predictions about the doctrinal form of Supreme Court decisions. If anything, the hierarchical branch of the strategic model predicts that the doctrinal form should vary over time with a complex array of frequently shifting variables, including the ideological diversity of the lower federal courts and the ideological distance between those courts and the Supreme Court. That is not what we see in the Court's modern Equal Protection decisions.

The legalist model poses a somewhat murkier question. It predicts that doctrinal form will reflect legal factors like the constitutional text, history, and judicial precedent. In the case of the Equal Protection Clause, however, both constitutional text and history seem to favor Justice Stevens's case-specific standard, rather than the categorical approach taken by the Court. There is, as Stevens suggests, but "one Equal Protection Clause," whose text makes no group or groups more equal than others. Both the fundamental-rights and suspect-classification doctrines, moreover, are pretty clearly innovations of the modern era. Of course, the history of the Fourteenth Amendment's drafting and ratification does suggest a special concern with the rights of formerly enslaved blacks, but that concern does not explain the Supreme Court's heightened scrutiny of racial classifications that benefit blacks. Nor does this history explain the heightened scrutiny the Court applies to other suspect classes or the virtually categorical deference the Court applies in cases not involving suspect classifications or fundamental rights. Judicial precedent does support the Court's categorical approach, but it certainly did not compel that approach in the first instance and thus cannot explain its emergence. Nor can judicial precedent explain why the Court's categorical approach has remained stable over such a long period, in the face of large-scale change in social conditions and in the ideological composition of the Court. The Court could have reversed itself at any point, but so far has not done so.[25]

Political-process theories, liberal and conservative, fare little better. For reasons elaborated above, those theories cannot readily explain the specific lines drawn by the Supreme Court's Equal Protection decisions. But neither can they explain why the Court has consistently opted for a categorical approach, rather than a Justice Stevens–style standard. Both special-interest dominance, emphasized by conservatives following public-choice theory, and political powerlessness, emphasized by liberals following defective pluralism, are matters of degree. A sliding-scale or all-things-considered approach to Equal Protection review would allow the Court to calibrate the stringency of its review accordingly. From the standpoint of the legalist model, its failure to do so remains a puzzle.[26]

The Judicial Capacity Model Applied

The Supreme Court has both the motive and opportunity to vigorously enforce the Equal Protection Clause, but it has consistently refused to do so for the past eighty years. The Court has also consistently cast its Equal Protection decisions in the form of narrow, categorical rules, with little textual or historical foundation. The judicial capacity model helps to explain both of these otherwise puzzling features of the Court's modern Equal Protection decisions.

As discussed in Chapter 2, the Court does not feel compelled to grant review of just any lower-court decision striking down government action as a violation of Equal Protection. Such cases frequently involve challenges to executive action, rather than legislation, and especially to executive action at the state and local levels, which generally affects a fairly limited population. All of these factors generally raise the Supreme Court's tolerance of disuniformity and thus reduce the percentage of cases it feels compelled to review.[27]

Even so, the Equal Protection Clause, which guarantees all persons "equal protection of the laws," has the potential to invite more litigation than the Supreme Court could handle while maintaining even a basic commitment to uniformity. In the terms of the judicial capacity model, this makes Equal Protection a high-volume domain. A robust reading of the Equal Protection Clause, articulated in the form of a vague standard like that advocated by Justice Stevens, would call into question much of the U.S. Code. It would also call into question innumerable state and local laws and a great number of administrative agency and other executive actions at all levels. The reason is straightforward and well-recognized by constitutional lawyers: All laws, indeed all government actions, treat some individuals differently from others.

This point has already been mentioned multiple times, but it requires special emphasis and further explanation here. The classic formulation comes from Joseph Tussman and Jacobus tenBroek in their 1949 article "The Equal Protection of the Laws": "The legislature, if it is to act at all, must impose special burdens upon or grant special benefits to special groups or classes of individuals." For example, local zoning laws permit some property owners to operate commercial or industrial establishments while denying this privilege to others. Federal labor law treats hourly workers differently from salaried professionals. Criminal law mandates lengthy incarceration for rapists, drug traffickers, and kidnappers, while permitting other offenders to escape with fines and community service. This process of differentiating or discriminating among classes of persons is conventionally known as "classification." Hence the truism that "all laws classify."[28]

This truism, however, creates a paradox: "The equal protection of the laws is a 'pledge of the protection of equal laws.' But . . . 'the very idea of classification is that of inequality.'" The Court has traditionally, and sensibly, resolved this paradox by construing the Equal Protection Clause to prohibit only unjustified or unreasonable classifications. This construction explains why not all laws violate Equal Protection, but it also makes the constitutionality of all laws turn on the persuasiveness of the legislative justifications standing behind them. By this logic, any law that makes arguably unjustified distinctions between persons is arguably unconstitutional. That covers pretty much all laws.[29]

The same goes for executive actions, which, like the laws they enforce, inevitably bestow benefits and burdens unequally. For example, the Defense Department awards major contracts to some contractors but not to others. The Social Security Administration automatically treats blindness but not migraine headaches as a qualifying disability. The Department of Justice vigorously prosecutes child pornographers but not purveyors of medical marijuana. State highway patrol officers ticket only a small fraction of vehicles traveling in excess of the posted speed limit.[30]

These lists of examples barely scratch the surface, but the point should be clear. Many, perhaps most, of these classifications are sensible and well-justified, but very few are inarguably so. Most, if not all, could be improved through more extensive deliberation and careful crafting. To subject all such classifications to rigorous or even meaningful Equal Protection review would therefore invite far more litigation than the federal court system, and in particular the Supreme Court, could handle, consistent with the justices' widely shared commitments to minimum professional standards and the uniformity of federal law.

Of course, as in other contexts, it is not only the quantity of threatened government action that determines the volume of potential litigation. It is also the magnitude of the benefits that such invalidation would generate for prospective plaintiffs and the number of prospective plaintiffs either collectively or individually capable of mustering the resources to litigate. Because the array of reasonably questionable government classifications is dizzyingly broad, so is the array of prospective plaintiffs who would stand to benefit from their invalidation. For present purposes, however, three groups suffice to demonstrate the vast number of potential plaintiffs with the motive and means to litigate Equal Protection challenges. Huge swaths of legislative and executive classifications implicate the interests of (1) regulated businesses or industries, which spend millions or billions of dollars on regulatory compliance; (2) landowners, with individually and collectively substantial real estate holdings; and (3) criminal defendants, who face substantial prison terms and are represented by government-funded counsel (or, in the case of many white-collar defendants, high-priced private defense lawyers). If this were not enough, a substantial and sophisticated pro bono bar stands ready to assist with high-profile constitutional litigation on behalf of indigent criminal defendants and small business and property owners.[31]

The upshot is straightforward. For most significant government classifications, and for many insignificant ones, some plaintiff will almost always have both the incentive and the resources to bring whatever constitutional challenges the Supreme Court's Equal Protection doctrine makes plausible. Some of these challenges will settle and some of them will never arise because the government actors in question will modify their behavior to avoid litigation. But if the Court subjects more than a handful of classifications to meaningful review, especially in the form of a vague standard, a vast number of these challenges will be litigated and appealed. The Court would not feel compelled to review every such challenge, but it would feel compelled to review enough—especially those involving federal legislation and administrative regulations—that Equal Protection qualifies as a high-volume domain. The judicial capacity model therefore predicts that the Court will feel compelled to adopt a strongly deferential approach, employ hard-edged categorical rules, or both.

This, in fact, is just what we see when we examine the Supreme Court's modern Equal Protection decisions. For the entire modern era, the Court has applied minimal rational-basis review to the great preponderance of government classifications. The vast majority of laws and executive actions are never challenged, not because they do not classify and not because the classifications they rely upon are obviously justified, but because the Court has signaled over and over again that it is almost always pointless to bring an Equal Protection challenge to government actions not implicating a fundamental right or suspect classification. Even for government actions that disproportionately burden a suspect class, such as racial minorities or women, it is pointless to bring an Equal Protection challenge unless those actions facially discriminate along racial or gender lines or are motivated by a discriminatory purpose. Not coincidentally, the Court's decisions—and lower-court decisions applying them—make it exceedingly difficult to demonstrate that a facially neutral government action is motivated by a discriminatory purpose.[32]

Obviously, judicial capacity is not the only factor that affects the Supreme Court's Equal Protection decisions. The ideology of the justices and their varying levels of concern about different types of government discrimination both matter greatly. Certainly it is difficult to explain the liberal–conservative divide in many of the Court's recent affirmative-action and same-sex marriage decisions without recourse to these factors. The conservative justices are simply much more troubled—constitutionally and, apparently, ideologically—by discrimination against white university and job applicants than are their liberal colleagues. Conversely, the liberal justices are much more troubled—again, constitutionally and, apparently, ideologically—by discrimination against gays and lesbians than the conservatives are.[33]

But the ways in which ideology influences the Supreme Court's constitutional decisions are strongly constrained by judicial capacity. The judicial capacity model does not explain the Court's decision to invalidate most race-based affirmative-action policies or its decisions to invalidate state bans on same-sex marriage or same-sex intimacy. But it does explain why conservative justices who oppose economic regulations of business and high tax rates on the wealthy as a matter of policy have resisted the temptation to subject such laws to serious Equal Protection review. The same goes for liberal justices and laws that burden—or fail to assist—workers, consumers, and the poor. The judicial capacity model also explains why the justices have pursued their ideological goals through a fairly rigid framework of tiered scrutiny that clearly marks off various narrow categories of government action for serious review, while subjecting all others to essentially categorical deference.

Like the Supreme Court's modern approach to the commerce power, this framework has two advantages from the standpoint of judicial capacity. First, it greatly limits the range of government action threatened by the Equal Protection Clause. Instead of prohibiting all unjustified government classifications, the Equal Protection Clause effectively prohibits only those classifications that burden fundamental rights or intentionally discriminate against a suspect class and cannot survive heightened scrutiny. This is by no means a trivial prohibition. States and localities burden the right to vote, limit access to courts, and intentionally or facially discriminate on the basis of race, gender, and other suspect or de facto suspect classifications (namely, sexual orientation) with some frequency. The Court's heightened scrutiny of these categories of government action certainly threatens a broader range of government action than the Court's recent commerce-power decisions. But this is nevertheless a tiny fraction of the government action that might plausibly trigger Equal Protection review. Moreover, because the great majority of that government action is state and local, the expected benefits of bringing suit are somewhat lower for prospective plaintiffs and the fraction of cases that the Court feels compelled to review is substantially smaller than it is for commerce-power cases. The resulting volume of litigation is easily manageable.

Second, the Supreme Court's tiered-scrutiny framework is crafted in clear and categorical terms, which reduces uncertainty for potential litigants and thus reduces the volume of litigation. In particular, it draws categorical lines between the discrete rights and suspect classifications that trigger meaningful Equal Protection review and everything else, clearly insulating virtually all of the latter against plausible constitutional challenge. This is not to say that tiered scrutiny will never cause confusion or debate; no categorical rule is that clear. In particular, what counts as a "burden" on a fundamental right, triggering heightened scrutiny, has given rise to real uncertainty. And the Court very occasionally feels compelled to put real teeth in rational-basis review—usually in the course of carving out a new discrete category of meaningful review, like gender, but every once in a while, on an ad hoc basis. But neither of these detracts from the broadly categorical character of the Court's tiered-scrutiny framework. Unlike other models of Supreme Court decision-making, the judicial capacity model explains why the Court would find such a framework attractive.[34]

Conversely, the judicial capacity model helps to explain the Supreme Court's reluctance to adopt anything resembling Justice Stevens's all-things-considered approach to Equal Protection review. That approach would have required the Court to assess the justification for government classifications on a case-by-case basis. From a textual, historical, and even an ideological standpoint, this test has much to recommend it. As explained above, it tracks the text of the Equal Protection Clause much better than tiered scrutiny and takes seriously the wide-ranging forms of unjustified government discrimination that clause was historically understood to embrace. Justice Stevens's approach would also give both liberal and conservative justices much greater flexibility to pursue their personal ideological views about which types of discrimination are justified and which are not.[35]

There is, however, one big problem. If applied with any real stringency, Stevens's nebulous standard would call into question a vast quantity of government action, generating an equally vast volume of litigation. In effect, the Court would be declaring itself open to reevaluating, on a case-by-case basis, the practical need justifying every government action significant enough for some plaintiff to bother bringing suit. Most of the government action challenged would be state and local, and much of it would ultimately be upheld as justified. But enough federal or important state legislation would be invalidated—or at least called into serious question—that the Supreme Court would feel compelled to review far more challenges than it could feasibly handle, consistent with its basic commitment to minimum professional standards. This is just what the judicial capacity model predicts the Court will be strongly constrained to avoid in high-volume domains like the Equal Protection Clause.

None of this is to suggest that the precise content and contours of the existing tiered-scrutiny framework were inevitable or that this framework is immune to change in the future. Here, as in other capacity-constrained domains, the limits of judicial capacity do not compel any one specific doctrinal formulation. Going forward, the Court might well scale back its review of one or more categories of discrimination that it currently subjects to heightened scrutiny. It might replace one of those categories with some new category or categories, or it might add some number of new categories to the current list. But whatever approach the Court ultimately takes will need to cleanly insulate the vast majority of government discrimination from serious constitutional review. This will require the Court to employ some combination of strong deference and narrow, categorical rules. Almost any approach that fits this description is likely to look, in broad brush, a lot like the existing tiered-scrutiny framework, though its particulars might be quite different.[36]

In sum, the judicial capacity model explains features of the Supreme Court's modern Equal Protection decisions that no other model readily can. Although the Court has both legal and ideological motives to engage in broad and meaningful Equal Protection review, the limits of judicial capacity prevent it from doing so except in carefully delimited categories. The Court also has legal and ideological motives to cast its Equal Protection review in the form of a context-specific standard, but its modern decisions have never done so. The judicial capacity model explains why. In these ways, it illuminates a crucially important area of constitutional law. In turn, the pattern of the Court's Equal Protection decisions provides additional evidence in its favor.

CHAPTER TEN

Takings

The Takings Clause of the Fifth Amendment is far less glamorous than the Equal Protection Clause, but its potential reach and import are comparably vast. Why this should be requires a bit of explanation. At first glance the Takings Clause appears to govern a fairly small corner of property law: "Nor shall private property be taken for public use without just compensation." As this text implies, the paradigmatic takings case involves the physical appropriation of private land, usually for a government infrastructure project such as a dam, road, or railroad. For this reason, the Takings Clause, which applies to both the federal government and the states, is sometimes known as "the Eminent Domain Clause."[1]

The name is deceiving. Nothing in the text or judicial construction of the Takings Clause limits its application to government condemnation of land, as opposed to other forms of property. Nor has the clause historically been understood as limited to physical appropriations. As courts and commentators have long recognized, government regulations affecting the use, disposition, and protection of property against incursion by other private actors can "take" the value of that property as effectually as direct physical appropriation. Both theoretically and in terms of their practical impact on property owners, such "regulatory takings" are very difficult to distinguish from physical appropriation.[2]

Once this logical step is taken, it is not easy to identify a stopping point. All, or virtually all, regulations affect the use, disposition, and protection of private property in some form or fashion, to the detriment of at least some property owners. Prohibition limited the permissible uses, and thereby reduced the value, of distilleries. The Clean Air Act and child labor laws did the same with dirty power plants and factories that previously employed children. Yet despite recognizing regulatory takings in principle, the Supreme Court has never made any serious attempt to police their full spectrum. Instead, the vast majority of regulations challenged under the Takings Clause are subject to the highly deferential test of *Penn Central Transportation Co. v. City of New York.* Where this test applies, the government almost always wins.[3]

The two narrow exceptions—"permanent physical invasion" and "complete elimination of a property's value"—are subject to clear-cut rules of per se invalidity. On the rare occasions when a challenged government regulation falls into one of these categories, the case is over; the government loses. There are occasional deviations from this pattern, typically short-lived, but in broad outline, modern takings law is a form of bifurcated review quite similar to that governing Equal Protection.[4]

This combination of narrow categorical limits and strong deference is puzzling for several reasons. First, from a legalist standpoint, there is little dispute that uncompensated regulatory takings, no less than uncompensated physical appropriations, are constitutionally prohibited. Second, also from a legalist standpoint, the Supreme Court's highly deferential approach to the vast majority of regulatory takings fails to track, even passably, any leading account of what the Takings Clause should be understood to prohibit.[5]

Third, from a cruder political standpoint, conservative justices should have a strong ideological motivation to expand serious constitutional review of regulatory takings. Like the nondelegation doctrine, unitary executive theory, and Equal Protection Clause, a robust Takings Clause would provide a potent tool for curtailing the regulatory state and for protecting business interests. If Supreme Court justices vote like legislators, as the attitudinal model posits, this is a result most or all conservative justices should favor to some substantial degree. Even liberal justices should be tempted to invalidate regulations that disproportionately burden the property interests of poor and minority citizens, as plenty of regulations unsurprisingly do. As in other contexts, the prospect of political backlash places some limit on the Court's ability to pursue either of these paths, but it cannot readily explain the Court's strong deference outside the narrow categories of permanent physical invasions and complete eliminations of a property's economic value.

None of the leading models of Supreme Court decision-making can readily explain these features of the Court's decisions, but the judicial capacity model can. In a nutshell, a robust regulatory takings doctrine, articulated in the form of a vague standard, would call into constitutional question an enormous quantity of federal regulatory legislation. It would also call into question innumerable state and local laws and a great number of administrative regulations and other executive actions at all levels. The reason is straightforward: Just as all laws classify, all regulations limit the use, disposition, or protection of some property interests, to the detriment of some property owners. To subject all such "takings" to serious review would invite far more litigation than the federal court system, and in particular the Supreme Court, could handle. The Court therefore only seriously scrutinizes regulatory takings when it can do so in the form of relatively narrow categorical rules that clearly insulate most governmental action from constitutional challenge.

The Pattern of Supreme Court Decisions

The core meaning of the Takings Clause has been clear and basically stable since the ratification of the Fifth Amendment in 1791: The government may not physically appropriate private land except for a public purpose and, even then, only with the payment of just compensation. Because the federal government seldom, if ever, attempted to condemn private land prior to the Civil War, and because the Supreme Court held the Fifth Amendment inapplicable to the states, this meaning was not much tested in court for almost a century. Many important nineteenth-century political figures did not even understand the federal government to possess the power of eminent domain outside the District of Columbia and the federal territories. But in 1875 the Supreme Court finally recognized a general federal eminent domain power, and in 1897 the Court extended the prohibition on uncompensated takings to states under the Due Process Clause of the Fourteenth Amendment. With these two developments, the Takings Clause began to show some real life as a constitutional limit on public condemnation of private land, which remains the paradigmatic application of the clause today.[6]

Even this stable core of the Takings Clause is not entirely free from ambiguity. What counts as a "public purpose" and who—or what institution—should decide that question has long been controversial and continues to be so today. The definition of "just compensation" can also be tricky, both conceptually and in particular applications. But if the Takings Clause implicated nothing more than traditional exercises of the eminent domain power over private land, mostly by state and local governments, it would be too narrow, too clear-cut, and of too little interest to the Supreme Court to have any place in this book. Only the expansion of the Takings Clause to embrace "regulatory takings" makes it fertile ground for the judicial capacity model.[7]

That expansion is conventionally traced to the Supreme Court's 1922 decision in *Pennsylvania Coal Co. v. Mahon,* which invalidated a Pennsylvania statute prohibiting the mining of coal "in such way as to cause the subsidence of, among other things, any structure used as a human habitation." The plaintiffs had sued under this statute, seeking to enjoin Pennsylvania Coal Company from mining under their house, even though the deed to their property expressly reserved this right to the company and waived all claims for damages that might result. In a famously cryptic opinion for the Court, Justice Oliver Wendell Holmes framed the constitutional issue as whether the regulation went "too far" to be sustained under the state's police power. If so, he said, it would be "recognized as a taking." He expressly recognized this inquiry as a "question of degree," which "therefore cannot be disposed of by general propositions." But in concluding that the Pennsylvania Act went too far, Holmes emphasized that the restrictions it imposed were the practical equivalent of "appropriating or destroying" the Company's "very valuable" right to mine coal.[8]

Bruce Ackerman described *Mahon* as "both the most important and the most mysterious writing in takings law." Carol Rose famously called it "a muddle." Certainly the decision has given rise to a fair amount of conceptual confusion about the criteria for distinguishing unconstitutional regulatory takings from valid exercises of the state police power or federal regulatory authority. But too often this confusion obscures the dominant fact about *Mahon:* The Supreme Court never again invalidated any state or local regulation under its vague "goes too far" standard. It has invalidated two federal regulations under this standard, but those decisions are very much the exception and involved highly peculiar facts that the Court relied upon to tightly circumscribe their reach. As a result of this broad deference, in the seventy years after *Mahon,* "the Takings Clause posed only a very limited threat to the state's regulatory power."[9]

Over this same period, a tolerably clear, if conceptually unsatisfying, doctrine emerged in *Mahon's* wake. Under this doctrine, regulations that involve permanent physical invasion or appropriation of private property are per se takings, invalid in all cases unless accompanied by adequate compensation. The same goes for regulations that deny all economically valuable or beneficial use of land. The best example of the former is *Loretto v. Teleprompter Manhattan CATV Corp.,* which invalidated a New York state statute requiring landlords to permit the installation of cable lines. The best example of the latter is *Lucas v. South Carolina Coastal Council,* which invalidated a South Carolina ban on construction within a designated coastal zone that deprived the plaintiff's two beachfront lots of "*all* economically beneficial use." This is sometimes known as the "total takings" doctrine.[10]

All regulations that fall outside these two narrow categories are subject to the deferential balancing test established in the 1978 case of *Penn Central Transportation Co. v. New York City.* In that now canonical case, the Supreme Court upheld the application of New York City's Landmarks Law to Grand Central Terminal. The effect of this application was to prohibit the construction of a planned fifty-story office building on the terminal site, which Penn Central challenged as an uncompensated regulatory taking of roughly $100 million in expected leasing revenues. Disclaiming any "set formula" for evaluating such claims, the Supreme Court instead "identified several factors that have particular significance." These include (1) the economic impact of a challenged regulation on the property owner; (2) the extent to which that regulation interferes with a property owner's "investment-backed expectations"; and (3) the "character of the government action."[11]

Apart from its rather cursory analysis upholding the New York Landmarks Law, the Supreme Court's opinion provides little guidance about how these factors relate to one another or how stringently its case-by-case test should be applied. In the lower courts, however, *Penn Central* balancing has been transformed into a highly deferential test. Commentators frequently equate this test to rational-basis review, and a recent empirical study showed that "fewer than 10 percent of regulatory takings claims [brought in state courts] are successful." As the authors of the study conclude, "courts almost always defer to the regulatory decisions made by government officials, resulting in an almost categorical rule that *Penn Central*-type regulatory actions do not amount to takings."[12]

At any time, the Supreme Court might have stepped in to put some real teeth in the *Penn Central* test or to adopt one of the many more theoretically rigorous alternatives proposed by academic commentators, but it has never done so. To the contrary, in the 2005 case of *Lingle v. Chevron, USA, Inc.*, a unanimous Court explicitly and emphatically disclaimed the application of any "heightened means-ends review" to regulations challenged under the Takings Clause. Indeed, the Court "has never applied [the *Penn Central* test] to invalidate a state or local regulation." The result is to make the highly deferential approach of the lower courts, for all practical purposes, the law of the land.[13]

Such is the modern law of takings in broad brush. This tidy summary obviously suppresses many nuances. In some cases, for instance, the line between a physical invasion (a per se taking) and a mere use regulation (subject to deferential *Penn Central* review) can become quite fine. Even *Loretto*, now the canonical physical invasion case, was something of a surprise when it was decided. In other cases, the "total takings" doctrine of *Lucas* raises difficult questions about the appropriate denominator for determining whether a challenged regulation eliminates all or only some fraction of the economic value of the plaintiff's property. But these are, in fact, nuances. At the end of the day, meaningful constitutional review of regulatory takings is confined to the usually clear categories of permanent physical invasions and total takings, both of which the Supreme Court and lower courts have defined quite narrowly. To the extent the boundaries of these categories are unclear, that ambiguity is almost always resolved in favor of challenged regulations. All other challenged regulations, which is to say the vast majority, are subject only to *Penn Central* review, which "has generally been fatal to regulatory takings claims." Frequent criticisms of regulatory takings doctrine as incoherent or arbitrary should not obscure this basic, and basically clear, doctrinal structure.[14]

It remains to consider the peculiar branch of takings doctrine governing "exactions," a generic term for conditions imposed on landowners in exchange for discretionary public benefits or regulatory forbearance. As elaborated in *Nollan v. California Coastal Comm'n* and *Dolan v. City of Tigard*, the Court's exactions doctrine represents a fairly straightforward application of the unconstitutional conditions doctrine. If the government is prohibited from taking private property without compensation, it must also be prohibited from demanding the surrender of such property as the price for obtaining a building permit or an exemption from zoning restrictions. Or so the Court's logic goes.[15]

This prohibition is not absolute. It can be overcome if the government demonstrates an "essential nexus" between the condition imposed and the benefit or regulatory forbearance offered in exchange, as well as a "rough proportionality" between the two. For instance, a development permit that would increase the risk of flooding could be conditioned on the permit seeker's dedication of a drainage channel for public use, so long as the dedication demanded was not disproportionate to the flooding risk that the development in question would create. As many commentators and the Court itself have observed, this amounts to a form of heightened scrutiny.[16]

Both the essential nexus and rough proportionality requirements are vague standards that have given rise to real uncertainty. Until recently, however, that uncertainty seemed to be bounded by the requirement that the challenged condition must have constituted a taking if unilaterally imposed. As such, an exaction could be constitutionally challenged only if the government demanded that a property owner, in exchange for a permit, variance, or the like, (a) submit to a physical invasion or appropriation;

or (b) surrender all economically viable uses of her property. Unless the state-imposed condition fell into one of these categories, it would be analyzed under the *Penn Central* test and would almost certainly not qualify as a taking.[17]

This changed with the Supreme Court's 2013 decision of *Koontz v. St. John's River Management District,* which extended the essential nexus and rough proportionality requirements to so-called monetary exactions. A monetary exaction is a requirement that a property owner pay a monetary fee—as opposed to surrendering land—in exchange for a discretionary state benefit or regulatory forbearance. Often the fee is ostensibly earmarked for offsetting the social costs of the sought-after benefit; sometimes it is dedicated to that purpose directly, rather than paid into government coffers. For instance, in *Koontz,* the defendant water management district offered to grant a building permit if the plaintiff agreed to pay for wetland restoration on district-owned land nearby.[18]

If this sounds a lot like an earmarked tax to support wetland restoration, that is because it is. Historically, such a tax would have been exempt from any takings scrutiny; it is hornbook law that taxes are not takings. But *Koontz* leaves the line between the two open to question. For this reason, the four *Koontz* dissenters and a host of academic commentators greeted the decision with alarm. Would all property taxes, permitting fees, and the like now be subject to heightened scrutiny?[19]

The *Koontz* majority emphatically says no but offers only vague hints as to the outer limits of its holding. Most notably, it declares that monetary exactions include only government-imposed financial obligations that "operate upon an identified property interest by directing the owner of a particular piece of property to make a monetary payment." This does little to distinguish property taxes and permitting fees, both of which are directed to the owners of particular pieces of property. It does, however, limit *Koontz* to monetary obligations imposed in connection with particular parcels of land and thus almost exclusively to the actions of local—and, more rarely, state—governments. In any event, the tidal wave of litigation predicted by *Koontz*'s many critics has thus far failed to materialize. I shall have more to say about this below.[20]

The Doctrinal Puzzle

The pattern of the Supreme Court's modern takings decisions, like its modern commerce-power and Equal Protection decisions, presents two distinct puzzles: First, why have those decisions exempted nearly all government regulations from meaningful takings review? Second, why has the Court limited the meaningful review it does engage in to a small handful of discrete categories, rather than embracing the more flexible case-by-case or sliding scale approaches advocated by so many commentators (and superficially suggested by decisions like *Mahon* and *Penn Central*)? No leading model of Supreme Court decision-making can readily answer these questions.

Post-Mahon *Deference*

Since deciding *Mahon* in 1922, the Supreme Court has upheld virtually every regulation it has considered under that decision's "goes too far" standard and the *Penn Central* test that succeeded it. Meanwhile, lower courts have turned the latter into a rule of categorical deference roughly equivalent to rational-basis review. This strong and persistent deference is puzzling because the Court has both legal and ideological motives for subjecting a wide range of government regulations to meaningful takings review and few strategic motives for deferring so comprehensively—or, what amounts to the same thing, permitting the lower courts to do so. Put in reverse, the legalist and attitudinal models both predict that the Court should have reviewed government regulation under the Takings Clause more aggressively than it has. The strategic model predicts that the Court will back off efforts to restrict regulatory takings that threaten serious political backlash, of the sort triggered by the Court's aggressive efforts to roll back the New Deal. But this prediction cannot readily explain why the Court has subjected so large a majority of government regulation to such highly deferential takings review.

The obvious exception is exactions. The attitudinal model does help to explain the conservative justices' embrace of heightened scrutiny for evaluating exactions as an effort to invalidate governmental interference with private property. But the attitudinal model cannot explain why those justices and their conservative predecessors have adopted such a deferential approach to regulatory takings generally.

Let us begin with the Supreme Court's legal motives for expanding review of regulatory takings. Despite the Court's long record of deference to most government regulations that negatively affect the value of private property, I am aware of no Supreme Court justice in the modern era who has openly urged a reversal of *Mahon* or contended that the Takings Clause protects only against physical appropriations. Some scholars have argued that the original meaning of the clause was limited in this way, but that view has attracted no support on the Court; nor has it ever been offered as a justification for reviewing regulatory takings deferentially. Indeed, the Court has now consistently read the Constitution to prohibit regulatory, as well as physical, takings for nearly a century.[21]

One reason for this, as Brannon Denning and Michael Kent have elegantly explained, is the Court's apparent concern to prevent evasion of the constitutional prohibition on uncompensated physical appropriations. But to effectually prevent such evasion would require a far broader and more rigorous regulatory takings doctrine than the Court has ever been willing to enforce. A great many regulations are close substitutes for—or functional equivalents to—physical appropriations. Indeed, many regulations the Supreme Court and lower courts have upheld under *Penn Central* review are far *more* burdensome than the physical appropriations they have invalidated under *Loretto*'s per se rule. The historic preservation statute upheld in *Penn Central* itself was credibly projected to cost Penn Central roughly $100 million, while the cost of the mandatory cable installation invalidated in *Loretto* was comparatively trivial. A principled legal concern with preventing evasion might explain the Court's expansion of takings review to encompass regulatory takings and the Court's recently expanded review of monetary exactions, but that concern cannot plausibly explain the extent of the Court's deference to the vast majority of challenged regulations.[22]

Of course, in 2017 the Supreme Court's broad deference to most government regulation is firmly entrenched in decades of case law, which counts as a legalist argument in its favor. But as in other contexts, this argument does not explain how the Court's deference came to be so entrenched, and because precedents can be overruled, it counts as only a partial explanation for why this deference has remained such a stable feature of the Court's decisions for the entire modern era. Precedent may be an even less satisfying explanation for the Court's deference to regulatory takings than for its deference in other contexts because the Court's leading regulatory takings decisions are not especially deferential on their face. At any point, the Court could easily have adopted a more rigorous approach to regulatory takings review without having to repudiate *Penn Central* or *Mahon*. And yet it has consistently failed to do so, effectively making the categorically deferential approach of the lower courts the law of the land. This failure cannot be explained by a legalist commitment to *stare decisis*.

Nor does the Court's categorical deference to all but a handful of carefully circumscribed classes of regulation plausibly track any leading academic account of regulatory takings. There are far too many such accounts to review them in a meaningful way here. Suffice it to say, few bodies of law are more widely and consistently abused in the academic literature than the Court's regulatory takings decisions. So frequent and widely rehearsed are the complaints that it has become almost a cliché to describe them as a cliché. But for present purposes, the point is not to complain. It is simply to note that legal theories developed by academics are no better able to explain the Court's regulatory takings doctrine than the other legalist factors canvassed up to this point.[23]

From a cruder political perspective, both liberal and conservative justices have strong ideological motives to review regulatory takings far more stringently. Because virtually all regulations negatively affect some property owners, a prohibition on uncompensated regulatory takings, like a prohibition on unjustified government classifications, is a highly potent—and highly malleable—tool for justices to invalidate disfavored regulations of virtually any stripe. If Supreme Court justices vote like legislators, as the attitudinal model posits, rigorous regulatory takings review would provide a ready vehicle for judicial conservatives to invalidate just about any federal, state, or local regulation that these justices oppose on policy grounds, which is plainly a large fraction of the regulatory universe. Since the New Deal and especially since the election of Ronald Reagan, few issues have been more central to American conservatism than the crusade to roll back economic regulation. This ideological hostility to regulation certainly helps to explain the motivations of the conservative justices to expand takings review of monetary exactions in *Koontz* and the votes of conservative justices in cases like *Lucas, Nollan,* and *Dolan.* Yet despite the soaring paeans to property rights in these decisions, no group of conservative justices has ever mounted a serious assault on the highly deferential *Penn Central* regime that has long applied to the vast majority of challenged regulations. From the standpoint of the attitudinal model, this is a genuine puzzle.[24]

For liberal justices, rigorous regulatory takings review should provide a powerful tool for shielding the socially and economically disadvantaged against the disproportionate regulatory burdens to which they are frequently subject. The constitutional prohibition on regulatory takings has come to be strongly associated with conservatism and libertarianism, but it is no coincidence that Justices William Brennan and Thurgood Marshall were among the most aggressive proponents of regulatory takings review during their tenure on the Court, nor that liberal constitutional scholar Frank Michelman was an important early advocate of a broad theory of takings. Regulations are a powerful tool for both special interests and popular majorities to enrich themselves at the expense of the politically powerless. Yet at no point in the modern history of the Court, even in the heyday of Warren Court liberalism, has any substantial number of liberal justices advocated the sort of rigorous approach to regulatory takings that would be necessary to correct this pathology. From the standpoint of the attitudinal model, this too is a genuine puzzle.[25]

As with the Commerce and Equal Protection Clauses, the strategic model is somewhat more helpful, but only somewhat. Fear of political recalcitrance might well explain why the modern Supreme Court has never pushed regulatory takings review to the hilt, in either a liberal or a conservative direction. To do so would effectively empower the Court to second-guess all regulatory decisions, which would surely provoke significant resistance from both Congress and state legislatures. But the strategic model cannot readily explain why the Court has circumscribed meaningful regulatory takings review to just a handful of discrete categories. More specifically, the strategic model cannot explain why the modern Court's conservatives have never been seriously tempted to exercise meaningful across-the-board review of economic regulations that would curb, but not overturn, the modern regulatory state. Nor can the strategic model explain why the Court's liberals have never seriously pushed for meaningful review of regulations that single out the politically powerless for disproportionate regulatory burden, which could stop considerably short of second-guessing all regulatory decisions.[26]

As in other contexts, neither of these steps seems likely to have provoked serious retaliation, especially when a sympathetic political party controlled one house of Congress or the presidency. Certainly the Court has taken and maintained far less popular stands in recent years, without triggering any effective political resistance. The strategic model, therefore, cannot persuasively explain the Court's failure to expand regulatory takings review.[27]

Preference for Categorical Rules over Standards

During the modern era, the Supreme Court has consistently refused to embrace the sort of vague regulatory takings standard superficially suggested by *Mahon* and *Penn Central* and championed, in one form or another, by a diverse array of academic commentators. Rather, both the physical invasion and the total takings branches of regulatory takings doctrine have been, since their inception, defined in categorical terms that clearly mark off the narrow lines within which uncompensated government regulation is per se invalid—and beyond which *Penn Central* review kicks in. The Court's deference in conducting that review has been similarly categorical, at least in practice. As noted above, the Supreme Court has never invalidated a state or local regulation under this test or its predecessors, and lower courts apply it much like the categorically deferential rational-basis test. The one exception is the Court's treatment of exactions, which especially after *Koontz*, appears to subject the vaguely defined class of government land-use bargains to the vague "essential nexus" and "rough proportionality" tests established in *Nollan* and *Dolan*.[28]

The leading models of Supreme Court decision-making cannot readily explain this pattern of decisions. As explained in earlier chapters, neither the attitudinal nor the strategic model makes any strong predictions about the doctrinal form of Supreme Court decisions. If anything, the hierarchical branch of the strategic model predicts that the doctrinal form should vary over time with a complex array of frequently shifting variables, including the ideological diversity of the lower federal courts and the ideological distance between those courts and the Supreme Court. By and large, that is not what we see in the Court's modern takings decisions. The attitudinal model might explain the conservative justices' embrace of a vague standard for evaluating exactions as an effort to invalidate ideologically disfavored governmental intrusions on private property interests, while preserving flexibility to uphold others. But that model cannot explain why those justices and their conservative predecessors have so long failed to embrace such a standard for regulatory takings generally, where the ideological incentives for doing so are precisely the same.

The legalist model, as usual, poses trickier questions. It predicts that doctrinal form will reflect legal factors like the constitutional text, history, and judicial precedent. In the case of the Takings Clause, however, none of these factors cuts particularly strongly in either direction. Both constitutional text and history might be read to support a hard, categorical distinction between physical and regulatory takings, with the former being per se forbidden without compensation and the latter per se permitted. But the Supreme Court has never embraced this view, treating at least one category of regulatory takings—total takings—as per se impermissible without compensation and refusing to hold other regulations immune from takings scrutiny, even as the Court comprehensively defers to them in practice. Precedent is similarly inconclusive. A long line of decisions treats uncompensated physical appropriations and invasions as per se impermissible, but a similarly long line of decisions suggests that regulatory takings present difficult questions of degree that courts should evaluate on an ad hoc basis. Yet the Supreme Court has never taken serious steps to prevent this vague standard from evolving into a rule of categorical deference in the lower courts. Some academic theories do support a categorical approach of one kind or another, but as explained above, the Court's approach does not closely, or even passably, track any of them.[29]

The Supreme Court's principled legal concern to prevent evasion of its takings decisions, discussed earlier, does help to explain the Court's departure from categorical rules in the context of exactions. The *Koontz* majority was quite explicit about this motivation. If the vaguely defined class of monetary exactions were exempted from heightened scrutiny, Justice Samuel Alito reasoned, "it would be very easy for land-use permitting officials to evade the limitations of *Nollan* and *Dolan*." The *Koontz* dissenters did not share this concern but thought it the principal driving force behind the majority's decision. As discussed earlier, however, this cannot explain the Court's categorical deference to a wide range of regulations that are close substitutes for—or functional equivalents of—physical takings.[30]

The Judicial Capacity Model Applied

The judicial capacity model helps to explain the Court's consistent failure to vigorously review regulatory takings. It also helps to explain why the Court has consistently cast its meaningful review of regulatory takings in the form of narrow, categorical rules, not compelled by text, history, or precedent. The judicial capacity model does not shed as much light on the Court's more robust and standard-like review of exactions. But on close examination, that review turns out to be at least consistent with its predictions, and the judicial capacity model helps to explain why the Court has not pursued a similar approach to regulatory takings more generally.

As discussed in Chapter 2, the Court does not feel compelled to grant review of just any lower-court decision invalidating government regulations under the Takings Clause. Such cases frequently involve challenges to executive action, rather than legislation, and especially to executive action at the local and state levels, which generally affects a fairly limited population—often only a single property owner. All of these factors generally raise the Supreme Court's tolerance of disuniformity and thus reduce the percentage of cases it feels compelled to review.[31]

Even so, once the Takings Clause is expanded beyond physical takings, it has the potential to invite more litigation than the Supreme Court could handle while maintaining even a basic commitment to uniformity and minimum professional standards. In the terms of the judicial capacity model, this makes the Takings Clause, like the Equal Protection Clause, a high-volume domain. A robust regulatory takings doctrine, articulated in the form of a vague standard like that superficially adopted by *Mahon* and *Penn Central,* would call into question a large fraction of the U.S. Code. It would also call into question innumerable state and local laws and a great number of administrative agency and other executive actions at all levels. The reason is straightforward: All regulations limit the use, disposition, or protection of property to the detriment of at least some property owners.

This point is hardly new. As usual, Carol Rose captures it well: "Every regulation has some winners and some losers, and to allow takings challenges to all of them in effect would turn the Takings Clause into an avenue for general taxpayer suits against governments, including the federal government." More colorfully, Rose writes, "the regulatory takings doctrine is at bottom an unfathomable well of antilegislative activism." Rose is predominantly a critic of robust regulatory takings review, as are most others who have made this point. But the most prominent proponent of such review, Richard Epstein, emphatically agrees with them: "It will be said that my position invalidates much of the twentieth-century legislation, *and so it does.*" Epstein, unsurprisingly, sees this as a feature, not a bug, of his proposal.[32]

As Rose and Epstein both recognize, the regulations imperiled by any robust regulatory takings review would not be limited to local land use and zoning ordinances, whose invalidation by lower courts the Supreme Court is usually content to leave unreviewed. Rather, the imperiled regulations would include many, if not most, federal regulations intended to protect workers, consumers, health, safety, the environment, and the national financial system. The Americans with Disabilities Act, the Civil Rights Act, the Endangered Species Act, the Controlled Substances Act, the Sherman Antitrust Act, the Lanham Act, the Federal Aviation Act, and the Fair Labor Standards Act all limit the rights of some property owners to use or dispose of their property, including land, personal property, and money. All of these regulations create losers as well as winners and therefore arguably constitute regulatory takings. The list of similar federal statutes could go on indefinitely, each encompassing dozens or hundreds of discrete provisions and many authorizing reams of important agency regulations. If these statutes, provisions, or regulations were invalidated by the lower courts, the Supreme Court would feel strongly compelled to grant review in almost every case.[33]

The point should be clear. To subject all such regulations to rigorous or even meaningful regulatory takings review, in the form of a vague standard, would invite far more litigation than the federal court system, and in particular the Supreme Court, could handle. Even an apparently categorical approach like Epstein's, which would treat virtually all regulations and progressive taxation as presumptively impermissible takings, would leave courts with much difficult work to do on a case-by-case basis. That is because Epstein's categorical prohibition on regulatory takings makes exceptions for cases in which regulation is necessary to protect the rights of other property owners, particularly their right to be free from common-law nuisances. Epstein also makes exceptions for cases where the property owner benefits at least as much as she loses, which he treats as a sort of in-kind compensation. As Neil Komesar has explained, evaluating the application of these exceptions on the scale Epstein envisions would be an enormous task. Because so many of the regulations in question are federal, this task would very likely overwhelm the limited capacity of the Supreme Court, which would feel compelled to review a large fraction of the resulting litigation.[34]

Of course, as in other contexts, it is not only the quantity of threatened government action that determines the volume of potential litigation. It is also the magnitude of the benefits that such invalidation would generate for prospective plaintiffs and the number of prospective plaintiffs either collectively or individually capable of mustering the resources to litigate. Because the array of reasonably questionable government regulations is practically infinite, so is the array of prospective plaintiffs who would stand to benefit from their invalidation. For present purposes, however, it suffices to note that huge swaths of federal regulations implicate large business and industrial interests, which spend millions or billions of dollars on regulatory compliance. Many federal regulations, and especially state and local regulations, also implicate the interests of landowners, with individually and collectively substantial real estate holdings, though the Court feels substantially less pressure to review the invalidation of state and local regulations. If this were not enough, a well-funded and sophisticated pro bono bar stands ready to assist with high-profile constitutional litigation on behalf of small business and property owners, at least in part as a stalking horse for subverting regulation of large businesses and industry.[35]

The upshot is straightforward. For most significant government regulations, and for many insignificant ones, some plaintiff or plaintiffs will almost always have both the incentive and the resources to bring whatever constitutional challenges the Supreme Court's regulatory takings doctrine makes plausible. Some of these challenges will settle and some of them will never arise because the government actors in question will modify their behavior to avoid litigation. But if the Court puts real teeth in its regulatory takings doctrine, especially in the form of a vague standard, a vast number of these challenges will be litigated and appealed. The Court will not feel compelled to review every such challenge, but it will feel compelled to review enough—especially those involving federal legislation and administrative regulations—that takings qualifies as a high-volume domain. The judicial capacity model therefore predicts that the Court will feel compelled to adopt a strongly deferential approach, employ hard-edged categorical rules, or both.

This, in fact, is just what we see when we examine the Supreme Court's modern regulatory takings decisions. As already mentioned numerous times, the Court has never invalidated a state or local regulation for "going too far" under *Mahon* or for failing *Penn Central*'s ad hoc balancing test. The vast majority of regulations are never challenged, not because they do not limit the use, disposition, or protection of private property, but because the Supreme Court has allowed lower courts to transform *Penn Central* into a rule of categorical deference. As a result, it is almost always pointless to bring a regulatory takings challenge to regulations that fall outside the per se rules against physical invasions and total takings. Not coincidentally, the Court's decisions—and lower-court decisions applying them—have construed these per se rules quite narrowly.[36]

Obviously, judicial capacity is not the only factor that affects the Supreme Court's regulatory takings decisions. The ideology of the justices and their varying levels of concern about different types of interference with private property both matter greatly. Certainly, it is difficult to explain the liberal-conservative divide in many of the Court's recent takings decisions without recourse to these factors. Today's conservative justices are simply much more troubled—constitutionally and, apparently, ideologically—by regulatory interference with private property. Conversely, today's liberal justices are much more concerned about unduly restricting the power of government regulators to protect the public interest.[37]

But the ways in which ideology influences the Supreme Court's constitutional decisions are strongly constrained by judicial capacity. The judicial capacity model does not explain the Court's decision to invalidate total takings or trivial physical invasions like the one at issue in *Loretto*. But it does explain why conservative justices who oppose much of the modern regulatory state as a matter of policy have resisted the temptation to subject any meaningful number of federal regulations to serious takings review, even when they impose far greater financial burdens than those invalidated in *Lucas* and *Loretto*. The same goes for liberal justices and laws that single out the politically powerless for disproportionate regulatory burdens. The model also explains why the justices have pursued their ideological goals through a fairly rigid framework of bifurcated scrutiny that clearly marks off two narrow categories of government regulation for per se invalidation, while subjecting all others to a rule of basically categorical deference.

Like the Supreme Court's modern approach to the commerce power and Equal Protection Clause, this framework has two advantages from the standpoint of judicial capacity. First, it greatly limits the range of government action threatened by the Takings Clause. Rather than casting a shadow over the entire regulatory state, the Takings Clause effectively prohibits only physical appropriations or invasions and total takings. This is by no means a trivial prohibition. States and localities routinely appropriate private property for infrastructure projects and other purposes and at least occasionally adopt regulations that involve a physical invasion or total taking of private property. The Court's per se prohibition of these categories of government action certainly threatens a larger quantity of government action than the Court's recent commerce power decisions. But this is nevertheless a tiny fraction of the regulation that might plausibly trigger takings review. More important, the great majority of the regulation threatened under the Court's current takings doctrine is local and state, rather than federal. That means the expected benefits of bringing suit are somewhat lower for prospective plaintiffs, because the incidence of the constitutionally vulnerable regulations is more limited. It also means that the fraction of cases that the Court feels compelled to review is dramatically smaller than it is for commerce-power cases.[38]

Second, the Supreme Court's bifurcated regulatory takings framework is crafted in clear and categorical terms, which reduces uncertainty for potential litigants and thus reduces the volume of litigation. In particular, it draws categorical lines around the narrow classes of regulation that are per se invalid without compensation, clearly insulating virtually all other regulations against plausible constitutional challenge. At the same time, the Court's categorical approach encourages settlement in cases where the per se rules apply, sharply limiting the volume of serious litigation that might require Supreme Court review. For physical appropriations of land, in particular, compensation is generally provided as a matter of course.[39]

This is not to say that the Court's bifurcated approach will never cause confusion or debate. As noted earlier, the per se rule against un-compensated physical invasions occasionally gives rise to difficult cases at the margin, and the total takings rule raises tricky question about the denominator for determining whether a particular taking is total or merely partial. And lower courts do occasionally invalidate gov-ernment regulations under *Penn Central*'s ad hoc balancing test. But no categorical rule is perfectly clear or predictable. And none of the low-level doctrinal ambiguities in the Court's takings jurisprudence detract from the broadly categorical character of its bifurcated approach. Un-like other models of Supreme Court decision-making, the judicial capacity model explains why the Court would find such a framework attractive.[40]

Conversely, it helps to explain the Supreme Court's reluctance to put real teeth in *Mahon*'s "goes too far" test or *Penn Central*'s ad hoc balancing test. From both a legal and an ideological standpoint, a stringent applica-tion of these tests has much to recommend it. At the very least, it would make fewer arbitrary distinctions between physical takings and regula-tory takings of equal or greater magnitude. In so doing, such an approach would make it more difficult for government regulators to evade the Con-stitution's clear prohibition on uncompensated physical takings. This approach would also give both liberal and conservative justices much greater flexibility to invalidate disfavored regulations and uphold favored ones.

There is one big problem. If applied with any real stringency, the nebulous standards of *Mahon* and *Penn Central* would call into question a vast quantity of regulation, with no clearly specified criteria for distinguishing the constitutionally permissible from the constitutionally impermissible. Most of the regulation challenged would be state and local, and much of it might ultimately be upheld as justified. But a huge quantity of federal regulation would also be called into question, enough that the Supreme Court would feel compelled to review far more challenges than it could feasibly handle. This is just what the judicial capacity model predicts the Court will be strongly constrained to avoid in high-volume domains like the Takings Clause.

Penn Central and *Mahon* have been widely and persuasively criticized for failing to specify criteria for determining when a regulation "goes too far." But the judicial capacity model also explains the Court's refusal to adopt more conceptually satisfying, but still vague and standard-like, approaches such as Frank Michelman's "demoralization cost" theory. That theory focuses on the special psychic costs to property owners of being arbitrarily singled out to bear a disproportionate regulatory burden. Although Michelman plausibly insists that these costs are different in kind from other types of harms, his approach would nevertheless require courts to identify and measure such costs, to evaluate the possibility that they have been adequately compensated in kind over the long run, and also to balance these costs against "settlement costs"—the costs of administering the compensation system. This is an extremely crude summary of Michelman's complex theory, but it captures the essential point for present purposes. To determine the permissibility of a challenged regulation under that theory would require an extremely intricate case-by-case evaluation. Michelman himself recognized the judicial capacity problems this would create and, on that basis, disclaimed "any idea that courts can or will decide each compensability case in accordance" with this theory.[41]

Other scholars have also recognized the constraints judicial capacity imposes on the Supreme Court's ability to engage in meaningful review of regulatory takings. The work of Neil Komesar and Carol Rose is especially illuminating on this point and deserves acknowledgment beyond the many citations throughout this chapter. What the judicial capacity model adds is the insight that judicial norms are crucial to understanding the constraining force of judicial capacity. In other words, it is not just the potential volume of litigation, emphasized by Komesar, Rose, and others, that constrains the Court's regulatory takings decisions. It is also the potential threat that those decisions pose to the validity of a large quantity of *federal* regulations, whose invalidation the Supreme Court would feel strongly compelled to review. This normative commitment to reviewing most, if not all, invalidations of federal law is the key factor distinguishing regulatory takings from other domains in which a large potential volume of litigation does not much constrain the Court because the Court is content to leave the vast majority of it unreviewed. Habeas corpus review of state criminal convictions, the Fourth Amendment, and Title VII are good examples.[42]

None of the foregoing is to suggest that the precise content and contours of the Supreme Court's current regulatory takings doctrine were inevitable or that this framework will not evolve in the future. Here, as in other capacity-constrained domains, the limits of judicial capacity do not compel any one specific doctrinal formulation. Going forward, the Court might well scale back one or both of its per se rules of invalidity. It might replace, or supplement, those rules with some new category or categories of prohibited regulations. More imaginatively, it might embrace William Fischel's proposal to categorically exempt federal regulations from meaningful takings scrutiny. But whatever approach the Court ultimately takes will need to cleanly insulate the vast majority of government regulation, especially federal regulation, from serious constitutional review. This will require the Court to employ some combination of strong deference and narrow, categorical rules. Almost any approach that fits this description is likely to look, in broad brush, a lot like the existing bifurcated review framework, though its particulars might be quite different.[43]

It remains to apply the judicial capacity model to exactions. Prior to the Court's recent decision in *Koontz,* this doctrine was generally—but not universally—understood as limited to conditions that would themselves constitute a taking. At first blush, this understanding might seem to have made exactions claims merely a smaller subset of takings claims, one whose potential volume would be effectively constrained by the same combination of narrow categorical rules and broad deference that limits the volume of takings claims generally. The reality is more complicated. Exactions are a ubiquitous feature of local land use practice, but unlike traditional exercises of the eminent domain power, which are also ubiquitous, exactions are subject to the hazy "essential nexus" and "rough proportionality requirements," which lower courts have applied with real bite. This combination of robust judicial review with vague standards would seem to make litigation far more likely and far more complicated than it is under the per se compensation requirement applicable to physical takings. In other words, even before *Koontz*, the Court's approach to exactions seemed to invite a very substantial volume of litigation. Instead of retrenching, *Koontz* extended that approach to a considerably larger universe of land use bargains.[44]

All of the above makes the Supreme Court's exactions doctrine the closest thing to a counterexample to the judicial capacity model's predictions that I am aware of. A closer examination, however, helps to reconcile the Court's exactions decisions with the model's predictions. The judicial capacity model cannot explain the Court's choice to take such an aggressive approach to the review of exactions, nor can it explain the Court's choice to cast that review in the form of a vague standard. But neither are these choices inconsistent with the model. Rather, exactions is best categorized as a normal domain in which the limits of judicial capacity do not strongly constrain the Court's decisions.

There are two decisive reasons for categorizing exactions as a normal domain. First, the land-use bargains that qualify as exactions almost all involve local and occasionally state, as opposed to federal, government action. As a result, the Court only feels compelled to review a tiny fraction of exactions challenges. This is dramatically illustrated by the nineteen years that passed between the Court's second exactions decision (*Dolan*) and its third (*Koontz*). During this period, the lower courts dealt with considerable exactions litigation, including on the precise questions presented by *Koontz*, but the Court clearly felt no urgency to grant review. Even so, all three of the Court's major exactions decisions triggered vigorous four-justice dissents resting in part on judicial capacity-related concerns.[45]

The local and state character of nearly all exactions is probably sufficient to explain the Supreme Court's willingness to invite substantial litigation in this domain. It does not, however, explain why no flood of exactions litigation ever materialized, either before or after *Koontz* expanded the *Nollan/Dolan* test to monetary exactions. This brings us to the second reason for categorizing exactions as a normal domain: The potential volume of exactions litigation is smaller than it first appears. One recent study counted only 1,400 state and local exactions cases in the two years prior to *Koontz* and 1,200 such cases in the two years starting six months after the *Koontz* decision. These are hardly trivial numbers. Indeed, if the exactions at issue involved federal laws, this volume of litigation would constitute something approaching a judicial capacity crisis. But since exactions almost never involve federal laws, 600 to 700 cases per year is far from the overwhelming onslaught of litigation that critics of the Court's exactions decisions, including the dissenting justices, predicted. Nor has there been any appreciable increase since *Koontz* was decided.[46]

A definitive explanation of why the predicted onslaught never materialized would require extensive study, but the existing literature suggests at least three plausible explanations. First, the Supreme Court's decisions might be deterring local governments from making the kinds of demands on developers that would trigger litigation. This would be the rational response in situations where the government predicts defeat in court but also in cases where projected litigation costs exceed the benefits of the bargain in question. Depending on the circumstances, this may lead local governments to permit development unconditionally or to prohibit development unconditionally.[47]

Second and relatedly, both local governments and large land developers have strong incentives to resolve exactions disputes through negotiation. Local governments benefit from promoting development, which increases their tax base, and repeat-player developers benefit from favorable relations with local governments, which remain free to deny permits, zoning variances, and other discretionary benefits unconditionally. Smaller, one-time property developers have less incentive to maintain good relations with local authorities. But in general, they are also less able to bear the costs of litigation, which will often exceed the cost of acceding to any particular governmental demand.[48]

Third, while some states provide a statutory damages remedy for unconstitutional exactions, *Koontz* refused to mandate any specific remedy as a matter of federal constitutional law. This leaves open the possibility that successful exactions plaintiffs might simply win the right to have their permit or variance denied unconditionally. Needless to say, this prospect significantly reduces the incentive to bring suit.[49]

Whatever the precise explanation, the Supreme Court has subjected exactions to meaningful judicial review in the form of a vague standard without triggering an avalanche of litigation that the Court itself feels compelled to review. That is not a necessary condition for exactions to qualify as a normal domain, but it is a fully sufficient one. The Court might decide to retreat from this approach at some point in the future, but barring a radical shift in the dynamics of exactions litigation, such a retreat will not be strongly compelled by the limits of judicial capacity. Beyond this, the judicial capacity model makes no predictions one way or another about the Court's use of deference or categorical rules in normal domains.

This analysis does suggest a sort of paradox. Normal domains can be definitively confirmed as such, but capacity-constrained domains cannot. If the Supreme Court adopts an aggressive approach to judicial review cast in the form of a vague standard, without triggering an avalanche of litigation that threatens the Court's basic normative commitments, the domain in question is definitively confirmed to be normal. But if the Court consistently employs some combination of deference and categorical rules, the volume of potential litigation that would result from abandoning this approach remains necessarily a matter of speculation. It can thus never be conclusively established that it is that volume, rather than some other factor, that explains the Court's consistently deferential or categorical approach. Instead, one must carefully compare the plausibility of competing explanations for this pattern of Supreme Court decisions. That is what all the chapters in this Part have sought to do.

To sum up, the judicial capacity model explains features of the Supreme Court's regulatory takings decisions that no other model readily can. Although the Court has both legal and ideological motives to engage in broad and meaningful takings review, the limits of judicial capacity prevent it from doing so except in carefully delimited categories. The Court also has legal and ideological motives to cast its regulatory takings review in the form of a context-specific standard, but its modern decisions have never done so. The judicial capacity model explains why. In these ways, it illuminates a crucially important area of constitutional law. In turn, the pattern of the Court's regulatory takings decisions provides additional evidence in its favor. The judicial capacity model sheds less light on the Court's exactions decisions, but those decisions are not inconsistent with it because exactions, unlike regulatory takings, is best categorized as a normal domain for judicial capacity purposes.

III

Positive and Normative Implications

The discussion to this point has been largely positive—that is, descriptive—and retrospective. The judicial capacity model helps to explain several persistent puzzles in the Supreme Court's past decisions across a wide range of constitutional domains. This is important in its own right and because it provides empirical support for the model's descriptive and predictive claims. As the preceding chapters have shown, that support is substantial and encompasses many of the most important domains of U.S. constitutional law. The implications of the judicial capacity model, however, go substantially beyond its power to explain constitutional doctrine. The model also has important implications for the power and limits of the courts as a vehicle for social reform, the comparative competence of courts relative to other decision-making institutions, and the democratic legitimacy of judicial review. It is no exaggeration to say that these are among the biggest questions in U.S. constitutional law.

This Part explores three of these implications, which have both positive and normative dimensions. First, the limits of judicial capacity constrain the Supreme Court's constitutional choice set. Lawyers, academics, and social activists who wish to invoke the aid of the courts in any project of social reform must consider whether their goals can be accomplished within the constraints imposed by judicial capacity. For the most ambitious goals, the answer will often be "no" or "not completely." Even where the answer is not categorically negative, it will often be helpful—or even imperative—to tailor proposed reforms to the limits of judicial capacity. These issues are explored in Chapter 11.

Second, the limits of judicial capacity also limit the ability of courts to reach reliably good results, otherwise known as judicial competence. In any given case, expanded protection of constitutional rights or enforcement of constitutional limits on government power might seem highly, even obviously, desirable in the abstract. After all, state and federal legislatures, administrative agencies, and executive officials make plenty of mistakes. But in many of the most important constitutional domains, the limits of judicial capacity will often require constitutional rights and limits to be cast in the form of crude, categorical rules, which protect both more and less than necessary. As a result, expanded judicial protection may do more harm than good. In this way, judicial capacity and judicial competence are deeply intertwined. These issues are explored in Chapter 12.

Third, the limits of judicial capacity substantially limit the Supreme Court's power to constrain democratic majorities, otherwise known as judicial independence. Constitutional decisions that block the will of national majorities for any substantial length of time across any substantial breadth of issues will usually generate substantial litigation. In many of the most important constitutional domains, the potential volume of litigation will be too great for the Court to handle, pushing the Court back to its default posture of broad deference, perhaps qualified by narrow, categorical limits at the margin. In this way, judicial capacity and judicial independence, like judicial capacity and judicial competence, are deeply intertwined. These issues are explored in Chapter 13.

Together, these implications demonstrate that the judicial capacity model is central to understanding the place of the courts, and in particular the Supreme Court, in the modern constitutional order. Judicial capacity constrains what the courts can do, how and how well they can do it, and their ability to persist in the face of democratic opposition. These questions are of acute interest to constitutional theorists, but they are also highly relevant to the work of social reformers and to perennial public debates about the role of courts in a democracy. All of these groups should take judicial capacity seriously.

CHAPTER ELEVEN

Judicial Capacity and the Constitutional Choice Set

Perhaps the most obvious implication of the judicial capacity model is that normative constitutional argument—argument about how judges *should* decide constitutional cases—must take account of institutional constraints on the judiciary. In particular, arguments that the Supreme Court should more stringently police government action in capacity-constrained domains must take account of judicial capacity, which sharply constrains both the extent to which the Court can intervene in these areas and the form in which it can do so. In a phrase, ought implies can. Proponents of aggressive judicial review, both academic theorists and practical reformers, ignore this simple proposition at their own risk.

This much is straightforward, but there is a subtler point. The limits of judicial capacity not only limit the extent of judicial review. They also limit the doctrinal tools available to the Supreme Court for policing government action—what I will call *the constitutional choice set*. In capacity-constrained domains, that set is likely to boil down to two choices: (1) a categorical rule of deference, which will inevitably require the Court to uphold some government action most observers would recognize as normatively unattractive, or (2) various categorical rules of invalidity, which will inevitably require the Court to invalidate some government actions that most observers would recognize as normatively attractive. For both academic theorists and practical reformers, the question is not whether either of these options is ideal but which is least bad.

The upshot is that the limits of judicial capacity require "second-best" thinking, in both the colloquial and the technical senses of that term. In the colloquial sense, "second-best" simply means nonideal. Judicial capacity limits will often require theorists and reformers to settle for nonideal constitutional results because capacity limits will often place ideal results off the table. In any capacity-constrained domain where the ideal or first-best result is not a categorical rule of deference or a categorical rule of invalidity, judicial capacity will necessitate second-best thinking in this colloquial sense. The judicial capacity model facilitates clear thinking of this sort by identifying the limits of the constitutional choice set. This point is particularly important for reformers, whose constitutional arguments are likely to face strong headwinds if they are not tailored to the limits of judicial capacity.

In the technical sense, "second-best" is a shorthand for the "general theory of the second best," originally developed by economists R. G. Lipsey and R. K. Lancaster. As summed up by Adrian Vermeule, that theory "holds that where it is not possible to satisfy all the conditions necessary for an economic system to reach an overall optimum, it is not generally desirable to satisfy as many of those conditions as possible." In other words, where the first-best result is unattainable, it will not always be desirable to approximate it as closely as possible. This theory, as Vermeule has elegantly shown, generalizes easily and widely beyond economics.[1]

The judicial capacity model provides an important example. If the ideal constitutional result is aggressive judicial review in the form of a vague standard, capacity constraints will often place that result off limits in capacity-constrained domains. In such cases, the closest approximation of the ideal result permitted by judicial capacity limits will often be a broad categorical rule of invalidity. But it is by no means clear—and it can certainly not be assumed a priori—that this is the best of the available alternatives. Depending on the context, such a broad rule of invalidity might be so over- and under-inclusive that both theorists and reformers would do better by giving up the game altogether and embracing a categorical rule of deference.

The same point holds if the ideal constitutional result is deferential judicial review cast in the form of a vague standard. In many capacity-constrained domains, capacity constraints will place that result off limits. The closest approximation permitted by the limits of judicial capacity will often be a categorical rule of deference. But again, it is by no means clear that this is the second-best approach. Depending on the context, such a broad rule of deference might permit such egregious government action, and so much of it, that both theorists and reformers would do better by embracing a relatively broad categorical rule of invalidity. This is second-best thinking in a nutshell.

Finally, the judicial capacity model raises the possibility that any success theorists and reformers achieve in securing their ideal constitutional results will be pyrrhic and short-lived. Because the limits of judicial capacity operate across the run of cases and do not strictly preclude the Supreme Court's ability to depart from deference or categorical rules in any individual case, it will sometimes be possible for proponents of aggressive judicial review in the form of a vague standard to obtain such results in individual cases. This may create the illusion that the constitutional choice set is unconstrained, but in capacity-constrained domains, that is never the case.

The Court is free to depart from deference and categorical rules occasionally, but it cannot do so often. When it does, the limits of judicial capacity force the Court to beat a quick retreat. Alternatively, the Court might passively permit the lower courts to transform its decision into a rule of categorical deference. Practically speaking, this amounts to the same thing. Either way, any apparent victory over the constraints of judicial capacity is short-lived, raising the question: Is the game worth the candle? This is a species of what Adrian Vermeule, following Albert Hirschman, has called a "futility argument." Such arguments will not always be persuasive in the context of judicial capacity, any more than they are elsewhere, but both theorists and reformers would do well to take them seriously.[2]

To recap, the limits of judicial capacity constrain both the extent of judicial review and the doctrinal tools available to the Supreme Court. These constraints require theorists and reformers to consider whether their constitutional goals are impossible, in whole or in part. The constraints of judicial capacity also require theorists and reformers to engage in second-best thinking. In particular, where the limits of judicial capacity place their ideal result outside the constitutional choice set, theorists and reformers must carefully consider whether the closest approximation of their ideal result is the best of the available alternatives. Often, it will not be. Regardless, theorists and especially reformers will benefit from tailoring their advocacy to the limits of judicial capacity. Finally, even where constitutional change is achievable in the short run, the judicial capacity model raises the possibility that reform efforts will prove futile in the long run. The remainder of this chapter elaborates these implications of the model through a series of illustrative examples drawn from the capacity-constrained domains discussed in Part II.

Ought Implies Can and the Second Best

In capacity-constrained domains, the judicial capacity model places many constitutional choices off limits. In so doing, it alters the normative calculus for both theorists and reformers, frequently in counterintuitive ways. This point is nicely illustrated by the Supreme Court's recent commerce-power decisions, especially *United States v. Lopez* and *United States v. Morrison*. In the realm of academic theory, Philip Hamburger's recent book *Is Administrative Law Unlawful?* provides another helpful illustration. This section will examine each in turn.[3]

The Supreme Court's Recent Commerce-Power Decisions

As explained in Chapter 5, *United States v. Lopez* invalidated the Gun-Free School Zones Act as beyond Congress's commerce power, principally on the ground that the Act's prohibition on possession of firearms in school zones was a regulation of noneconomic, rather than economic, activity. Three years later, *United States v. Morrison* reaffirmed *Lopez* but went one step further, clarifying that the rule for noneconomic regulation is one of virtually per se invalidity. That is to say, federal regulations of noneconomic activities will virtually always be held invalid, without regard to their impact on interstate commerce or the quality of the legislative record. On this basis, *Morrison* invalidated the Violence Against Women Act's civil remedy for victims of "gender-motivated crimes of violence." At the same time, the Court made clear that federal regulations of economic activity remain subject to highly deferential review.[4]

Many critics of these decisions are willing to concede that the Gun-Free School Zones Act and even the Violence Against Women Act might exceed the federal commerce power, yet they routinely savage the categorical distinction the Court used to strike them down. There is simply no defensible basis, the argument goes, for restricting federal power under the Commerce Clause to regulations of economic activity. Not all economic regulations address the kind of national problems Congress should be empowered to address, and plenty of noneconomic regulations do address such problems. In other words, the economic/noneconomic distinction is both over- and under-inclusive relative to the purpose that the Supreme Court itself has said that American federalism is meant to serve—distinguishing the "truly national" from the "truly local."[5]

Once we consider capacity constraints, however, the Supreme Court's approach looks much more defensible. A vague standard requiring that federal statutes respond to a sufficiently serious national problem, would invite an avalanche of litigation if applied with any stringency. What federal statute would not be open to challenge under this formulation? Yet, if applied without any stringency, such a standard could not produce the result the majority reached in *Lopez* and *Morrison*. It would amount effectively to the rational-basis test endorsed by the dissenters in those cases, which in practice is a rule of categorical deference.

Thus, the Court's categorical distinction between economic and non-economic activity had a fair amount going for it. It achieved a result that many critics concede to be right or at least reasonable—the invalidation of two federal statutes that did not respond to any obvious national problem the states could not resolve on their own. Because the distinction was both categorical and quite deferential to Congress, it achieved this result without calling into question a giant swath of federal legislation. Or so the majority in these cases might reasonably have believed.

At the same time, the judicial capacity model also sheds helpful and favorable light on the position of the *Lopez* and *Morrison* dissenters. It may be true that the Gun-Free School Zones and Violence Against Women

Acts were merely congressional grandstanding that solved no serious national problems. But if a normatively indefensible categorical distinction was the only way to invalidate them, consistent with the limits of judicial capacity, the position of the dissenters has a strong appeal. Invalidating a broad array of socially desirable noneconomic regulations—of pandemic disease, interstate environmental problems, etc.—seems a hefty price to pay just to invalidate two unnecessary but relatively innocuous federal statutes. Certainly, a reasonable person might conclude, as the dissenters did, that the costs of such an approach outweighed the benefits.

To put all of this in terms of the second-best, judicial capacity constraints put the first-best rule advocated by many of the Supreme Court's critics off the table. A vague standard requiring that federal statutes respond to a sufficiently serious national problem would invite more litigation than the Court could handle, consistent with its basic normative commitments. If ought implies can, the Court cannot be faulted for failing to embrace such an unworkable approach. Nor should theorists or reformers advocating such a rule hope to have much success in persuading the Court to adopt it. In the commerce power and other capacity-constrained domains, the limits of judicial capacity routinely place the optimal constitutional results off the table. Thus, the only options available to the Court are second-best in the colloquial sense of nonideal.

More subtly, the unavailability of this first-best alternative forced the Supreme Court to choose between second-best alternatives—some kind of crude categorical limit akin to the economic / noneconomic distinction or the categorically deferential rational-basis test—that were very far from the first-best alternative that theorists and reformers might both prefer. Few would argue that either of these rules was optimal, and reasonable people might disagree about which was preferable, but they were the rules that defined the Court's constitutional choice set.

For theorists, the principal lesson is that any non-utopian normative appraisal of the Court's work—or the best practically achievable constitutional law of federalism—ought to focus on a comparison of these second-best alternatives. The best alternative, moreover, may not be the one that most closely approximates the first-best result. For reformers, the principal lesson of the judicial capacity model is that efforts to establish constitutional limits on the federal commerce power are unlikely to meet with much success. They would simply produce too much litigation. If these efforts have any chance, however, their success likely depends on the ability of their proponents to formulate categorical rules that clearly insulate most government actions from scrutiny, while providing clear notice to prospective parties and clear guidance to lower courts. The activity-inactivity distinction embraced by five justices in *NFIB v. Sebelius* is a good example. By contrast, reformers opposed to expanded judicial review of the commerce power should focus their efforts on demonstrating the crudity of categorical rules—their inevitable over- and under-inclusiveness—and their consequent undesirability. Many of the most forceful arguments made against the activity/inactivity distinction in *NFIB* took essentially this form.[6]

Philip Hamburger's Is Administrative Law Unlawful?

In the realm of academic theory, Philip Hamburger's recent book *Is Administrative Law Unlawful?* is another excellent illustration of the judicial capacity model's implications for the constitutional choice set. Alternately hailed as "brilliant" and dismissed as "disheartening [and] irresponsible," Hamburger's massive, hyperbolic, and richly historical broadside against the modern administrative state is centrally concerned with delegations of legislative power. Perhaps more than any other feature of the American administrative state, Hamburger identifies such delegations as the root of a "modern revival of absolute power." True to the uncompromising logic of his position, Hamburger is not content to argue for a more rigorous nondelegation doctrine. As he sees it, the problem is not merely that administrative agencies wield too much power to "fill up [statutory] details" or that the "intelligible principles" governing congressional delegations are too broad. Rather, the problem is that Congress is permitted to delegate the power to make binding rules—defined as rules that alter the legal rights and obligations of private parties—*at all*. To remedy this despotic state of affairs, as he sees it, Hamburger calls on the courts to invalidate all such delegations, as well as the regulations flowing from them, which he dubs "extralegal legislation."[7]

This prescription would obviously unsettle an extraordinary volume of legislation and administrative regulation. There are thousands of congressional statutes that vest executive or independent agencies with the authority to issue binding rules and tens or hundreds of thousands of agency regulations adopted in the exercise of this authority. Yet Hamburger, like many constitutional scholars, barely pauses to consider the "concerns about . . . judicial practicalities" that his approach would raise. Had he done so, he would have encountered a powerful objection grounded in judicial capacity, as well as an interesting potential response.[8]

The objection is straightforward. Without abandoning its commitment to uniformity and minimum professional standards, the Supreme Court lacks anything like the bandwidth necessary to aggressively review so much legislation and regulation in an area where it would feel strongly compelled to decide a large fraction of cases itself. If ought implies can, Hamburger's argument fails. Certainly this is an objection Hamburger could and should have taken more seriously. His failure to do so is one of several reasons "it would be the easiest thing in the world to dismiss Hamburger's book with the glib observation that it will change nothing."[9]

That would be too quick. Hamburger's proposed rule is far more hard-edged and categorical than most proposed versions of the nondelegation doctrine, which generally require courts to figure out how much delegation is too much. As discussed in Chapter 8, this is a difficult, uncertain, and fact-sensitive enterprise. Like Hamburger's approach, it would threaten a wide swath of legislation and regulation. But it would also produce a great deal of uncertainty, increasing the volume of litigation and producing divergent rulings in the lower courts that the Supreme Court would feel compelled to resolve.

By contrast, Hamburger's proposal is relatively straightforward, predictable, and categorical. It would merely require courts to identify which delegations and regulations purport to bind private parties, a far more clean-cut inquiry. Unlike other categorical rules the Supreme Court has established in capacity-constrained domains, Hamburger's approach would not insulate much governmental action from challenge, but it would produce far less uncertainty and might well be enforceable on lower courts largely through summary decisions.

None of this is to endorse Hamburger's argument. Indeed, the judicial capacity objection is almost certainly more powerful than the response. There are also many other reasons to believe Hamburger's project impractical or undesirable. But for present purposes, the merits of that project are unimportant. The crucial point is that the judicial capacity model illuminates both the significant constraints on judicial action and the affirmative capacities of the Court to act. Any approach to constitutional law that ignores judicial capacity is missing something quite important. In short, we must attend closely not only to what the Court cannot do, but also to what it can do and why.

Again, there is a subtler point. Considered without reference to judicial capacity limits, Hamburger's argument has suffered from its apparent extremism. Even those readers who share his skepticism of the administrative state's expansive reach and lack of accountability are likely to be unsettled by Hamburger's call for its complete demolition. Surely, such readers will think, there must be some middle way that would effectively curtail the worst excesses of the federal bureaucracy without returning us to the primitive constitutional arrangements of seventeenth-century England.

Proceeding from certain normative and empirical priors, such a middle way—on the nondelegation doctrine, presidential administration, and so on—might indeed be the first-best constitutional approach. But as explained at length in Chapters 7 and 8, the judicial capacity model largely places such an approach off limits. Because of the difficulty of drawing rule-like distinctions to limit congressional delegations of power or interference with presidential administration, the practical alternative to Hamburger's extreme approach might not be the middle way imagined by his moderate critics but instead the categorical deference of rational-basis review.

Most theorists and reformers, even those uneasy about the modern administrative state, would probably still blanch at the extravagance of Hamburger's approach. Others might attempt to formulate narrower categorical limits on the administrative state consistent with the limits of judicial capacity. For present purposes, we need not resolve this question. The important point is that the analysis looks considerably different once we recognize that judicial capacity eliminates the first-best constitutional rule—by hypothesis, a moderate version of the nondelegation doctrine, cast in the form of a vague standard—from the constitutional choice set.

As with the Supreme Court's recent commerce-power decisions, the principal lesson for theorists is that any non-utopian normative analysis should focus on a comparison of the choices practically available to the Court, and those choices are constrained by the limits of judicial capacity. A choice that at first appears obviously inferior to an imagined first-best alternative may look better when compared to the actual constitutional choice set. The best choice, moreover, may not be the one that most closely resembles the first-best result.

The principal lesson for reformers also mirrors the lesson of the Supreme Court's recent commerce-power decisions. Simply put, most efforts to reinvigorate the nondelegation principle or unitary executive theory are unlikely to meet with much success. They would produce too much litigation. If these efforts stand any chance, however, their success likely depends on the ability of their proponents to formulate categorical rules that clearly insulate most government actions from scrutiny, while providing clear notice to prospective parties and clear guidance to lower courts. The *Clinton* and *Chadha* decisions, discussed in Chapters 7 and 8, are good examples of this. Another good example is the recent challenge to the Consumer Financial Protection Bureau, seeking a per se prohibition on for-cause removal restrictions as applied to agencies headed by a single director.[10]

By contrast, reformers opposed to expanded judicial scrutiny of the administrative state should focus their efforts on demonstrating the crudity of categorical rules—their inevitable over- and under-inclusiveness—and their consequent undesirability. To make the point more concrete, do proponents of the unitary executive theory wish to give up the independence of the Federal Reserve and administrative law judges, along with that of PCAOB and the FTC? Do opponents of delegation wish to give up EPA's authority to regulate arsenic in drinking water along with its authority to regulate greenhouse gases?

Finally, reformers should consider the possibility that some truly sweeping reforms like Hamburger's might be consistent with the limits of judicial capacity, due to their starkly categorical character, but nevertheless worse than the disease they were intended to cure. Again, the point is not to endorse any particular side in these debates. It is simply to demonstrate the ways in which judicial capacity alters the constitutional choice set and the sort of second-best thinking that this necessarily requires. In this respect, the Supreme Court's recent commerce-power decisions and Philip Hamburger's attack on the modern administrative state are merely illustrative. The same point extends to every capacity-constrained domain discussed in Part II.

Futility

In addition to placing many first-best constitutional rules off the table, the limits of judicial capacity provide an important additional metric against which to assess the decisions of the Supreme Court in capacity-constrained constitutional domains. All else equal, constitutional decisions that exceed the limits of judicial capacity are inferior to decisions that remain within those limits. That is because constitutional decisions that invite more litigation than the Court can handle are likely to be *futile* in the sense that they fail to secure their objectives in the long-term, while consuming substantial public and private resources in the process.

I do not, for present purposes, mean to endorse judicial norms that underlie the limits of judicial capacity. Those norms strike me as perfectly sensible, but the futility argument that is my focus here does not depend on that view. It depends only on the descriptive observation that judges are already committed to such norms. Taking that commitment as given, decisions that exceed the limits of judicial capacity are problematic not because—or at least not only because—they threaten the norms underlying judicial capacity. Rather, they are problematic because the limits of judicial capacity will eventually force the Supreme Court to retreat from any decision exceeding those limits. Such decisions will therefore invite a large volume of litigation, with all of the costs that entails for both courts and private litigants, while providing no compensating social benefit.

Here again, the Supreme Court's recent commerce-power decisions helpfully illustrate the point. We can distinguish between three different objections to the Court's decisions in *United States v. Lopez* and *United States v. Morrison*. One is a first-best normative argument that the statutes those decisions invalidated should have been upheld. Another is the second-best argument discussed above—that rational-basis review is normatively superior to the majority's categorical distinction between economic and noneconomic activity, even if rational-basis review requires the Court to uphold some socially undesirable statutes like the ones invalidated in *Lopez* and *Morrison*. A third objection is that the majority's apparently categorical rule—even if functionally superior to rational-basis review—is insufficiently hard-edged and will in fact break down under the pressure of litigation. When it does, the result will be to invite an avalanche of litigation that the judiciary is unprepared to handle, at which point the Court will have to retreat anyway. If that is the case, why bother trying? The rule established will not survive long enough to do meaningful good—even from the perspective of its proponents—and the avalanche of litigation it invites will consume considerable resources, both private and public. This is a classic futility argument.

The same sort of argument played a prominent role in the first wave of legal challenges to the Affordable Care Act, though it was not widely recognized as a claim about judicial capacity. This argument held that the activity/inactivity distinction pressed by the Act's challengers was too difficult for courts to apply consistently in practice. For purposes of argument, one could accept the challengers' position that the Affordable Care Act was socially undesirable. Even if one does not accept that position, one could accept that the activity/inactivity distinction was preferable to the toothless rational-basis test of the Supreme Court's other modern commerce-power decisions. Even so, if the activity/inactivity distinction was insufficiently sturdy to provide guidance to lower courts and potential litigants under the pressure of litigation, that would have been a powerful reason to reject it. This is not just because courts might make mistakes in applying the test. It is also because, by employing such an unsteady test, they would risk inviting an avalanche of litigation that would force the Supreme Court to retreat in short order, in which case the game would not have been worth the candle.[11]

In the Affordable Care Act litigation, there was an additional wrinkle, which may also apply in some other high-profile cases. Had the Court invoked the activity/inactivity distinction to strike down the Act only to retreat from that distinction shortly thereafter, this may have given its decision the kind of nakedly political appearance that tends to undermine the Court's legitimacy. Even in the absence of such an appearance, the capacity-compelled retreat from a recently established constitutional rule may upset the interests of those who reasonably relied upon the Court's original decision. Thus, legitimacy costs and reliance interests must be added to the downsides of short-lived constitutional decisions that exceed the limits of judicial capacity.[12]

Of course, in retrospect, the futility arguments against the activity-inactivity and economic-noneconomic distinctions look decidedly over-blown. As discussed in Chapter 5, the version of the activity-inactivity distinction embraced by the Supreme Court seems to have been deliber-ately cast in exceedingly narrow terms, and there has been no flood of commerce-power challenges in the aftermath of *NFIB v. Sebelius* seeking to expand its reach. The story is similar with respect to *Lopez* and *Mor-rison,* except that the volume of ensuing litigation was somewhat larger and the Court partially retreated from the economic-noneconomic dis-tinction—or at least retrenched—in *Gonzales v. Raich,* decided eight years after *Morrison.* This demonstrates that futility arguments are not always empirically well-founded, but it does not undermine their essential logic.[13]

A more fundamental objection to futility arguments based on the judi-cial capacity model is that no constitutional decision is truly permanent. Even if the limits of judicial capacity eventually compel the Supreme Court to retreat from a decision, that decision might well do substantial good in the meantime. This is clearly true, and it requires a slight modifica-tion in the definition of futility. A decision is not futile merely because the Court eventually retreats from it. It is futile only if the social costs of es-tablishing and retreating from the decision exceed the social benefits it produces while it remains in force. Whether this is true of any given de-cision is a function in part of the time it remains in place—or, if the ques-tion is posed ex ante, the time it is likely to remain in place. It is also a function of the decision's normative merits and the quantity and magni-tude of the reliance interests disrupted by its reversal. Notwithstanding these complications and qualifications, the essential point remains: All else equal, decisions that exceed the limits of judicial capacity are infe-rior to decisions that remain within those limits. This is true not just for the commerce power but across all capacity-constrained domains.

For theorists, the lesson is straightforward. An otherwise desirable con-stitutional decision or doctrinal change may be rendered unsustainable by the limits of judicial capacity even if the Supreme Court can be convinced to embrace it in the short run. Since the establishment and retreat from a new constitutional rule has various social costs, this may militate in favor of maintaining the status quo, though these costs should be weighed against the social benefits a new rule might produce during the time it remains in force. For practical reformers, the lesson is very similar. The key difference is that practical reformers must think not only, or even principally, about the social costs and benefits of their reform efforts. They must also, and primarily, think about their own limited resources and the opportunity costs of pursuing a reform strategy that is likely to prove unsustainable in the long-run, even if that strategy has some prospect of succeeding in the short-run. This will often militate in favor of pursuing narrower and more rule-like constitutional reforms that are consistent with the limits of judicial capacity and thus likely to prove more durable. If such narrow reforms are too small-bore to justify the effort, the futility of strategies that challenge the limits of judicial capacity might also increase the attraction of nonlegal, or at least nonconstitutional, reform strategies.

The broader point is that neither constitutional theorists nor practical reformers can afford to ignore the limits of judicial capacity. In a wide range of important constitutional domains, those limits will often place the first-best result outside the Supreme Court's constitutional choice set. Among the remaining choices, the best may or may not be the one that most closely approximates the first-best result placed off the table by judicial capacity limits. Even where the first-best result is achievable in the short run, the limits of judicial capacity may make it unsustainable—and thus futile—in the long-run. For all of these reasons, judicial capacity should occupy a prominent place both on the agenda of constitutional theory and in the toolkits of practical reformers.

CHAPTER TWELVE

Judicial Capacity and Judicial Competence

In addition to defining the realm of the possible, the judicial capacity model has important implications for the competence of the Supreme Court in capacity-constrained constitutional domains. Judicial competence, of course, is a perennial preoccupation of the academic literature on constitutional law. In fact, apart from judicial independence, addressed in the next chapter, it is difficult to think of another single topic that has attracted more sustained attention from constitutional scholars over the past half century. Judicial competence also plays an important role in the Court's own jurisprudence and in constitutional arguments made before the Court.[1]

To take just two examples, commentators advocating judicial deference to congressional delegations of power to administrative agencies routinely emphasize the Supreme Court's comparative incompetence to decide how much delegation is too much. Advocates of deference to congressional interference with presidential administration frequently make very similar arguments. As Justice Breyer put it in his *Free Enterprise Fund v. PCAOB* dissent, "Compared to Congress and the President, the Judiciary possesses an inferior understanding of the realities of administration, and the manner in which power, including and most especially political power, operates in context." Similar statements can be found throughout the U.S. Reports.[2]

Ubiquitous as they are, both academic and judicial claims of judicial incompetence are chronically under-theorized. It is true that Supreme Court justices, in the main, are less experienced than legislators with the day-to-day operations of both Congress and the administrative state. They also lack anything like the staff or budget that Congress and the President can devote to evaluating the constitutional questions that come before them. But there is clearly another side to the story. The justices are substantially insulated from many of the political pressures that might cause legislators and presidents to use—or ignore—their expertise and fact-finding resources against the public interest. Justices also have access to the entire legislative record, and much additional factual input in the form of amicus briefs, all tested through an adversarial process. Of course, powerful interests are well represented in that process, just as they are in the political process. On the other hand, the marginal value of interest-group expenditures is probably lower in the courts than it is in the political process.[3]

None of this is to suggest that courts are necessarily more competent than legislatures and executive agencies, but the case is closer and more complicated than the conventional wisdom assumes. Or rather, it would be if courts were free to spend unlimited time and energy considering every constitutional issue on a case-by-case basis. But of course, the courts are not free to take this approach. As the judicial capacity model demonstrates, the Supreme Court in particular is strongly constrained from taking anything like this approach in many of the most important constitutional domains. Instead, capacity limits force the Court to choose between hard-edged, categorical limits on governmental action and highly deferential standards. This choice, in turn, controls the constitutional decisions of all lower courts.

The implications for judicial competence are substantial and have been largely unappreciated. Hard-edged categorical limits are inevitably over- and under-inclusive relative to their underlying purposes and may well make things worse rather than better. Highly deferential standards tend in practice to collapse into rules of categorical deference, which are the practical equivalent of no judicial review at all. This limited and unattractive menu of options is certainly not the only reason to question the competence of courts in capacity-constrained constitutional domains, but it provides much needed ballast for the chronically under-theorized conventional wisdom that courts, including the Supreme Court, are generally less competent than legislatures and executive agencies.[4]

This insight has both positive and normative implications. On the positive side, some versions of the legalist model predict that the Supreme Court will defer to the political process, at least some of the time, because the justices believe courts are less competent than legislatures, administrative agencies, and so on. The relative incompetence of the courts thus provides a possible legalist explanation for at least some of the Supreme Court's strong deference to the political process in capacity-constrained domains. The role of judicial capacity in undermining judicial competence suggests that these explanations of judicial decision-making are not competing but complementary. In some contexts, the Supreme Court may well be hesitant to aggressively review government action due to doubts about its own competence. But if those doubts are a product of the Court's limited capacity—at least in part—this counts for the judicial capacity model, not against it.[5]

On the normative side, judicial competence is a constant theme in arguments against more stringent judicial review in capacity-constrained domains. The typical reasons offered for doubting judicial competence are plausible but not especially impressive. The judicial capacity model bolsters the case against the courts by identifying an additional and largely unappreciated reason to doubt judicial competence. At least in capacity-constrained domains, the Supreme Court may simply lack the capacity to engage in significantly more robust review. Even if it possesses the capacity, it will often be constrained to employ crude categorical rules that would be worse than no judicial review at all. Judicial capacity will not be decisive in every debate over judicial competence, but it is an important factor in the balance that has received almost no sustained attention to date. Given the prominent role that judicial competence plays in both academic and judicial argument, this is another reason for both constitutional theorists and practical reformers to take judicial capacity seriously.

The remainder of this Chapter elaborates each of these points, the positive and the normative, using examples drawn from Part II.

Judicial Competence and the Explanatory Power
of the Judicial Capacity Model

The explanatory power of the judicial capacity model is a function of its ability to explain important features of the Supreme Court's past decisions that other models cannot. One of those features is the Court's strong and systematic deference to the political process in capacity-constrained domains. As Part II demonstrated, no other leading model of Supreme Court decision-making can readily explain this feature of the Court's decisions across a broad range of capacity-constrained domains. That includes the legalist model, whose principal prediction is that judicial decisions will be consistent with the traditional legal materials in any given constitutional domain.

Some versions of the legalist model, however, also emphasize the predictive power of principled legal commitments that cut across legal domains. One of these is a commitment to judicial restraint, premised on concerns about limited judicial competence. Part II did not consider this variant of the legalist model for two reasons. First, its predictions are the same across all constitutional domains. It therefore would have been highly repetitive to discuss those predictions in every constitutional domain explored in Part II. Second, as Chapter 4 emphasized, this variant of the legalist model predicts only that most judges will sometimes act on the basis of a principled commitment to judicial restraint, among various other legal factors. The model does not predict that this commitment will systematically constrain the Supreme Court to embrace a strongly deferential approach. Nor does it predict that the Court will be willing to depart from that approach only in the form of hard-edged categorical rules. In each of these respects, the judicial capacity model explains important features of the Court's decisions that the legalist model cannot.[6]

On the other hand, there is obviously some overlap between the predictions of the judicial-restraint variant of the legalist model and the predictions of the judicial capacity model. The legalist model does not predict systematic deference that the judicial capacity model does, but it does predict some meaningful measure of judicial deference. To the extent that this prediction overlaps with the predictions of judicial capacity model, it represents a case of observational equivalence. The evidence is consistent with both models and is therefore uniquely explained by neither. The upshot is that some—though not all—of the Supreme Court's deference in capacity-constrained domains might be the product of a principled legalist commitment to judicial restraint, premised on the limits of judicial competence. Alternatively, it might be the product of judicial capacity limits, or it might be the joint product of both. The available evidence is consistent with all of these possibilities.

If this were all that could be said, the judicial capacity model would still stand alone in its power to explain the Supreme Court's systematic deference in capacity-constrained domains and the Court's unwillingness to depart from such deference except in the form of hard-edged categorical rules. It would simply have to acknowledge that some of the Court's deference is equally well explained by a variant of the legalist model. The same, of course, holds in reverse. If some of the Court's deference is equally consistent with the predictions of the legalist model and the judicial capacity model, neither model can claim victory over the other. More evidence would be needed to fully disentangle the two or to confirm that both are operating simultaneously. Simply highlighting this uncertainty about the causal efficacy of judicial competence, a time-worn legalist explanation for judicial deference, would be an important contribution.

In fact, the judicial capacity model allows us to go considerably further. If the legalist commitment to judicial restraint is waning in force or is likely to do so in the near future, it is of pressing importance to determine whether other constraints, such as judicial capacity, will continue to push the Supreme Court toward deference in the areas where the two models overlap. Many prominent scholars have argued that judicial restraint is undergoing—or has already undergone—exactly this kind of decline. Others have pointed to cyclical fluctuations in levels of judicial restraint over time. The constraints of judicial capacity, by contrast, rest on long-standing and widely held judicial norms that seem unlikely to erode substantially any time soon. Thus, in the face of cyclical fluctuations—or even a secular decline—in the legalist commitment to judicial restraint, the judicial capacity model provides theoretically and empirically compelling reason to believe that the Supreme Court will remain strongly constrained to employ some combination of deference and categorical rules in capacity-constrained domains.[7]

This still leaves the most intriguing possible explanation for the overlap between the judicial capacity model and the judicial-restraint variant of the legalist model. The predictions of the judicial capacity model might overlap with those of the legalist model because the causal forces underlying the legalist model are endogenous to limited judicial capacity. (In theory, the reverse could also be true, but it is difficult to come up with a plausible account on which judicial capacity could be endogenous to a legalist commitment to judicial constraint.) I have already explained the basic logic. The legalist model predicts that judges will defer to the political process because they are appropriately humble about the limits of judicial competence. The judicial capacity model predicts that the justices of the Supreme Court will defer to the political process because they are constrained to do so by the limits of judicial capacity. But if the limits of judicial competence underlying the legalist commitment to judicial restraint are at least partly a function of judicial capacity—because capacity limits force the Supreme Court to choose among a narrow and unattractive menu of options—then a commitment to judicial restraint is itself a by-product of the limits of judicial capacity. This would make the legalist model and the judicial capacity model partial complements, rather than competitors.

So is judicial competence endogenous to the limits of judicial capacity? This is not a question that can be readily answered on the basis of the empirical evidence. By definition, in areas where the predictions of the two models overlap, both are equally consistent with the available evidence. But there are strong theoretical reasons for concluding that judicial capacity is an important factor limiting judicial competence in capacity-constrained domains, substantially contributing to the appeal of a legalist commitment to judicial restraint.

These reasons are well illustrated by the nondelegation doctrine. Opponents of a judicially enforced nondelegation doctrine routinely emphasize the difficulty of determining how much delegation of power to administrative agencies is too much. Judges, they argue, are particularly ill-suited to answer this question because they lack the fact-finding and investigatory tools available to Congress and, for the most part, have no day-to-day experience in either the legislative or executive branch on which to base their decisions. Proponents of a judicially enforced non-delegation doctrine counter that judges engage in similarly difficult line-drawing exercises in many other areas of law without hesitation. They also point out the political motivation to avoid accountability for hard decisions and the distorting effect that this seems likely to exert on legislative judgment. Finally, they point out the risks to political accountability of transferring decision-making authority from the relatively more transparent legislative process to the more arcane and convoluted processes of administrative rule-making—risks that are not lost on the politically influential special interests that pressure Congress into delegating power.[8]

This is obviously a simplified and stylized summary of a large and long-running debate. The essential point, however, should be clear. There is nothing like a clear and decisive case against the competence of courts to enforce the nondelegation doctrine. This, alone, raises questions about the sufficiency of judicial competence to explain any meaningful subset of the Supreme Court's deference in nondelegation cases. More important is the weight that judicial capacity adds to the argument against judicial competence. If the constraints of judicial capacity permit the Court to enforce the nondelegation doctrine only in the form of a crude categorical rule, the intelligence, impartiality, experience, and access to information of judges are largely beside the point. If the constraints of judicial capacity permitted courts to examine the how-much-is-too-much question on a case-by-case basis, they might be able to do a perfectly passable job, at least compared to the highly compromised political process. But the constraints of judicial capacity do not permit this. Instead, they force the Supreme Court to choose between doing nothing and making a delicate and nuanced distinction in the form of a crude categorical rule, which all lower courts would then be compelled to follow. This is at least as strong as, and quite possibly stronger than, any other argument against the competence of courts to enforce the nondelegation doctrine. Thus, even if legalist concerns about judicial competence are behind some of the Court's deference to congressional delegations, there is strong reason to believe that this concern is at least partially endogenous to judicial capacity. In this respect, the judicial capacity model both complements the legalist model and helps to illuminate the causal mechanism on which its judicial-restraint variant is premised.

Judicial Competence and the Normative Case for Limiting Judicial Review

Judicial competence plays an important role in positive accounts of Supreme Court decision-making, but the role it plays in normative arguments about the proper scope of judicial review is nothing short of dominant. This makes sense. Judicial review in effect substitutes the decisions of courts for the decisions of legislatures, executive agencies, and other political institutions. In evaluating the desirability of such a substitution, it is almost impossible to avoid the basic question: Which of these institutional alternatives would do a better job? Or, put slightly differently, which of these institutional alternatives can be most reliably entrusted with the power in question? As Neil Komesar has forcefully insisted, these questions are irreducibly comparative. Thus, constitutional theorists, judges, and practical reformers all spend enormous time and energy comparing the competence of courts to that of more democratically accountable institutions, particularly legislatures and administrative agencies.[9]

The sophistication and rigor of these comparisons varies widely. All too often, a serious malfunction in one of the alternatives is presented as a sufficient justification for preferring another, without meaningful comparison of the two. Even genuinely comparative analyses, however, often treat the courts as quite obviously unfit to be trusted with the great majority of governmental decisions. Something like this view may, in the end, be correct. But as explained above, the conventional justifications offered for it are decidedly underwhelming, at least if we confine ourselves—as most versions of the argument do—to the competence of the individual officials who staff the relevant institutions, the fact-finding tools at their disposal, and the political incentives shaping their decisions. In fact, considering only these factors, it is possible to make a plausible case for the superiority of judges over other alternative decision-makers in many constitutional domains. At the very least, the argument is nowhere near as lopsided as is frequently and casually assumed.[10]

My point is not that the conventional wisdom is necessarily wrong, merely that it is incomplete. It is incomplete because it overlooks the impact of judicial capacity limits on judicial competence. In many of the most important constitutional domains, in which the proper scope of judicial review is most hotly contested, the Supreme Court may simply lack the capacity to engage in meaningful review. Even if it possesses the capacity, it will often be constrained to employ crude categorical rules that would be worse than no judicial review at all. This is not to say that capacity will always provide a satisfying reason for the Court to defer to other actors. Sometimes the options consistent with the limits of judicial capacity will be reasonably good. Even when they are not, the pathologies of the alternative decision-making institutions may be even more severe. Either way, capacity is a crucial and largely overlooked determinant of judicial competence.

This point is well illustrated by the preceding discussion of the nondelegation doctrine. The difficulty of determining how much delegation is too much might explain why the Supreme Court has applied the nondelegation doctrine so deferentially. It might also *justify* the Court's deferential posture. But for that to be the case, the Court and defenders of its nondelegation decisions would have to be right that the political process is more competent to make decisions about the scope of congressional delegations than are the courts. As explained above, the conventional arguments for this view are plausible but far from decisive. The judicial capacity model, however, adds significant weight to the argument against judicial competence. If the constraints of judicial capacity force the Supreme Court to choose between doing nothing and making a delicate and nuanced distinction in the form of a crude categorical rule, they may well do best by embracing a rule of categorical deference.

The Equal Protection Clause provides another vivid illustration. Opponents of expansive Equal Protection review routinely emphasize the difficulty of determining which government classifications are well justified. Unlike legislatures and executive agencies, courts are not set up to receive input from the full array of interests affected by the government classifications that broad Equal Protection review would call upon them to evaluate. Think only of allocation of public school funding, distribution of the tax burden, or the differential generosity of public benefits and public works programs. All of these might be subject to equal-protection challenge, and all would require enormously complicated and information-intensive analysis to evaluate intelligently, much less to reform. Just as clearly, judicial intervention in any of these areas would have far-reaching effects on interests not represented before the courts.[11]

Proponents of broad Equal Protection review counter that the political process systematically ignores or undervalues the interests of many groups and does so not just through overt facial classifications but also through government actions that impose a disproportionate burden on disfavored groups. Absent serious Equal Protection review that extends to unequal impacts, as well as facial discrimination, the interests of these groups are sure to be perennially shortchanged. As for the informational deficit of courts, judges have access to the full legislative and administrative record and are probably better suited by training and intellectual ability to tackle hard policy questions than most elected officials. In any case, what good is a mountain of data or an army of experts if elected decision-makers have no practical political incentive to consider the interests of the poor or the disabled or of racial minorities—or, worse, if they have a positive incentive to sacrifice the interests of these groups in favor of those with more political clout?[12]

Again, this is obviously a highly simplified summary of a large and long-running debate, but the essential point should be clear. There is nothing like a decisive normative case against the competence of courts to evaluate the legitimacy of a broad range of government classifications. Once we consider judicial capacity, however, that case becomes considerably stronger. If the constraints of judicial capacity permit the Supreme Court to enforce the Equal Protection Clause only in the form of crude categorical rules, the intelligence, impartiality, training, and access to information of judges are largely beside the point. If the constraints of judicial capacity permitted courts to evaluate government classifications on a case-by-case basis, they might be able to do a perfectly passable job of setting tax policy or apportioning public school funding or making infrastructure appropriations. But the constraints of judicial capacity do not permit this. Instead, they force the Supreme Court to choose between doing nothing and establishing crude rules of categorical invalidity. This is at least as strong as, and quite possibly stronger than, any other argument against the competence of courts to engage in broad Equal Protection review.

To repeat, this is not to suggest that judicial capacity will always provide a satisfying reason for the Supreme Court to reject Equal Protection challenges that push the limits of the existing tiered-scrutiny framework. Sometimes the options consistent with the limits of judicial capacity will be reasonably good. Even when they are not, the pathologies of the alternative decision-making institutions may be even more severe. But either way, no careful analysis of judicial competence can afford to overlook judicial capacity.

To recap, in a wide range of important constitutional domains, judicial capacity limits constrain the Supreme Court to choose from a small menu of unattractive choices. This helps to explain why the justices themselves might question the Court's competence to improve on the decisions made by other institutional actors. It also adds much-needed support to the conventional wisdom that the Court *should* leave most decisions to other institutional actors—a view that plays a prominent role in both academic debates and practical constitutional argument but has been chronically under-theorized. For all of these reasons, judicial capacity should occupy a prominent place both on the agenda of constitutional theory and in the toolkits of practical reformers.

CHAPTER THIRTEEN

Judicial Capacity and
Judicial Independence

In addition to defining the realm of the possible and enriching standard accounts of judicial competence, the judicial capacity model also has important implications for judicial independence. As I use the term here, judicial independence refers to the capacity—or inclination—of the judiciary to produce social change against the tide of dominant political forces. So understood, judicial independence, like judicial competence, is a perennial preoccupation of the academic literature on constitutional law. Indeed, in one form or another, these two topics have dominated the agenda of constitutional theory over the past half century. Judicial independence also plays an important role in the Supreme Court's own jurisprudence, in constitutional arguments made before the Court, and in frequently heated public debates over the proper role of the courts in a democracy.

To take just two recent examples, the dissenting justices in both *Obergefell v. Hodges,* the same-sex marriage case, and *Shelby County v. Holder,* an important voting-rights case, bitterly decried the Supreme Court's willingness to invalidate recently enacted laws adopted by sizable legislative or public majorities. The majority opinions in these cases responded by forcefully insisting on the Court's vital role as a check on majoritarian political processes. At oral argument in *Shelby*

County, Justice Scalia went so far as to suggest that the overwhelming congressional support for renewing the Voting Rights Act of 1965 was a reason for the Court to scrutinize that legislation more stringently. These debates over the desirability of judicial independence are but the most recent and vivid examples of a much longer running debate over the democratic legitimacy of counter-majoritarian judicial review that encompasses virtually all of the capacity-constrained domains discussed in this book.[1]

Over the past two decades, a substantial literature has grown up that undercuts the empirical underpinnings of this debate. This literature greatly downplays the extent of judicial independence—both in terms of the judiciary's inclination to act contrary to political consensus and in terms of its ability to overcome political resistance when it does act. The work in this vein is rich and varied but its central thrust is that "the Court [is] so tightly cabined in by 'majoritarian forces' as to be little more than a reflection of pre-existing majoritarian preferences." Not surprisingly, proponents of this claim have been broadly dismissive of familiar normative debates over the democratic legitimacy of judicial review. If the Supreme Court has no significant capacity to act contrary to dominant social and political forces, both hopes and fears of counter-majoritarian judicial review are unfounded. The Court can neither act as a bulwark against tyranny of the majority nor establish a nightmarish "government by judiciary."[2]

This school of thought has largely carried the day. On both the descriptive and the normative fronts, it has become the new orthodoxy. Like the conventional wisdom about judicial competence, however, this conventional understanding of judicial independence has been chronically undertheorized. For example, Barry Friedman relies on the Court's institutional memory of costly retaliations past to explain the Court's generally majoritarian decisions. But the examples of such retaliations are so few and far between that it seems implausible that they would strike substantial fear into the heart of rational justices. Other possible mechanisms for explaining the Court's pattern of deference are somewhat more plausible. The politics of judicial appointments in particular almost certainly ensures some rough congruence between the views of the court and the political branches. But as Richard Pildes has persuasively shown, neither the appointments process nor any other mechanism identified in the literature appears to constrain the Court very strongly or reliably. Nor is there any certainty that these constraints will operate as effectually in the future as they have in the past. Indeed, Pildes offers good reasons to believe the opposite is the case. If he is right, the counter-majoritarian difficulty may still have real bite.[3]

I cannot do full justice to this contest here. But again, my point is not that the conventional view is wrong—at least not as far wrong as Pildes's important account suggests. Rather, that view has ignored an important limit on the Supreme Court's power to challenge dominant political forces: judicial capacity. Even in the absence of *any* effective political constraints, the limits of judicial capacity would significantly constrain the Court's ability to challenge majoritarian views. The reason is straightforward. Any decision that constrains governmental power increases the expected benefits of constitutional litigation. And any decision that does so in the teeth of strongly held majority views is quite likely to involve a high-stakes, if not a high-volume, domain in which the Court feels compelled to grant review in a large fraction of cases. These, of course, are the domains in which the constraints of judicial capacity have real force. Some of this litigation might be settled before it reaches the Supreme Court, or the government might acquiesce to constitutional limits in anticipation of legal challenges. But settlement and acquiescence are both less likely if strong popular majorities—national or local—support the government action in question. Massive resistance to *Brown v. Board of Education,* the school prayer cases, and *Roe v. Wade* are good illustrations.[4]

In some contexts the Supreme Court may be able to manage this capacity problem by employing hard-edged categorical rules to reduce disuniformity in the lower courts and encourage settlement. But as the pre-1937 Commerce Clause cases demonstrate, the clarity and determinacy of such rules often breaks down under the pressure of litigation. Even if the rules do not break down, the over- and under-inclusiveness of any categorical rule that would seriously constrain democratic majorities may well dissuade the Court from adopting this course. We should therefore generally expect the Court to refrain (or quickly retreat) from serious intervention in areas that the public really cares about—not because it fears political opposition or because the justices' views systematically track the public's, but because the Court lacks the capacity to take such issues on in large numbers.[5]

This is not to suggest that a capacity-constrained Court will never make counter-majoritarian decisions. It obviously will. The point is simply that the limits of judicial capacity are essential to understanding the actual extent of judicial independence and whatever normative conclusions may follow from it. Any account that focuses exclusively on political constraints, ignoring capacity limits, is likely to overstate the extent of the Court's independence, perhaps quite substantially.

This insight has both positive and normative implications. On the positive side, the reluctance of the Supreme Court to challenge dominant political forces is frequently cited as an explanation for judicial deference. Indeed, that is the core prediction of the strategic model. The reluctance of the Court to challenge political majorities thus provides a possible strategic explanation for at least some of the Court's strong deference to the political process in capacity-constrained domains. The role of judicial capacity in limiting the Court's ability to challenge political majorities suggests that these explanations of judicial decision-making are not competing but complementary. It may well be, in some contexts, that the Court is hesitant to aggressively challenge dominant political forces. But if that reluctance is—at least in part—a product of the Court's limited capacity, this counts for the judicial capacity model, not against it.[6]

On the normative side, the point is more straightforward. Once again, ought implies can. The typical mechanisms offered to explain the Supreme Court's timidity in the face of democratic majorities are not especially convincing. But the judicial capacity model identifies an important additional mechanism limiting the Court's capacity to effect social change in the teeth of political opposition. If this mechanism is effective, both hopes and fears of a powerful counter-majoritarian judiciary are to a large extent misplaced. In most capacity-constrained domains, would-be reformers should consider whether the game is worth the candle. At a minimum, they should focus their efforts on formulating attractive categorical rules that cleanly insulate most governmental action from constitutional challenge. Opponents of aggressive judicial review, by contrast, should mostly rest easy, though a capacity-constrained Court remains capable of challenging dominant political forces within narrow bounds.

The remainder of this chapter elaborates each of these points, the positive and the normative, using examples drawn from Part II.

Judicial Independence and the Explanatory Power of the Judicial Capacity Model

As emphasized throughout this book, the explanatory power of the judicial capacity model is a function of its ability to explain important features of the Supreme Court's past decisions that other models cannot. One of those features is the Court's strong and systematic deference to the political process in capacity-constrained domains. As Part II demonstrated, no other leading model of Supreme Court decision-making can readily explain this feature of the Court's decisions across a broad range of capacity-constrained domains. That includes the strategic model, which predicts that the Supreme Court will defer to the political process only when there is reason for the justices to fear significant political opposition. The model does not predict that this fear will systematically constrain the Supreme Court to embrace a strongly deferential approach. Nor does it predict that the Court will be willing to depart from that approach only in the form of hard-edged categorical rules. In each of these respects, the judicial capacity model explains important features of the Court's decisions that the strategic model cannot.

On the other hand, there is obviously some overlap between the predictions of the strategic model and the predictions of the judicial capacity model. The strategic model does not predict the systematic deference that the judicial capacity model does, but it does predict some judicial deference to the political branches. In this respect, the strategic model stands in the same relation to the judicial capacity model as the judicial restraint variant of the legalist model. Any overlap between the predictions of the strategic model and the predictions of the judicial capacity model represents a case of observational equivalence. If these predictions prove correct, the evidence is consistent with both models and is therefore uniquely explained by neither. The upshot is that some—though not all—of the Supreme Court's deference in capacity-constrained domains might be the product of a strategic fear of political opposition. Alternatively, it might be the product of judicial capacity limits, or it might be the joint product of both. The available evidence is consistent with all of these possibilities.

If this were all that could be said, the judicial capacity model would still stand alone in its power to explain the Supreme Court's systematic deference in capacity-constrained domains and the Court's unwillingness to depart from such deference except in the form of hard-edged categorical rules. It would simply have to acknowledge that some of the Court's deference is equally well explained by the strategic model. As with the judicial restraint variant of the legalist model, the same holds in reverse. If some of the Court's deference is equally consistent with the predictions of the strategic model and the judicial capacity model, neither model can claim victory over the other. More evidence would be needed to fully disentangle the two or to confirm that both are operating simultaneously. Simply highlighting this uncertainty about the causal efficacy of the strategic model, a timeworn explanation for judicial deference, would be an important contribution.

In fact, the judicial capacity model allows us to go considerably further. If the mechanisms underlying the Court's strategic timidity are waning in force or are likely to do so in the near future, it is of pressing importance to determine whether other constraints, such as judicial capacity, will continue to push the Supreme Court toward deference in the areas where the two models overlap. As discussed above, Richard Pildes has persuasively argued that the mechanisms underlying the strategic model (and other closely related explanations for the Supreme Court's majoritarian tendencies) are either weak to begin with or likely to weaken in the relatively near future. The constraints of judicial capacity, by contrast, rest on long-standing and widely held judicial norms that seem unlikely to erode substantially any time soon. Thus, even if Pildes is correct, as I believe he is, the judicial capacity model provides theoretically and empirically compelling reason to believe that the Supreme Court will remain strongly constrained to employ some combination of deference and categorical rules in capacity-constrained domains.[7]

This still leaves the most intriguing possible explanation for the overlap between the judicial capacity model and the strategic model. The predictions of the judicial capacity model might overlap with those of the strategic model because the causal forces underlying the strategic model are endogenous to limited judicial capacity. Here, too, the strategic model stands in precisely the same relation to the judicial capacity model as the judicial restraint variant of the legalist model. The strategic model predicts that judges will defer to the political process because they fear political opposition. The judicial capacity model predicts that the justices of the Supreme Court will defer to the political process because they are constrained to do so by the limits of judicial capacity. But if the fear of political opposition underlying the strategic model is at least partly a function of judicial capacity—because significant political opposition tends to produce a high volume of litigation that taxes the limits of judicial capacity—then the fear of political opposition is itself a by-product of the limits of judicial capacity. This would make the strategic model and the judicial capacity model partial complements, rather than competitors.

So is the fear of political opposition endogenous to the limits of judicial capacity? This is not a question that be readily answered on the basis of the empirical evidence. By definition, in areas where the predictions of the two models overlap, both are equally consistent with the available evidence. But there are strong theoretical reasons for concluding that judicial capacity is an important factor behind the Supreme Court's fear of political opposition in capacity-constrained domains, substantially contributing to the Court's hesitancy to oppose dominant political forces.

Those reasons are well illustrated by the Supreme Court's modern commerce- and spending-power decisions. Unlike the judicial capacity model, the strategic model does not predict that the Court will be compelled to defer systematically to the political branches in these areas, except where it casts constitutional limitations in the form of narrow, categorical rules. But the strategic model does predict that the Court will defer to the political branches when doing so is necessary to avoid triggering serious political opposition. This prediction is frequently offered to explain why the Court has never returned to anything like its early New Deal approach to the commerce and spending powers: By invalidating many popular aspects of the modern regulatory and welfare states, including federal minimum wage laws, environmental regulations, civil rights laws, and much more, such an approach would almost certainly have triggered enormous political opposition at any point since 1937. This is just what the strategic model predicts the Court will feel constrained to avoid.[8]

There are two major reasons the strategic model makes this prediction. First, Congress and the States might overturn the Court's decisions by constitutional amendment. Alternatively, Congress and the President might refuse to enforce or abide by them, rendering the whole enterprise futile. If that is the case, why would the justices waste their scarce resources trying? Second, Congress and the President might retaliate against the Court by cutting its budget, shrinking its jurisdiction, or passing some modern analogue of Franklin Roosevelt's Court-packing plan that would seriously undercut the Court's institutional legitimacy and independence. If that is the case, an effort to roll back the commerce and spending powers may not only be futile but may also have serious costs for the Court as an institution.[9]

There are a couple of significant problems with this theory. First, as Pildes has ably explained, the prospects of serious and sustained political retaliation against the Supreme Court seem extremely remote. Constitutional amendments are, under modern conditions, virtually guaranteed to fail. Public support for the Court as an institution has proved remarkably stable over a long period of time, even when the Court has made highly unpopular decisions. In part for this reason, "Congress has not effectively retaliated or even credibly threatened to retaliate against the Court in generations." The clearest example of such retaliation in modern history is Franklin Roosevelt's Court-packing plan. But that plan ultimately failed, and it might well have done so even if the Court had not beat a wholesale retreat in 1937. Either way, the closeness of the question and the significant political capital that this episode cost Roosevelt— an enormously popular President facing down a deeply unpopular Court in a time of severe economic crisis—underscores the strength of the Court's position vis-à-vis the political branches. As Pildes concludes, "only . . . the most extraordinary circumstances will provoke politics and public opinion into imposing major constraints on the modern Court."[10]

Second, apart from the remote prospect of direct attacks on the Supreme Court or a constitutional amendment, it is not clear how or why political opposition—even of a strong and sustained character—would lead the Court to defer to the political branches. If Congress keeps passing commerce- and spending-power legislation that the Court views as unconstitutional, the persons burdened by those laws (or some subset of them) will keep filing suit. But when confronted with such suits, the courts can and presumably will keep issuing injunctions and holding federal officials who violate them in contempt. The same goes for presidential defiance. This depends, of course, on the existence of prospective plaintiffs with the motives and means to sue and to overcome the collective action problem of determining who will bear the costs of doing so. But as discussed in Chapters 5 and 6, such plaintiffs are in ample supply in both the commerce-power and spending-power contexts. It also depends on the Court sustaining enough popular legitimacy to survive prolonged conflict with the political branches, even when its individual decisions are unpopular. But the New Deal episode and the long and stable public support the Court has enjoyed for many decades suggests that it has large reserves of legitimacy to spend.

I do not mean to suggest that the risk of political retaliation is zero. Past may not be prologue. New and dynamic features of the American political landscape, such as accelerating partisan polarization or loss of trust in public institutions, might well cause a contemporary constitutional crisis to play out differently. As such, no terribly confident prediction can be ventured about the sort of political response that the Supreme Court would precipitate by returning in 2018 or 2025 to its pre-1937 approach to the commerce and spending powers. The essential point is simply this: While the strategic model undoubtedly contains elements of truth, it fails to supply anything like a fully satisfying explanation of why we should expect the Court to shrink from challenging dominant political forces in constitutional cases. Indeed, the modern era offers precious little evidence that a rational Court had, or has, much to worry about in the way of political resistance to its constitutional decisions.[11]

Enter the judicial capacity model. If the constraints of judicial capacity permit the Supreme Court to limit the commerce and spending powers only in the form of narrow categorical rules or one-off applications of extremely deferential standards, the prospect of meaningful political retaliation is largely beside the point. The limits of judicial capacity will generally stop the Court far before it reaches the point where such retaliation becomes a serious possibility. The same goes for political defiance of judicial decisions. This may help to explain why Congress has made no serious attempt to retaliate against the Court since the New Deal crisis. The limits of judicial capacity have largely prevented the Court from acting boldly enough to make such a dramatic response necessary.

Even if the limits of judicial capacity fail to deter the Court from challenging dominant political forces, political defiance of a serious and sustained character would quickly overwhelm the Court's limited capacity, at least in capacity-constrained domains. If Congress keeps passing laws that violate constitutional limits imposed by the Court, the Court will have to keep invalidating them, in addition to whatever other, similar statutes are already on the books. If the executive branch refuses to abide by the Court's decisions or insists on construing them narrowly, the Court will be forced to keep hearing new cases, issuing new injunctions, and holding more officials in contempt. As Chapters 5 and 6 demonstrate, the constraints of judicial capacity starkly limit the Court's ability to do this in the commerce- and spending-power contexts.

That does not mean such a course is outright impossible. But to manage it, the Supreme Court would have to leave many lower-court invalidations of federal law unreviewed or cast its own decisions in the form of broad categorical rules, which could be applied more or less summarily to invalidate broad swaths of commerce- and spending-power legislation. It may well have to do both, and even these approaches may not be enough, given the tendency of categorical rules to break down under the pressure of sustained litigation. Even if it were possible for the Court to craft sturdy enough categorical rules to survive under these conditions, the crudity of those rules may well make them substantively unpalatable to some or all of the justices. This further decreases the likelihood that the Court will be willing to mount a sustained challenge to dominant political forces.[12]

The predictions of the judicial capacity model closely track the events of the New Deal constitutional showdown recounted in Chapter 5. During 1935 and 1936 the Court undertook to invalidate a broad swath of laws in areas that were just beginning to become capacity-constrained domains due to the proliferation of New Deal commerce- and spending-power legislation. To do so, the Court employed a variety of categorical approaches such as the manufacturing/commerce distinction and the direct/indirect effects test discussed in Chapter 5. Ordinarily such rules might have been expected to send a clear signal about what was constitutional and what was not, limiting uncertainty and thus the volume of litigation. But these were not ordinary circumstances. The quantity of affected legislation, the number of potential plaintiffs, and the intensity of political opposition were all sufficiently large that the Court's approach invited an extraordinary volume of litigation challenging the constitutionality of a wide array of federal statutes. This, in turn, put great strain on the predictability and coherence of the Court's categorical rules, further increasing uncertainty and inviting more litigation. As McNollgast explains, "The number of cases threatened to overwhelm the judicial system, and the Supreme Court in particular."[13]

This is just what the judicial capacity model predicts the Supreme Court will feel strongly compelled to avoid, and in fact, the Court retreated in very short order. The conventional wisdom, of course, is that this retreat was motivated by fear of Roosevelt's Court-packing plan. Other scholars have attributed the retreat to legalist factors, such as an improvement in the government's lawyering, or to an ideological shift produced by Roosevelt's new appointments to the Court in 1937–1940. The judicial capacity model does not contradict any of these explanations. Rather, it complements them by suggesting that, even in the absence of Roosevelt's Court-packing plan, better government lawyering, or an ideological infusion of liberal justices, the Supreme Court could not long have sustained its crusade against the New Deal without overwhelming the limits of its capacity. That is to say, the Court could not long have sustained this course without sacrificing its deeply rooted commitments to minimum professional standards and reviewing virtually all lower-court invalidations of federal laws.[14]

More generally, the judicial capacity model supplies an alternative mechanism to explain the Court's reluctance to challenge dominant political forces, one that should be expected to operate even in the absence of a serious threat of political retaliation or any other effective mechanism—such as the appointments process—keeping the Court reliably in line with majoritarian views. Thus, even if a strategic concern about political opposition is behind some of the Court's deference to the political branches in capacity-constrained domains, there is strong reason to believe that this concern is at least partially endogenous to judicial capacity. In this respect, the judicial capacity model both complements the strategic model and helps to illuminate the causal mechanism on which it is premised.

This is emphatically not to suggest that a capacity-constrained Supreme Court will never challenge dominant political forces. It obviously will. The New Deal constitutional showdown is a clear example, and it would not be difficult to list others. Pildes is clearly right to insist on this fact and to insist on its importance. But the limits of judicial capacity are essential to understanding the actual extent of judicial independence and whatever normative conclusions may follow from it. Any account that focuses exclusively on political constraints, ignoring capacity limits, is likely to overstate the power of the Court to challenge political majorities, perhaps dramatically so.

Judicial Capacity and the Counter-Majoritarian Difficulty

Judicial independence plays an important role in positive debates about Supreme Court decision-making, but like judicial competence, the role it plays in normative arguments about the proper scope of judicial review is nothing short of dominant. This makes sense. Judicial review in effect substitutes the decisions of unelected judges and justices for the decisions of more democratically accountable institutions. In evaluating the desirability of such a substitution, it is almost impossible to avoid two basic questions: Why should nine unelected lawyers have the final say on vexed moral questions about which they disagree along roughly the same lines as everyone else? On the other hand, how can the fundamental rights of political minorities be left to a majority vote? As Barry Friedman has shown, these questions, which he aptly calls "the threat" and "the hope" of judicial review, have dominated debates over the Supreme Court throughout American history.[15]

Constitutional theorists have offered many ingenious responses to both questions and continue to churn them out at an impressive rate. But

Friedman and others have called the relevance of this debate into serious question by challenging its empirical premises. While critics and defenders of strong judicial review reach diametrically opposite conclusions, they both assume, implicitly or explicitly, that the Supreme Court is capable of standing up to dominant political forces in a meaningful way. If the Court is not politically independent in this sense, the whole debate is essentially hypothetical, like a couple of teenagers debating whether a real-life Superman would be a force for good or evil. This is just what Friedman and others have argued. Their view has largely carried the day, to the point that the leading cliché of modern constitutional scholarship is arguably no longer handwringing over the counter-majoritarian difficulty but cheerful dismissal of such handwringing as "naïve or passé."[16]

Such dismissal remains widespread, but as I have already explained, Richard Pildes's important critique calls it into very serious question. The key point is simply that the mechanisms behind the majoritarian thesis do not appear especially strong upon close examination. There is also good reason to suspect that they will operate with even less force going forward. If Pildes is right about this, the counter-majoritarian difficulty retains real bite and cannot easily be brushed aside or transcended. Recent Supreme Court decisions striking down major federal statutes, such as *Citizens United v. FEC* (the Bipartisan Campaign Finance Reform Act), *Shelby County v. Holder* (the Voting Rights Act), *NFIB v. Sebelius* (the Affordable Care Act), and *United States v. Windsor* (the Defense of Marriage Act), have lent significant ballast to Pildes's critique, triggering yet another round of intense debate over the counter-majoritarian difficulty. Liberal anxiety in particular has been heightened by the possibility that the retirement of one or two elderly justices could produce the most solidly conservative Supreme Court the United States has seen since 1937.[17]

The issue is thus squarely joined: Is the counter-majoritarian difficulty naïve and passé? Or is it more acute and morally urgent than ever? The judicial capacity model suggests an intermediate response. Judicial capacity imposes significant constraints on the Supreme Court's ability to challenge dominant forces, but it does so only in capacity-constrained domains. Even in those domains, the Court retains the power to impose constitutional limits if it can do so in the form of categorical rules, especially narrow categorical rules that insulate most federal legislation from constitutional challenge. The Court also retains the power to invalidate federal laws through one-off—or simply very rare—applications of extremely deferential standards. Outside of capacity-constrained domains, Pildes's critique applies with full force, casting serious doubt on the mechanisms underlying strong forms of the majoritarian thesis. Within capacity-constrained domains, the judicial capacity model suggests an alternative and more robust mechanism constraining the Court's power to challenge dominant political forces. This mechanism should serve to mute both the threat and the hope of counter-majoritarian judicial review, but mute does not mean eliminate.[18]

The point is well illustrated by the Supreme Court's commerce-power decisions. Ever since the New Deal, critics of expansive commerce-power review have pressed trenchant objections to its democratic legitimacy. Defenders of expansive commerce-power review have defended its necessity and urged the Court to engage in far more of it. Both sides assume that the Court could take a far more robust approach to commerce-power review if it wanted to. The judicial capacity model suggests this is not the case. For the Court to take such an approach, especially in the form of a vague standard, would call into question the constitutionality of a vast number of federal statutes, triggering an avalanche of litigation that the Court would itself feel compelled to decide. The judicial capacity model suggests that this course is extremely unlikely.[19]

To this extent, both the hopes and fears of expansive judicial review of federal commerce legislation are misplaced. But that is not to suggest they have no place whatever. The Court's near invalidation of the entire Affordable Care Act based on a narrow categorical distinction between activity and inactivity vividly illustrates the power that the Court retains, even in capacity-constrained domains, to invalidate major legislation adopted by more democratically accountable institutions. The Gun-Free School Zones Act, invalidated in *United States v. Lopez,* and the civil remedy provision of the Violence Against Women Act, invalidated in *United States v. Morrison,* were clearly less important than the Affordable Care Act, they were probably also more popular. The key point is simply this: The constraints that judicial capacity imposes on the Court's power to engage in aggressive commerce-power review do not obviate the need to justify the real power the Court continues to exercise. At the same time, it matters greatly whether such decisions are the exception or the norm, and the judicial capacity model strongly suggests that they will be the exception.

What follows? Advocates of more aggressive commerce-power review need not despair, but the judicial capacity model suggests that they should temper their expectations and craft their arguments for expanded judicial review in the form of narrow categorical rules similar to the ones embraced by the Court in *Lopez, Morrison,* and *NFIB.* Practical reformers seeking to invalidate particular statutes might have real success with this strategy. Principled proponents of more robust federalism should question whether the categorical constitutional limits consistent with judicial capacity constraints are sufficiently significant or sufficiently attractive to represent an improvement over the status quo. Opponents of more aggressive commerce-power review, by contrast, should recognize that their worst fears are almost certainly unfounded. Instead, they should focus their efforts on demonstrating the crudity and instability of the narrow categorical limits that are likely to hold the greatest appeal for the Court. They may lose this battle in particular cases, with perhaps quite significant consequences, but they are unlikely to lose the war.

The Equal Protection Clause provides another excellent and somewhat contrasting illustration. Opponents of expansive Equal Protection review routinely emphasize the democratic illegitimacy of unelected and unaccountable judges second-guessing the decisions of more democratically accountable actors. Democratic arguments were advanced with great vigor and indignation by opponents of *Brown v. Board of Education,* and they have been strongly pressed by opponents of Equal Protection review ever since. Historically, supporters of expanded Equal Protection review typically countered that counter-majoritarian review is appropriate and necessary to protect the rights of groups inadequately protected by the political process. Some arguments of this sort attempted to weave judicial protection of minority rights into the definition of democracy; others simply argued that the claims of democracy have their limits. More recently, many supporters of expanded Equal Protection review have embraced a variant of the majoritarian thesis and argued that such review is generally, perhaps even inevitably, majoritarian. On this view, of course, the counter-majoritarian difficulty is no difficulty at all.[20]

Many participants in this debate have assumed that the Supreme Court could take a far more robust approach to Equal Protection review if it wanted to—for instance, by extending heightened scrutiny to discrimination against the poor or to government action that merely has a disparate impact on women and racial minorities. Others have urged the Court to subject all government classifications to the same open-ended review in the form of a vague standard and assumed that the Court could take this path if it so chose. The judicial capacity model suggests this is not the case. For the Court to seriously expand Equal Protection review in any of these ways, especially in the form of a vague standard, would call into question the constitutionality of a vast number of statutes, many of them federal, triggering an avalanche of litigation that the Court would itself feel compelled to decide. The judicial capacity model suggests that this course is extremely unlikely.[21]

To this extent, both the hopes and fears of expansive Equal Protection review are misplaced, just as they are with respect to the commerce power. But there the similarity ends. Because much of the government action implicated by the Equal Protection Clause is state and local, and because the Supreme Court has managed to craft relatively attractive categorical rules for subjecting discrimination against racial minorities, women, and others to heightened scrutiny, the Court's modern approach to Equal Protection is considerably more robust than its modern approach to the commerce power. The Court's invalidation of school segregation and other aspects of the Jim Crow system, of numerous government classifications based on sex, and of same-sex marriage bans in a majority of U.S. states were all highly consequential exercises of power requiring some form of normative justification. I do not question that such a justification exists, nor do I take any position for present purposes on what the best justification might be. I merely note that the question remains a live one despite the constraints of judicial capacity.[22]

What does all of this mean for theorists and practical reformers seeking to expand Equal Protection review? The Supreme Court does have some flexibility to do more in this area but that flexibility has real limits. In particular, the Court is very unlikely to embrace an open-ended standard that would call into question the constitutionality of a broad range of government classifications. The Court is also fairly unlikely to add to the current list of suspect classifications, out of fear that opening this door would encourage an avalanche of litigation by groups aspiring to this status. The best approach for practical reformers, therefore, may well be to make their case under rational-basis review, as did the plaintiffs in the recent gay rights cases. Most such challenges will necessarily fail. Otherwise, rational-basis review would be transformed into an open-ended standard rather than a rule of categorical deference, but some small number may succeed. Principled proponents of heightened scrutiny for the poor or disparate impact claims or open-ended Equal Protection review of all government classifications are likely to fare less well and should consider directing their energies elsewhere.[23]

Theorists and practical reformers opposed to aggressive Equal Protection review should recognize that their worst fears are probably unfounded. They should also remain vigilant because the Supreme Court has meaningful flexibility to engage in broader Equal Protection review, so long as it preserves the very deferential character of rational-basis review and does not encourage an avalanche of litigation from new groups seeking suspect class status. Lower courts have similar flexibility, and perhaps even more, since the Supreme Court does not feel compelled to review an especially large fraction of Equal Protection cases. As such, opponents of expanded review should emphasize the risk that invalidating legislation under rational-basis review will transform that categorically deferential approach into an open-ended standard. They should also emphasize the risk that expanding the list of suspect classifications will invite an avalanche of litigation from groups seeking to add themselves to the list. Opponents of Equal Protection review may lose this battle in particular cases, with perhaps quite significant consequences. But like opponents of expansive commerce-power review, they are unlikely to lose the war.

The broader point is that no careful analysis of judicial independence can afford to overlook judicial capacity. In a wide range of important constitutional domains, the limits of judicial capacity help to explain why the Supreme Court is often reluctant to challenge dominant political forces. As such, the judicial capacity model both complements the strategic model and helps to illuminate the causal mechanism underlying it. It also helps to clarify where and when the Court is able to challenge dominant political forces and thus where and when the counter-majoritarian difficulty still has meaningful bite. Finally, the judicial capacity model provides guidance to practical reformers about how to leverage the limits of judicial capacity to their advantage in advocating for or against counter-majoritarian judicial review. It also suggests that some practical reformers should direct their energies elsewhere. For all of these reasons, judicial capacity should occupy a prominent place both on the agenda of constitutional theory and in the toolkits of practical reformers.

Conclusion

Judicial capacity has been too long misunderstood and too long neglected. It is a central institutional characteristic of the federal judiciary, which has significantly influenced the development of American constitutional law across many of the most important constitutional domains. It is impossible to fully understand the modern constitutional law of federalism, separation of powers, or individual rights without considering the constraining force of judicial capacity.

Judicial capacity also has significant implications for the forward-looking work of constitutional scholars, legal reformers, and practicing lawyers. If capacity limits preclude the Supreme Court from robustly policing government action in the most important constitutional domains, it is difficult to fault the Court for failing to do so. Nor should would-be reformers waste their energy trying to prod the Court into action.

Even more important, both scholars and legal reformers must recognize that, when the Court acts, the options at its disposal are often constrained by the limits of judicial capacity. Taking these constraints into account may well alter their assessment of when and whether judicial review of government action is ultimately desirable. At the very least, the limits of judicial capacity should inform the tactical decisions of lawyers and activists on both sides—those who want the Court to do more and those who do not. Understanding the limits of the possible is crucial to effective advocacy.

For all of these reasons, judicial capacity deserves a central place on the agenda of constitutional theory, on par with that accorded to judicial competence and judicial independence. Indeed, judicial capacity is crucial to a full understanding of both of these much-discussed institutional features of the judiciary. The limits of judicial capacity frequently force the Supreme Court to employ crude categorical rules or defer to other government actors. The former undermines the Court's ability to produce reliably good results; the latter constrains its ability to challenge dominant political forces. Often, the limits of judicial capacity force the Court to do both.

Judicial capacity is thus essential to understanding the role of the Supreme Court in American government. That role is not unimportant. The Court can and does issue occasional decisions that affect the lives of millions of people. The Court can and does occasionally thwart the will of democratic majorities and their political representatives. But the Court is nothing like the omnipotent force imagined by both its admirers and its detractors. Compared to the governmental machinery of Congress, the federal executive branch, and the fifty state governments, the Court is a tiny institution, capable of resolving only a small fraction of the constitutional issues generated by American government. It is bound by the limits of judicial capacity. Anyone interested the Supreme Court and the U.S. Constitution must take those limits seriously.

Methods

Chapter 4 and the introduction to Part II describe the methodological approach of this book in nontechnical terms. This brief appendix provides additional technical background and explanation of the choices behind this methodological approach.

A Multiple-Case Study Framework

One of the most venerable approaches to qualitative empirical research, a multiple-case study research design involves in-depth and comparative analysis of multiple cases, performed for the purpose of testing a causal theory or model. As applied to the judicial capacity model, this approach raises two distinct but related methodological issues. The first is how to select constitutional domains—the cases of interest—for analysis. The second is how to draw causal inferences from the pattern of the Supreme Court's decisions in particular constitutional domains.[1]

Any consideration of these questions must start with the crucial premise that case studies employ a different kind of causal inference from that employed by statistical analysis. Rather than patterns of covariation across independent and dependent variables, causal inference in case research is based on "the match between what empirical evidence we would hypothesize that the [causal] mechanism should leave and what we actually find in the case." This explains why some case-study researchers prefer the terms "causal condition" and "outcome" to "independent variable" and "dependent variable." Within a given case, neither the value of the causal condition nor the value of the outcome actually varies. Instead, a causal condition, such as limited judicial capacity, either does or does not cause a particular outcome, such as deference or categorical rules.[2]

Case Selection

From this account of "within-case" causal inference, it follows that the rationale for studying multiple cases is not to examine variation across cases—for instance, in the frequency of categorical rules or deferential decisions across high-stakes and low-stakes (or high-volume and low-volume) domains. Instead, the reason for studying multiple cases is to identify the bounds of the population in which a given causal inference—made within individual cases, rather than across them—holds. For this purpose, the only relevant cases are those in which the causal condition (or the corresponding value of the independent variable) is present. Here that means the capacity-constrained domains in which the model predicts that the limits of judicial capacity will strongly constrain Supreme Court decision-making.[3]

Within this category, the qualitative methods literature recommends studying as broad and diverse a range of cases as possible. The greater the number and diversity of cases in which a causal inference holds, "the better we are able to infer [that] what was found in the chosen cases should also be present in other typical cases throughout the population." As such, the case studies in Part II encompass a broad and diverse range of capacity-constrained domains, but no normal domains, because the causal condition on which the judicial capacity model is premised is not present in those domains. This method of case selection does not produce selection bias because its goal is not to generate a representative sample of the general population of cases, but instead to identify the subset of that population in which a causal inference drawn from individual cases holds.[4]

Causal Inference

So much for case selection. The more difficult issue is how to make causal inferences about the influence of judicial capacity from the pattern of Supreme Court decisions within any given constitutional domain. The standard approach, variously known as congruence testing, pattern-matching, or implication analysis, boils down to two essential questions: First, is the pattern of the Supreme Court's decisions consistent with the model's predictions? Second, can the judicial capacity model explain important aspects of that pattern that other models of judicial decision-making cannot? Put more formally, are the predictions of the judicial capacity model "theoretically unique"? The logic is straightforward. If the empirical evidence is consistent with the judicial capacity model but inconsistent with—or simply unexplained by—the most plausible alternative models, then that lends strong support to the judicial capacity model. This is the same essential logic by which judges and juries can and do make inferences of guilt beyond a reasonable doubt based solely on the evidence of the single case before them. Chapter 4 describes this approach at length, so I need not elaborate further here.[5]

Qualitative vs. Quantitative Methods

The qualitative case-study design employed in this book draws on a rich array of contextual information that no quantitative research design could hope to capture. Of course, qualitative and quantitative analysis are not mutually exclusive, and in theory, the judicial capacity model should be quantitatively testable. In practice, however, such testing is difficult or impossible because the dependent variables of the model—deference and doctrinal form (rules versus standards)—are both continuous, which is to say matters of degree, and highly context-specific. In other words, it is possible to characterize particular decisions as more or less deferential and more or less rule-like, but not simply as deferential or rule-like full stop. Furthermore, what counts as deferential or rule-like (or the opposite) for purposes of the judicial capacity model varies by context and depends on many factors outside the four corners of the Supreme Court's opinions. That is because the model does not predict that the Court's decisions in high-volume and high-stakes domains will be deferential or rule-like in some abstract or absolute sense. Rather, it predicts that those decisions will be sufficiently deferential or rule-like to avoid triggering an overwhelming volume of litigation.[6]

What that amounts to in any given constitutional domain depends heavily on context-specific factors like the universe of government actions covered by the Court's decision and the fraction of those actions the Court's decision would render invalid or call into question. It also depends on the ease and certainty with which litigants and lower-court judges can be expected to predict the application of various doctrinal formulations (the difference between a rule and standard being largely a function of clarity and predictability to the relevant audience of judges and litigants, which cannot be determined a priori).[7]

To make matters even more complicated, the practical effects of the Supreme Court's decisions can be altered dramatically by the way in which lower courts apply them. For example, a decision that looks standard-like or nondeferential on its face can be transformed, intentionally or otherwise, into a categorical rule of deference in the lower courts. If the Supreme Court does not intervene to correct this misapplication, the approach of the lower courts becomes, for all practical purposes, the prevailing law—one that the Court tacitly condones through its passivity. Examples of this phenomenon are discussed in Chapters 5 and 11.

All of this makes the dependent variables of the judicial capacity model extremely difficult to measure validly (in a way that accurately captures the phenomena of interest) or reliably (in a way that produces consistent results across coders) using the sort of scalable coding techniques required by large-N statistical methods. The amount of relevant information outside the four corners of Supreme Court decisions—the usual dataset for quantitative analysis of judicial behavior—may make such measurement impossible. This makes the judicial capacity model more amenable to qualitative testing, which "creates opportunities to develop more valid measures of concepts instead of having to rely on often crude, indirect proxies in large-N research."[8]

In sum, the qualitative, multiple case-study approach employed in this book draws on an enormous quantity of context-specific information that a quantitative approach would necessarily leave on the cutting room floor. This is not to disparage quantitative analysis in general or to suggest that it has no possible role in testing the judicial capacity model. Indeed, I hope to pursue the possibility of quantitative testing further in the future. But given the context-specific predictions of the judicial capacity model, the multiple-case-study research design employed in this book has very substantial advantages.[9]

Notes

Introduction

1. Pamela S. Karlan, "Foreword: Democracy and Disdain," 126 *Harv. L. Rev.* 1, 68 (2012); Keith E. Whittington, *Political Foundations of Judicial Supremacy: The Presidency, the Supreme Court, and Constitutional Leadership in U.S. History* (2007), 7; Laurence H. Tribe, "*Erog v. HSUB* and Its Disguises: Freeing *Bush v. Gore* from Its Hall of Mirrors," 115 *Harv. L. Rev.* 170, 288 (2001); J. Harvie Wilkinson III, *Cosmic Constitutional Theory* (2012), 4; United States v. Windsor, 133 S. Ct. 2675, 2698 (2013) (Scalia, J., dissenting); Shelby County v. Holder, 133 S. Ct. 2612, 2648 (2013).

2. *Windsor,* 133 S. Ct. at 2698 (Scalia, J., dissenting); Office of Mgmt. & Budget, Exec. Office of the President, *Budget of the United States Government, Fiscal Year 2017* (2016); Central Intelligence Agency, *GDP (Purchasing Power Parity), The World Factbook* (2016), https://www.cia.gov/library/publications/the-world-factbook/rankorder /2001rank.html; Admin. Office of the U.S. Courts, *The Judiciary FY 2017 Congressional Budget Summary* (2016), http://www.uscourts.gov/sites/default/files/fy_2017 _federal_judiciary_congressional_budget_summary_0.pdf; Bureau of Econ. Analysis, U.S. Dept. of Commerce, *Gross Domestic Product by Metropolitan Area, 2016* (2017), 12, https://www.bea.gov/newsreleases/regional/gdp_metro/2017/pdf/gdp_metro0917 .pdf.

3. Raoul Berger, *Government by Judiciary: The Transformation of the Fourteenth Amendment* (1977).

4. 247 U.S. 251 (1918); Adrian Vermeule, *Judging under Uncertainty: An Institutional Theory of Legal Interpretation* (2006), 281; 410 U.S. 113 (1973); Mary C. Segers and Timothy A. Byrnes, "Introduction, Abortion Politics in American States," in

Abortion Politics in American States, ed. Mary C. Segers and Timothy A. Byrnes (1995), 5; Rachel Garfield and Anthony Damico, *The Coverage Gap: Uninsured Poor Adults in States That Do Not Expand Medicaid,* Kaiser Family Foundation (Oct. 2016), 2, http://files.kff.org/attachment/Issue-Brief-The-Coverage-Gap-Uninsured-Poor -Adults-in-States-that-Do-Not-Expand-Medicaid.

5. United States v. Windsor, 133 S. Ct. 2675, 2698 (2013) (Scalia, J., dissenting).

1. Structural and Normative Underpinnings

1. Peter L. Strauss, "One Hundred Fifty Cases Per Year: Some Implications of the Su-preme Court's Limited Resources for Judicial Review of Agency Action," 87 *Colum. L. Rev.* 1093, 1099 (1987); Neil K. Komesar, *Imperfect Alternatives: Choosing Institutions in Law, Economics, and Public Policy* (1994), 144–145; Komesar, *Law's Limits: The Rule of Law and the Supply and Demand of Rights* (2001), 40–41; Richard A. Posner, *The Federal Courts: Challenge and Reform* (1996), 133–134; Lee Epstein et al., *The Be-havior of Federal Judges: A Theoretical and Empirical Study* (2013, ebook), 871.

2. Keith E. Whittington, "Once More unto the Breach: Postbehavioralist Approaches to Judicial Politics," *Law and Social Inquiry* 25 (2000): 601, 628; Lawrence Baum, *The Puzzle of Judicial Behavior* (1997), 61.

3. Judith Resnik, "Tiers," 57 *S. Cal. L. Rev.* 837, 849 (1984); Adrian Vermeule, *Judging under Uncertainty: An Institutional Theory of Legal Interpretation* (2006), 268; Mar-garet Meriwether Cordray and Richard Cordray, "The Supreme Court's Plenary Docket," 58 *Wash. & Lee L. Rev.* 737, 745–746 (2001).

4. Cordray and Cordray, "Supreme Court's Plenary Docket," 740 (emphasis added); Posner, *The Federal Courts,* 4; Amanda Frost, "Overvaluing Uniformity," 94 *Va. L. Rev.* 1567, 1631–1635 (2008); H. W. Perry Jr., *Deciding to Decide: Agenda Setting in the United States Supreme Court* (1991), 251; "Justice Elena Kagan on Supreme Court and Constitutional Law," C-SPAN (Aug. 31, 2016), https://www.c-span.org/video/ ?414445-1/justice-elena-kagan-supreme-court-constitutional-law; Perry, *Deciding to Decide* (1991) (ebook), 2949–2950; Robert L. Stern et al., *Supreme Court Practice,* 8th ed. (2002), 244, 246–247, 271–272; Michael F. Sturley, "Observations on the Su-preme Court's Certiorari Jurisdiction in Intercircuit Conflict Cases," 67 *Tex. L. Rev.* 1251, 1254 (1989).

5. Administrative Office of the U.S. Courts, "Table A-1—Supreme Court of the United States Judicial Business," United States Courts (Sept. 30, 2016), http://www.uscourts .gov/sites/default/files/supcourt_a1_0930.2016.pdf (showing that the Supreme Court granted review to 66, 93, 76, 71, and 82 cases each year in 2011–2015, respectively).

6. Jeff Shesol, *Supreme Power: Franklin Roosevelt vs. the Supreme Court* (2010), 169; Mc-Nollgast, "Politics and the Courts: A Positive Theory of Judicial Doctrine and the Rule of Law," 68 *S. Cal. L. Rev.* 1631, 1672 (1995).

7. Posner, *The Federal Courts,* 128.

8. Vermeule, *Judging under Uncertainty,* 268; Cordray and Cordray, "Supreme Court's Plenary Docket," 740.

9. Andrew Coan and Nicholas Bullard, "Judicial Capacity and Executive Power," 102 *Va. L. Rev.* 765, 766–767 (2015); Vermeule, *Judging under Uncertainty,* 268.

10. Posner, *The Federal Courts,* 4, 133; Komesar, *Imperfect Alternatives,* 145; Akhil Reed Amar, "A Neo-Federalist View of Article III: Separating the Two Tiers of Federal Jurisdiction," 65 *B.U. L. Rev.* 205, 268 n.213 (1985); Samuel Estreicher and John E. Sexton, "A Managerial Theory of the Supreme Court's Responsibilities: An Empirical Study," 59 *N.Y.U. L. Rev.* 681, 693–94 (1984); Arthur D. Hellman, "Caseload, Conflicts, and Decisional Capacity: Does the Supreme Court Need Help?," 67 *Judicature* 28, 39–40 (1983).

2. The Judicial Capacity Model

1. Richard A. Posner, *The Federal Courts: Challenge and Reform* (1996), 95–96, 98–99, 369; Neil K. Komesar, *Imperfect Alternatives: Choosing Institutions in Law, Economics, and Public Policy* (1994), 147–148.

2. Komesar, 147; Aziz Z. Huq, "Judicial Independence and the Rationing of Constitutional Remedies," 65 *Duke L.J.* 1 (2015); Posner, *The Federal Courts,* 178, 369; Lawrence M. Friedman, "Legal Rules and the Process of Social Change," 19 *Stan. L. Rev.* 786, 819–20 (1967); Russell B. Korobkin, "Behavioral Analysis and Legal Form: Rules vs. Standards Revisited," 79 *Or. L. Rev.* 23, 32 (2000); Bell Atlantic Corp. v. Twombly, 550 U.S. 544, 570 (2007); Ashcroft v. Iqbal, 556 U.S. 662 (2009); Arthur R. Miller, "From *Conley* to *Twombly* to *Iqbal:* A Double Play on the Federal Rules of Civil Procedure," 60 *Duke L.J.* 1, 54 n.206 (2010); Andrew B. Coan, "Is There a Constitutional Right to Select the Genes of One's Offspring?," 63 *Hastings L.J.* 233, 263 (2011); Peter L. Strauss, "One Hundred Fifty Cases Per Year: Some Implications of the Supreme Court's Limited Resources for Judicial Review of Agency Action," 87 *Colum. L. Rev.* 1093, 1102 (1987).

3. U.S. Const. art. III, §2; Judiciary Act of 1925, Pub. L. No. 68-415, 43 Stat. 936 (codified as amended in scattered sections of 28 U.S.C.); *Ex parte* McCardle, 74 U.S. 506 (1868); Sheldon v. Sill, 49 U.S. 441 (1850); U.S. Const. art. I, §8, cl. 18; Rules Enabling Act, 28 U.S.C. §2072 (2006); McNollgast, "Politics and the Courts: A Positive Theory of Judicial Doctrine and the Rule of Law," 68 *S. Cal. L. Rev.* 1631, 1649 (1995); Posner, *The Federal Courts,* 96; Komesar, *Imperfect Alternatives,* 143.

4. Cannon v. U. of Chicago, 441 U.S. 677, 709 (1979); Pickering v. Board of Ed., 391 U.S. 563, 568 (1968).

5. Louis Kaplow, "Rules versus Standards: An Economic Analysis," 42 *Duke L.J.* 557, 577 (1992).

6. Gary Goertz, *Multimethod Research, Causal Mechanisms, and Case Studies* (2017); Derek Beach and Rasmus Brun Pedersen, *Causal Case Study Methods: Foundations and Guidelines for Comparing, Matching, and Tracing* (2016) (ebook), 1323, 1992–1993.

7. Komesar, *Imperfect Alternatives,* chap. 1, 128–133; Keith E. Whittington, "Congress before the *Lochner* Court," 85 *B.U. L. Rev.* 821, 835 (2005); Vanessa A. Baird, "The

Effect of Politically Salient Decisions on the U.S. Supreme Court's Agenda," *Journal of Politics* 66 (2004): 755, 769.

8. U.S. Const. amend. V; Kermit Roosevelt, *The Myth of Judicial Activism* (2008), 18; Loving v. Virginia, 388 U.S. 1, 10 (1967); Chicago, B. & Q. R. Co. v. City of Chicago, 166 U.S. 226 (1897); Bolling v. Sharpe, 347 U.S. 497, 498–499 (1954); Richard A. Primus, *"Bolling Alone,"* 104 *Colum. L. Rev.* 975, 976 (2004).

9. See Chapter 1.

10. Komesar, *Imperfect Alternatives,* 251; Washington v. Davis, 426 U.S. 229, 248 (1976).

11. Komesar, *Imperfect Alternatives,* 251; Suzanne B. Goldberg, "Equality without Tiers," 77 *S. Cal. L. Rev.* 481, 485 (2004); Casey L. Dwyer, "An Empirical Examination of the Equal Protection Challenge to Contingency Fee Restrictions in Medical Malpractice Reform Statutes," 56 *Duke L.J.* 611, 618 (2006); Gerald Gunther, "The Supreme Court, 1971 Term—Foreward: In Search of an Evolving Doctrine on a Changing Court: A Model for A Newer Equal Protection," 86 *Harv. L. Rev.* 1, 12 (1972); 438 U.S. 104 (1978). Adam Winkler, "Fundamentally Wrong about Fundamental Rights," 23 *Const. Comment.* 227, 233 (2006); Basil H. Mattingly, "Forum over Substance: The Empty Ritual of Balancing in Regulatory Takings Jurisprudence," 36 *Willamette L. Rev.* 695, 699 (2000); Lingle v. Chevron U.S.A. Inc., 544 U.S. 528, 538 (2005).

12. Chavez v. Martinez, 538 U.S. 760, 775 (2003); Komesar, *Imperfect Alternatives,* 259–260; United States v. Morrison, 529 U.S. 598 (2000) Civil Rights Cases, 109 U.S. 3 (1883); Christian Turner, "State Action Problems," 65 *Fla. L. Rev.* 281 (2013); Posner, *The Federal Courts,* 317; Randy E. Barnett, "Why Popular Sovereignty Requires the Due Process of Law to Challenge 'Irrational or Arbitrary' Statutes," 14 *Geo. J. L. & Pub. Pol'y* 355, 372 (2016); Clark Neily, "Litigation without Adjudication: Why the Modern Rational Basis Test Is Unconstitutional," 14 *Geo. J. L. & Pub. Pol'y* 537 (2016); Richard A. Epstein, *The Classical Liberal Constitution* (2014), 311; Erwin Chemerinsky, "Rethinking State Action," 80 *NW. U. L. Rev.* 503, 506 (1985); Robert J. Glennon Jr. and John E. Nowak, "A Functional Analysis of the Fourteenth Amendment 'State Action' Requirement," 1976 *Sup. Ct. Rev.* 221, 221; Charles L. Black Jr., "The Supreme Court, 1966 Term—Foreword: 'State Action,' Equal Protection, and California's Proposition 14," 81 *Harv. L. Rev.* 69, 95 (1967).

13. Posner, *The Federal Courts,* 98; Barry Friedman, "A Tale of Two Habeas," 73 *Minn. L. Rev.* 247, 329–340 (1988); Larry W. Yackle, "The Origins of Habeas Corpus," in *Postconviction Remedies* (West 2011), §4:6; Toby J. Heytens, "Doctrine Formulation and Distrust," 83 *Notre Dame L. Rev.* 2045, 2102 (2003); *compare* Schneckloth v. Bustamonte, 412 U.S. 218, 273 (1973) (Blackmun, J., concurring) *with* Schriro v. Landrigan, 550 U.S. 465, 499 (2007) (Stevens, J., dissenting).

14. *See* Chapter 1.

15. David C. Thompson and Melanie F. Wachtell, "An Empirical Analysis of Supreme Court Certiorari Petition Procedures: The Call for Response and the Call for the Views of the Solicitor General," 16 *Geo. Mason L. Rev.* 237 (2009).

16. Erwin Chemerinsky, *Constitutional Law: Principles and Policies,* 2d ed. (2002), 238; John E. Nowak and Ronald D. Rotunda, "Treatise on Constitutional Law: Substance

and Procedure," §4.8(d) (West 2017); Laurence H. Tribe, *American Constitutional Law,* 2d ed. (1988), 305–306.

3. Refining the Model

1. Lee Epstein and Jack Knight, "Reconsidering Judicial Preferences," 16 *Ann. Rev. Pol. Sci.* 11, 14 (2013); Michael A. Bailey and Forrest Maltzman, *The Constrained Court: Law, Politics, and the Decisions Justices Make* (2011) (ebook), 158, 868.
2. 561 U.S. 477 (2010).
3. Stephen Skowronek, "The Conservative Insurgency and Presidential Power: A Developmental Perspective on the Unitary Executive," 122 *Harv. L. Rev.* 2070, 2073 (2009); Jud Mathews, "Minimally Democratic Administrative Law," 68 *Admin. L. Rev.* 605, 631 (2016); Barry Friedman, "Taking Law Seriously," *Perspectives on Politics* 4, no. 2 (2006): 261, 266; *compare* Free Enterprise Fund v. Public Company Accounting Oversight Board, 561 U.S. 477, 477–514 (Roberts, C.J.) *with id.* at 514–549 (Breyer, J., dissenting).
4. *Supreme Court Decision-Making: New Institutionalist Approaches,* ed. Cornell W. Clayton and Howard Gillman (1999) (collecting new institutionalist perspectives on Supreme Court decision-making); Keith E. Whittington, "Once More unto the Breach: Postbehavioralist Approaches to Judicial Politics," 25 *Law and Social Inquiry* 25, no. 2 (2000): 601, 615 (quoting Cornell W. Clayton, "The Supreme Court and Political Jurisprudence: New and Old Institutions," in *New Institutionalist Approaches,* 15, 30); Ryan C. Black and Ryan J. Owens, "Agenda Setting in the Supreme Court: The Collision of Policy and Jurisprudence," *Journal of Politics* 71 (2009): 1062 (attempting to identify and disentangle the legal and political influences on Supreme Court agenda-setting); Bailey and Maltzman, *The Constrained Court,* 42; Jeffrey R. Lax, "The New Judicial Politics of Legal Doctrine," *Annual Review of Political Science* 14 (2011): 131, 132; Lee Epstein and Jack Knight, "Reconsidering Judicial Preferences," *Annual Review of Political Science* 16 (2013): 11, 24.
5. Whittington, "Once More unto the Breach," 615; James G. March and Johan P. Olsen, "The New Institutionalism: Organizational Factors in Political Life," *American Political Science Review* 78 (1984): 734, 739.
6. Kathleen F. Brickey, "Criminal Mischief: The Federalization of American Criminal Law," 46 *Hastings L.J.* 1135, 1154 (1995); For a discussion of Chief Justice Rehnquist's dire (but probably exaggerated) predictions to this effect, see Fred Strebeigh, *Equal: Women Reshape American Law* (2009), 362–363.
7. Robert L. Stern et al., *Supreme Court Practice,* 8th ed. (2002), 247–248; Matthew Diller and Nancy Morawetz, "Intracircuit Nonacquiescence and the Breakdown of the Rule of Law: A Response to Estreicher and Revesz," 99 *Yale L.J.* 801, 809–810 (1990).
8. Lawrence M. Friedman, "Legal Rules and the Process of Social Change," 19 *Stan. L. Rev.* 786, 808 (1967); Bert I. Huang, "Lightened Scrutiny," 124 *Harv. L. Rev.* 1109 (2011) (empirically demonstrating an example of this process in action); Richard A.

Posner, *The Federal Courts: Challenge and Reform* (1996), 160–162; Jeffrey O. Cooper and Douglas A. Berman, "Passive Virtues and Casual Vices in the Federal Courts of Appeals," 66 *Brook. L. Rev.* 685, 688 (2001); William M. Richman and William L. Reynolds, *Injustice on Appeal: The United States Courts of Appeals in Crisis* (2012), 115.

9. Marcelo Neves, lecture at the International Seminar on Institutional Theory at the National Federal University of Rio de Janeiro: "Institutional Limits of the Supreme Federal Court Practice Enlightened by the Brazilian Constitution" (Nov. 5, 2014) (transcript on file with author).

10. Barry Friedman, "Taking Law Seriously," 271.

11. Judith Resnik, "Whither and Whether Adjudication?," 86 *B.U. L. Rev.* 1101, 1104 (2006); Federal Magistrates Act, Pub. L. No. 90-578, 82 Stat. 1108, 1108–1114 (1968); Act of June 27, 1988, Pub. L. No. 100-352, 102 Stat. 662 (1988).

12. Tara Leigh Grove, "Tiers of Scrutiny in a Hierarchical Judiciary," 14 *Geo. J.L. & Pub. Pol'y* 475 (2016); Robert Post, "The Supreme Court Opinion as Institutional Practice: Dissent, Legal Scholarship, and Decisionmaking in the Taft Court," 85 *Minn. L. Rev.* 1267, 1287 (2001).

4. Testing the Model

1. Derek Beach and Rasmus Brun Pedersen, *Causal Case Study Methods: Foundations and Guidelines for Comparing, Matching, and Tracing* (2016), 182; John Gerring, *Case Study Research: Principles and Practices* (2007), 1–5, 118; Gary King et al., *Designing Social Inquiry: Scientific Inference in Qualitative Research* (1992) 38.

2. Michael Bailey and Forrest Maltzman, *The Constrained Court: Law, Politics, and the Decisions Justices Make* (2011), 7; Adrian Vermeule, *Law's Abnegation: From Law's Empire to the Administrative State* (2016), 1–3; Lee Epstein et al., *The Behavior of Federal Judges: A Theoretical and Empirical Study* (2013), 2.

3. Epstein et al., *Behavior of Federal Judges,* 11; Antonin Scalia, "The Rule of Law as a Law of Rules," 56 *U. Chi. L. Rev.* 1175, 1187 (1989); Richard A. Posner, "The Rise and Fall of Judicial Self-Restraint," 100 *Cal. L. Rev.* 519, 520; Aziz Z. Huq, "When Was Judicial Self-Restraint?," 100 *Cal. L. Rev.* 579, 581 (2012).

4. Epstein et al., *Behavior of Federal Judges;* Harry T. Edwards and Michael A. Livermore, "Pitfalls of Empirical Studies That Attempt to Understand the Factors Affecting Appellate Decisionmaking," 58 *Duke L.J.* 1895, 1947–1949 (2009); Gregory C. Sisk, "The Quantitative Moment and the Qualitative Opportunity: Legal Studies of Judicial Decision Making," 93 *Cornell L. Rev.* 873, 884 (2008).

5. Lee Epstein et al., *Behavior of Federal Judges,* 25–30, 69. The most influential articulation of the attitudinal model is Jeffrey A. Siegel and Harold J. Spaeth, *The Supreme Court and the Attitudinal Model Revisited* (2002); Joshua B. Fischman and David S. Law, "What Is Judicial Ideology, and How Should We Measure It?," 29 *Wash. U. J.L. & Pol'y* 133, 133–134 (2009); Michael C. Dorf, "Whose Ox Is Being Gored? When Attitudinalism Meets Federalism," 21 *St. John's J. Legal Comment.* 497, 498–499 (2007);

Jeffrey A. Segal and Harold J. Spaeth, *The Supreme Court and the Attitudinal Model* (1993), 65; Lee Epstein and Jack Knight, "Documenting Strategic Interaction on the U.S. Supreme Court," 3 (Annual Meeting of the American Political Science Association, Political Science Paper No. 275, 1995), http://epstein.wustl.edu/research/conference papers.1995APSA.pdf; Bailey and Maltzman, *The Constrained Court,* 6, 29.

6. Epstein and Knight, *Documenting Strategic Interaction,* 15; Bailey and Maltzman, *The Constrained Court,* 4; Lawrence B. Solum, "The Positive Foundations of For-malism: False Necessity and American Legal Realism," 127 *Harv. L. Rev.* 2464, 2475-2776 (2014); Jonathan P. Kastellec and Jeffrey R. Lax, "Case Selection and the Study of Judicial Politics," *Journal of Empirical Legal Studies* 5 (2008): 407, 410; Frederick Schauer, "Judging in a Corner of the Law," 61 *S. Cal. L. Rev.* 1717, 1725 (1988); Jeffrey R. Lax, "The New Judicial Politics of Legal Doctrine," 14 *Ann. Rev. Polit. Sci.* 131, 148 (2011) (quoting Jeffrey A. Segal and Harold J. Spaeth, *Attitudinal Model Revisited* (2002)); Bailey and Maltzman, *The Constrained Court,* 67.

7. Barry Friedman, "Taking Law Seriously," *Perspectives on Politics* 4 (2006): 261, 267; Epstein and Knight, *Documenting Strategic Interaction,* 3-4; Lax, "New Judicial Politics," 49; Kastellec and Lax, 438; Dorf, "Whose Ox Is Being Gored?," 497, 505; Peter J. Smith, "Federalism, Instrumentalism, and the Legacy of the Rehnquist Court," 74 *Geo. Wash. L. Rev.* 906, 909 (2006); United States v. Lopez, 514 U.S. 549, 560 (1995); Gonzales v. Raich, 545 U.S. 1, 41 (2005).

8. Tonja Jacobi, "The Impact of Positive Political Theory on Old Questions of Consti-tutional Law and the Separation of Powers," 100 *Nw. U. L. Rev.* 259, 264 (2006); Lee Epstein et al., "The Supreme Court as a Strategic National Policymaker," 50 *Emory L.J.* 583, 592 (2001); Lee Epstein and Jack Knight, *The Choices Justices Make* (1997). Bailey and Maltzman, *The Constrained Court,* chaps. 6-7; Mario Bergara et al., "Modeling Supreme Court Strategic Decision-Making: The Congressional Constraint," 28 *Leg. Stud. Q.* 247 (2003); Epstein and Knight, *Documenting Stra-tegic Interaction,* 12; Epstein et al., *Behavior of Federal Judges;* Jeffrey A. Segal et al., "Congress, the Supreme Court, and Judicial Review: Testing a Constitutional Separation of Powers Model," *American Journal of Political Science* 55 (2011): 89, 89-90.

9. Epstein and Knight, *Documenting Strategic Interaction,* 4-7, as an example; Bailey and Maltzman, *The Constrained Court,* 97-98; Frank B. Cross and Blake J. Nelson, "Strategic Institutional Effects on Supreme Court Decisionmaking," 95 *Nw. U. Law Rev.* 1437, 1446-1447 (2001); Anna Harvey and Barry Friedman, "Pulling Punches: Congressional Constraints on the Supreme Court's Constitutional Rulings, 1987-2000," 31 *Legis. Stud. Q.* 533, 562 (2006).

10. Bailey and Maltzman, *The Constrained Court,* 5.

11. Scott Baker and Pauline T. Kim, "A Dynamic Model of Doctrinal Choice," 4 *J. Leg. Anal.* 329, 333-335 (2012); Frank Cross et al., "A Positive Political Theory of Rules and Standards," 2012 *U. Ill. L. Rev.* 1, 10-12; Jeffrey R. Lax, "Political Constraints on Legal Doctrine: How Hierarchy Shapes the Law," *Journal of Politics* 74, no. 3 (2012): 765, 766; McNollgast, "Politics and the Courts: A Positive Theory of Judicial Doctrine

and the Rule of Law," 68 *S. Cal. L. Rev.* 1631, 1636–1637 (1994); Lax, "Political Constraints," 766; Baker and Kim, "A Dynamic Model," 329.

12. Lax, "Political Constraints," 779; Cross et al., "A Positive Political Theory," 4; Baker and Kim, "A Dynamic Model," 355–356.

13. Beach and Pedersen, *Causal Case Study Methods,* 183; Ryan C. Black and Ryan J. Owens, "Agenda Setting in the Supreme Court: The Collision of Policy and Jurisprudence," *Journal of Politics* 71 (2009): 1062, 1064; Jeffrey R. Lax and Kelly T. Rader, "Legal Constraints on Supreme Court Decision Making: Do Jurisprudential Regimes Exist?," *Journal of Politics* 72 (2010): 273, 274; Mark J. Richards and Herbert M. Kritzer, "Jurisprudential Regimes in Supreme Court Decision Making," 96 *American Political Science Review* 96 (2002): 305; Gordon Silverstein, *Law's Allure: How Law Shapes, Constrains, Saves, and Kills Politics* (2009), 15; Mark A. Graber, "The Countermajoritarian Difficulty: From Courts to Congress to Constitutional Order," *Annual Review of Law and Social Science* 4 (2008): 361, 363–365; *Supreme Court Decision-Making: New Institutionalist Approaches,* ed. Cornell W. Clayton and Howard Gillman (1999); *The Supreme Court in American Politics: New Institutionalist Interpretations,* ed. Cornell W. Clayton and Howard Gillman (1999); Lax, "New Judicial Politics," 133; Jeb Barnes, "Bringing the Courts Back In: Interbranch Perspectives on the Role of Courts in American Politics and Policy Making," *Annual Review of Political Science* 10 (2007): 25, 31.

14. Fischman and Law, "What Is Judicial Ideology," 147.

15. Ibid., 147; Lawrence Baum, *The Puzzle of Judicial Behavior* (1997), 20.

16. Richard H. Pildes, "Is the Supreme Court a 'Majoritarian' Institution?," *Sup. Ct. Rev.* 103, 157 (2010); Bailey and Maltzman, *The Constrained Court,* 2, 18–20.

II. The Judicial Capacity Model Applied

1. Derek Beach and Rasmus Brun Pedersen, *Causal Case Study Methods: Foundations and Guidelines for Comparing, Matching, and Tracing* (2016), 292.

2. Erwin Chemerinsky, *Constitutional Law,* 5th ed. (2017), 731–732; Randy E. Barnett, "Scrutiny Land," 106 *Mich. L. Rev.* 1479, 1481 (2008); Steven Menashi and Douglas H. Ginsburg, "Rational Basis with Economic Bite," 8 *N.Y.U. J. L. & Liberty* 1055, 1057 (2014); Andrew B. Coan, "Judicial Capacity and the Substance of Constitutional Law," 122 *Yale L.J.* 422, 438 n.44 (2012); Neil K. Komesar, *Imperfect Alternatives: Choosing Institutions in Law, Economics, and Public Policy* (1994), 257; Reno v. Flores, 507 U.S. 292, 302 (1993); Beach and Pedersen, *Causal Case Study Methods,* 100; Gary Goertz, *Multimethod Research, Causal Mechanisms, and Case Studies: An Integrated Approach* (2017), 66.

Federalism

1. David Schwartz, "A Question Perpetually Arising: Implied Powers, Capable Federalism, and the Limits of Enumerationism," 59 *Ariz. L. Rev.* 573, 620 (2017).

2. William J. Novak, *The People's Welfare: Law and Regulation in Nineteenth-Century America* 59 (1996); Anuj C. Desai, "Wiretapping before the Wires: The Post Office and the Birth of Communications Privacy," 60 *Stan. L. Rev.* 553, 556 (2007); Anuj C. Desai, "The Transformation of Statutes into Constitutional Law: How Early Post Office Policy Shaped Modern First Amendment Doctrine," 58 *Hastings L.J.* 671, 672–673 (2007).

3. Novak, *The People's Welfare*, 241; Jack M. Balkin, "Commerce," 109 *Mich. L. Rev.* 1, 50 (2010); Lawrence Lessig, "Translating Federalism: *United States v. Lopez*," 1995 *Sup. Ct. Rev.* 125, 140–143 (1995); Howard Gillman, "Reconnecting the Modern Supreme Court to the Historical Evolution of American Capitalism," in *The Supreme Court in American Politics: New Institutionalist Interpretations*, ed. Howard Gillman and Cornell Clayton (1999), 235, 241–246; Susan Low Bloch and Vicki C. Jackson, *Federalism: A Reference Guide to the U.S. Constitution* (2013), 277; Bruce Ackerman, *We the People*, vol. 2: *Transformations* (1998), 407; Robert Post, "Federalism in the Taft Court Era: Can It Be 'Revived'?," 51 *Duke L.J.* 1513, 1517 (2002); Keith E. Whittington, "Dismantling the Modern State? The Changing Structural Foundations of Federalism," 25 *Hastings Const. L.Q.* 483, 483 (1998); Stephen M. Griffin, "Constitutional Theory Transformed," 108 *Yale L.J.* 2115, 2130 (1999); Lynn A. Baker and Ernest A. Young, "Federalism and the Double Standard of Judicial Review," 51 *Duke L.J.* 75, 75 (2001); Robert D. Cooter and Neil S. Siegel, "Collective Action Federalism: A General Theory of Article I, Section 8," 63 *Stan. L. Rev.* 115, 130 (2010); Jeff Shesol, *Supreme Power: Franklin Roosevelt vs. the Supreme Court* (2010), 454; Cass R. Sunstein, "Constitutionalism after the New Deal," 101 *Harv. L. Rev.* 421, 425 (1987).

4. Samuel H. Beer, "The Modernization of American Federalism," 3 *Publius* 49, 51; Gary Lawson, "The Rise and Rise of the Administrative State," 107 *Harv. L. Rev.* 1231, 1236 (1994); Schwartz, "A Question Perpetually Arising," 645; Whittington, "Dismantling the Modern State?," 486–487; Lynn A. Baker, "Putting the Safeguards Back into the Political Safeguards of Federalism," 46 *Vill. L. Rev.* 951, 952 (2001); Neal Devins, "The Judicial Safeguards of Federalism," 99 *Nw. U. L. Rev.* 131, 144 (2004); John O. McGinnis and Ilya Somin, "Federalism vs. States' Rights: A Defense of Judicial Review in a Federal System," 99 *Nw. U. L. Rev.* 89, 90 (2004); Nicole Huberfeld et al., "Plugging Into Endless Difficulties: Medicaid and Coercion in *National Federation of Independent Business v. Sebelius*," 93 *B.U. L. Rev.* 1, 50 (2013); Lawrence B. Solum, "How *NFIB v. Sebelius* Affects the Constitutional Gestalt," 91 *Wash. U.L. Rev.* 1, 2 (2013).

5. The Commerce Power

1. U.S. Const. art. I, §8, cl. 8; Kenneth R. Thomas, Cong. Res. Serv., *The Power to Regulate Commerce: Limits on Congressional Power* (2014), 1–2, https://fas.org/sgp/crs/misc/RL32844.pdf; Gary Lawson, "The Rise and Rise of the Administrative State," 107 *Harv. L. Rev.* 1231, 1236 (1994); Barry Friedman and Genevieve Lakier,

"To Regulate," Not "To Prohibit": Limiting the Commerce Power," 2012 *Sup. Ct. Rev.* 255, 255–256 (2012); Richard Primus, "The Limits of Enumeration," 124 *Yale L.J.* 576, 642 (2014).

2. David Lightner, *Slavery and the Commerce Power: How the Struggle against the Interstate Slave Trade Led to the Civil War* (2006); Paul Finkelman, "Teaching Slavery in American Constitutional Law," 34 *Akron L. Rev.* 261, 263 (2000); Lawrence M. Friedman, *A History of American Law,* 3d ed. (2005), 120; Michael J. Klarman, "How Great Were the 'Great' Marshall Court Decisions?," 87 *Va. L. Rev.* 1111, 1132 (2001); Norman R. Williams, "*Gibbons,*" 79 *N.Y.U. L. Rev.* 1398, 1482 (2004).

3. Keith E. Whittington, "Congress before the *Lochner* Court," 85 *B.U. L. Rev.* 821, 823 (2005); Jeff Shesol, *Supreme Power: Franklin Roosevelt vs. the Supreme Court* (2010), 454; William E. Leuchtenburg, "FDR's Court-Packing Plan: A Second Life, a Second Death," 1985 *Duke L.J.* 673 (1985); McNollgast, "Politics and the Courts: A Positive Theory of Judicial Doctrine and the Rule of Law," 68 *S. Cal. L. Rev.* 1631, 1672 (1994); Shesol, *Supreme Power,* 168.

4. Daniel E. Ho and Kevin M. Quinn, "Did a Switch in Time Save Nine?," 2 *J. Legal Analysis* 69 (2010).

5. Lee Epstein et al., "The Judicial Common Space," *Journal of Law, Economics, & Organization* 23 (2007): 303, 312 (showing a consistently conservative Supreme Court since the early 1970s); Andrew D. Martin et al., "The Median Justice on the United States Supreme Court," 83 *N.C. L. Rev.* 1275, 1302 tbl.4 (2005) (presenting data showing that the last liberal median justice was Thurgood Marshall in 1968); Alicia Parlapiano and Margot Sanger-Katz, "A Supreme Court with Merrick Garland Would Be the Most Liberal in Decades," *New York Times,* Mar. 16, 2016, https://www .nytimes.com/interactive/2016/02/18/upshot/potential-for-the-most-liberal-supreme -court-in-decades.html; Jefferson Cowie, *The Great Exception: The New Deal and the Limits of American Politics* (2016), 206–207; Eliot A. Rosen, *The Republican Party in the Age of Roosevelt: Sources of Anti-Government Conservatism in the United States* (2014), 1; J. M. Balkin, "Too Good to Be True: The Positive Economic Theory of Law," 87 *Colum. L. Rev.* 1447, 1454 (1987); Federal Arbitration Act, chap. 392, Pub. L. No. 80-282, 61 Stat. 669 (1947) (codified as amended at 9 U.S.C. §§1–16, 201–208, 301–307 (2012)); Class Action Fairness Act of 2005, Pub. L. No. 109-2, 119 Stat. 4–14 (codified as amended at 28 U.S.C. §§1332(d), 1453, 1711–1715 (2012)); Comprehensive Drug Abuse Prevention and Control Act of 1970, Pub. L. No. 91-513, 84 Stat. 1236– 1296 (codified as amended at 21 U.S.C. §801 et seq. (2012)).

6. 22 U.S. 1, 189 (1824); *compare* Jack M. Balkin, "Commerce," 109 *Mich. L. Rev.* 1, 50 (2010) *with* Randy Barnett, "Jack Balkin's Interaction Theory of 'Commerce,'" 2012 *U. Ill. L. Rev.* 623 (2012).

7. *Gibbons,* 22 U.S. at 194; 17 U.S. 316, 409, 422, 423 (1819); *Gibbons,* 22 U.S. at 14; *McCulloch,* 17 U.S. at 405; *Gibbons,* 22 U.S. at 19; *McCulloch,* 17 U.S. at 366–367.

8. Letter from James Madison to Spencer Roane (Sept. 2, 1819); *Richmond Enquirer,* Mar. 30, 1819, at 3, col. 3, reprinted in 2 *John P. Branch Historical Papers of Randolph-Macon College* 2, no. 1, ed. W. Dodd (1905): 51–63; "Opinion on Bill for Establishing a National Bank," in The Thomas Jefferson Papers at the Library of Congress

(Feb. 15, 1791), http://lcweb2.loc.gov/service/mss/mtj//mtj1/013/013_0984_0990.pdf; Lawrence Lessig, "Translating Federalism: *United States v. Lopez*," *Sup. Ct. Rev.* 125, 145 (1995); David P. Currie, *The Constitution in the Supreme Court: The Second Century, 1888–1986* (1994), 206; William E. Leuchtenberg, *The Supreme Court Reborn: The Constitutional Revolution in the Age of Roosevelt* (1996), 215; Shesol, *Supreme Power*.

9. 298 U.S. 238, 299, 307–308 (1936); Lessig, "Translating Federalism," 152; Lawrence Lessig, "Understanding Federalism's Text," 66 *Geo. Wash. L. Rev.* 1218, 1225 (1998).

10. United States v. Morrison, 529 U.S. 598, 640 (2000) (Breyer, J., dissenting); *Carter Coal Co.*, 298 U.S. at 327 (Cardozo, J., dissenting); Robert D. Cooter and Neil S. Siegel, "Collective Action Federalism: A General Theory of Article I, Section 8," 63 *Stan. L. Rev.* 115, 130 (2010), at 130; Lessig, "Translating Federalism," 177; *Carter Coal Co.*, 298 U.S. at 295–296.

11. *Id.* at 327–328 (Cardozo, J., dissenting).

12. NLRB v. Jones & Laughlin Steel Corp., 301 U.S. 1, 37 (1937).

13. Letter from Justice Robert H. Jackson to Judge Sherman Minton (Dec. 21, 1942) (unsigned carbon copy of typed letter), in Robert H. Jackson Papers, Library of Congress, Manuscript Division, Washington, DC, box 125, folder 8; Pamela S. Karlan, "Foreword: Democracy and Disdain," 126 *Harv. L. Rev.* 1, 43 (2012); Primus, "The Limits of Enumeration," 642.

14. 379 U.S. 294, 303–304 (1964); Primus, "The Limits of Enumeration," 642; Karlan, "Foreword: Democracy and Disdain," 43.

15. United States v. Lopez, 514 U.S. 549, 567 (1995); *Morrison*, 529 U.S. at 610, 613.

16. Andrew B. Coan, "Judicial Capacity and the Substance of Constitutional Law," 122 *Yale L.J.* 422, 444 (2012); Gary Lawson, "Making a Federal Case Out of It: *Sabri v. United States* and the Constitution of Leviathan," *Cato Sup. Ct. Rev.*, 2004, at 119, 139; Ernest A. Young, "Dual Federalism, Concurrent Jurisdiction, and the Foreign Affairs Exception," 69 *Geo. Wash. L. Rev.* 139, 160 (2001); Gonzales v. Raich, 545 U.S. 1, 25 (2005); *id.* at 49 (O'Connor, J., dissenting).

17. Nat. Fed. Indep. Bus. v. Sebelius, 567 U.S. 519, 552, 588 (2012) (Roberts, C.J.); *id.* at 647 (Scalia, Kennedy, Thomas, Alito, Js., dissenting).

18. *Id.* at 549 (Roberts, C.J.); *id.* at 662 (Scalia, Kennedy, Thomas, Alito, Js., dissenting).

19. Andrew Coan, "Implementing Enumeration," 57 *Wm. & Mary L. Rev.* 1985, 1989–1990 (2016); Primus, "The Limits of Enumeration," 587; David Schwartz, "A Question Perpetually Arising: Implied Powers, Capable Federalism, and the Limits of Enumerationism," 59 *Ariz. L. Rev.* 573, 580 (2017); Gregory v. Ashcroft, 501 U.S. 452, 459 (1991) (O'Connor, J.); United States v. Lopez, 514 U.S. 549, 552 (1995) (Rehnquist, C.J.); Printz v. United States, 521 U.S. 898, 918–922 (1997) (Scalia, J.); U.S. Term Limits, Inc. v. Thornton, 514 U.S. 779, 838 (1995) (Kennedy, J.); Griswold v. Connecticut, 381 U.S. 479, 501 (1965) (Douglas, J.); United States v. Morrison, 529 U.S. 598, 655–656 (2000) (Breyer, J., dissenting); BMW of N. Am., Inc. v. Gore, 517 U.S. 559, 607 (1996) (Ginsburg, J., dissenting); Gov't Publ. Office, *Supreme Court Decisions Overruled by Subsequent Decision* (2014), https://www.gpo.gov/fdsys/pkg/GPO

-CONAN-2002/pdf/GPO-CONAN-2002-12.pdf (compiling 233 overruled Supreme Court decisions between 1810 and 2010).

20. *See* sources collected at *supra* note 4; Gonzales v. Raich, 545 U.S. 1, 32–33; Erwin Chemerinsky, *Enhancing Government: Federalism for the 21st Century* (2008), 231–245; Roderick M. Hills Jr., "Against Preemption: How Federalism Can Improve the National Legislative Process," 82 *N.Y.U. L. Rev.* 1, 3 (2007).

21. *See* sources collected at *supra* notes 16 and 18 and accompanying text.

22. Ilya Somin, "Closing the Pandora's Box of Federalism: The Case for Judicial Restriction of Federal Subsidies to State Governments," 90 *Geo. L.J.* 461, 495 (2002); Citizens United v. Fed. Election Comm'n, 558 U.S. 310 (2010); Gary Langer, "In Supreme Court Ruling on Campaign Finance, the Public Dissents," ABC News (Feb. 17, 2010), http://blogs.abcnews.com/thenumbers/2010/02/in-supreme-court-ruling-on -campaign-finance-the-public-dissents.html; United States v. Eichman, 496 U.S. 310 (1990); Texas v. Johnson, 491 U.S. 397 (1989); Peter Hanson, "Flag Burning," in *Public Opinion and Constitutional Controversy,* ed. Nathaniel Persily et al. (2008) (collecting contemporaneous public opinion polls showing opposition to *Johnson* approaching 80 percent); Sch. Dist. of Abington Twp. v. Schempp, 374 U.S. 203 (1963); Engel v. Vitale, 370 U.S. 421 (1962); Lauren Maisel Goldsmith and James R. Dillon, "The Hallowed Hope: The School Prayer Cases and Social Change," 59 *St. Louis U. L.J.* 409, 430 (2015); Michael A. Bailey and Forrest Maltzman, *The Constrained Court: Law, Politics, and the Decisions Justices Make* (2011), 107–108; *compare* Barry Cushman, *Rethinking the New Deal Court: The Structure of a Constitutional Revolution* (1998) *with* Ho and Quinn, "Switch in Time."

23. U.S. Const. art. I, §8, cl. 8; United States v. Morrison, 529 U.S. 598, 617 (2000); United States v. Lopez, 514 U.S. 549, 567 (1995); *Morrison,* 529 U.S. at 610–611; 567 U.S. at 550 (2012) (Roberts, C.J.).

24. See *supra* note 7 and accompanying text; 545 U.S. 1, 34–35 (2005) (Scalia, J., concurring).

25. See *supra* note 11 and accompanying text.

26. *Lopez,* 514 U.S. at 567–568; *Morrison,* 529 U.S. at 617–618; *NFIB,* 567 U.S. at 536; Coan, "Implementing Enumeration," 1997–1998; Cooter and Siegel, "Collective Action Federalism," 164, 172, 184; *compare* Barnett, "Jack Balkin's Interaction Theory," 147, *with* Cooter and Siegel, 160.

27. *See supra* note 10 and accompanying text.

28. Robert H. Bork and Daniel E. Troy, "Locating the Boundaries: The Scope of Congress's Power to Regulate Commerce," 25 *Harv. J.L. & Pub. Pol'y* 849, 885–893 (2002); Thomas, *Power to Regulate Commerce,* 66.

29. Jeffrey L. Fisher, "A Clinic's Place in the Supreme Court Bar," 65 *Stan. L. Rev.* 137, 142–143 (2013); Richard J. Lazarus, "Advocacy Matters before and within the Supreme Court: Transforming the Court by Transforming the Bar," 96 *Geo. L.J.* 1487, 1557 (2008); Nancy Morawetz, "Counterbalancing Distorted Incentives in Supreme Court Pro Bono Practice: Recommendations for the New Supreme Court Pro Bono Bar and Public Interest Practice Communities," 86 *N.Y.U. L. Rev.* 131, 144–145 (2011).

30. Keycite search of *Gonzales v. Raich,* Westlaw, https://1.next.westlaw.com/Related Information/I4dd5a05fd69411d99439b076ef9ec4de/kcNegativeTreatment.html ?docSource=2cd6aed3b5b74a9082275dafdce8b22e&pageNumber=1&transitionType =ListViewType&contextData=(sc.UserEnteredCitation).

31. *See supra* note 11 and accompanying text.

32. *See supra* note 3 and accompanying text; Thomas, *Power to Regulate Commerce*; Lawson, "The Rise and Rise of the Administrative State."

33. Gonzales v. Raich, 545 U.S. 1, 58 (2005) (Thomas, J., dissenting); United States v. Lopez, 514 U.S. 549, 584 (1995) (Thomas, J., concurring).

34. *Raich,* 545 U.S. at 37 (Scalia, J., concurring); *Lopez,* 514 U.S. at 569 (Kennedy, J., concurring).

6. The Spending Power

1. "Federal Net Outlays as Percent of Gross Domestic Product," Fed. Reserve Econ. Data, https://fred.stlouisfed.org/series/FYONGDA188S (last updated July 28, 2017) (displaying federal net outlays as a fraction of gross domestic product); Maureeen Constantino and Leigh Angres, Cong. Budget Off., *The Federal Budget in 2015* (2016), https://www.cbo.gov/sites/default/files/cbofiles/images/pubs-images/50xxx/51110 -Land_Overall.png (pie chart breaking down categories of 2015 federal spending to-taling $3.7 trillion); Alex Kozinski and Steven A. Engel, "Recapturing Madison's Constitution: Federalism without the Blank Check," in *James Madison and the Future of Limited Government,* ed. John Samples (2003), 23; Lynn A. Baker, "Conditional Federal Spending and States' Rights," *Annals of the American Academy of Political and Social Science* 574 (2001): 104, 105; David E. Engdahl, "The Spending Power," 44 *Duke L.J.* 1, 2 (1994); Illya Somin, "Closing the Pandora's Box of Federalism: The Case for Judicial Restriction off Federal Subsidies to State Governments," 90 *Geo. L.J.* 461, 462 (2002).

2. Agricultural Adjustment Act, Pub. L. No. 73-10, 48 Stat. 31 (codified as amended at 7 U.S.C. §§601–624 (2012)); Laurie Ristino and Gabriela Steier, "Losing Ground: A Clarion Call for Farm Bill Reform to Ensure a Food Secure Future," 42 *Colum. J. Envtl. L.* 59, 80 (2016); Agricultural Act of 2014, Pub. L. No. 113-79, 128 Stat. 649, 659; Renee Johnson, *Specialty Crop Provisions in the 2014 Farm Bill* (P.L. 113-79), Cong. Res. Serv. (2014), http://nationalaglawcenter.org/wp-content/uploads/assets /crs/R43632.pdf; Anthony Kammer, "Cornography: Perverse Incentives and the United States Corn Subsidy," *Journal of Food Law and Policy* 8 (2012), 1, 20; 23 U.S.C. §158 (2012); Dakota v. Dole, 483 U.S. 203, 205 (1987); 42 U.S.C. §2000d (2012); Eloise Pasachoff, "Conditional Spending after *NFIB v. Sebelius:* The Example of Fed-eral Education Law," 62 *Am. U. L. Rev.* 577, 642–643 (2013); Ann Carey Juliano, "The More You Spend, the More You Save: Can the Spending Clause Save Federal Anti-Discrimination Laws?," 46 *Vill. L. Rev.* 1111, 1163–1167 (2001); Brian Galle, "The Tragedy of the Carrots: Economics and Politics in the Choice of Price Instruments,"

64 *Stan. L. Rev.* 797, 801 (2012); Gerrit De Geest and Giuseppe Dari-Mattiacci, "The Rise of Carrots and the Decline of Sticks," 80 *U. Chi. L. Rev.* 341, 354-355 (2013).

3. Kozinski and Engel, "Recapturing Madison's Constitution." 19; Lynn A. Baker, "Constitutional Ambiguities and Originalism: Lessons from the Spending Power," 103 *N.W. U. L. Rev.* 495, 511-515 (2009); Engdahl, "The Spending Power," 26-27; Alison L. LaCroix, "The Interbellum Constitution: Federalism in the Long Founding Moment," 67 *Stan. L. Rev.* 397, 410; Andrew Coan, "Judicial Capacity and the Conditional Spending Paradox," 2013 *Wis. L. Rev.* 339, 340; 297 U.S. 1 (1936); Laurence H. Tribe, *American Constitutional Law*, 3d ed. (2000), §5-b, at 836; 567 U.S. 519 (2012); Richard M. Re, "On 'A Ticket Good for One Day Only,'" 16 *Green Bag* 2d 155, 155 (2013).

4. Morton Grodzins, *The American System: A New View of Government in the United States* (1984), 60-71; Philip J. Weiser, "Towards a Constitutional Architecture for Cooperative Federalism," 79 *N.C. L. Rev.* 663, 696-698 (2001). Sally F. Goldfarb, "The Supreme Court, the Violence Against Women Act, and the Use and Abuse of Federalism," 71 *Fordham L. Rev.* 57, 79-80 (2002); sources collected at *supra* note 1.

5. U.S. Const. art. I, §8, cl. 1; United States v. Butler, 297 U.S. 1, 65 (1936); Engdahl, "The Spending Power," 26-27.

6. 297 U.S. 1 (1936). One reason it took so long was the difficulty of bringing challenges to spending legislation under then-prevailing notions of justiciability. Massachusetts v. Mellon, 262 U.S. 447, 480-489 (1923); *Butler,* 297 U.S. at 13; Pub. L. No. 73-10, 48 Stat. 31 (codified as amended at 7 U.S.C. §§601-624 (2012)); *Butler,* 297 U.S. at 65-66, 74; Engdahl, "The Spending Power," 26-35; Anuj C. Desai, "Filters and Federalism: Public Library Internet Access, Local Control, and the Federal Spending Power," 7 *U. Pa. J. Const. L.* 1, 86-89 (2004).

7. 301 U.S. 619 (1937); 301 U.S. 548 (1937); Pub L. No. 74-271, 49 Stat. 620 (codified as amended 42 U.S.C. §§301-1397 (2012)); *Helvering,* 301 U.S. at 645-646; *Steward Mach. Co.,* 301 U.S. at 598; Jack M. Balkin, "Commerce," 109 *Mich. L. Rev.* 1, 2-3 (2010); Desai, "Filters and Federalism." 87-90.

8. 483 U.S. 203, 211-12 (1987); 23 U.S.C. §158 (2012); *Dole,* 483 U.S. at 207; Lynn A. Baker, "Conditional Federal Spending after *Lopez*," 95 *Colum. L. Rev.* 1911, 1959-1960, 1966-1967 (1995); *Dole,* 483 U.S. at 211 (quoting Steward Mach. Co. v. Davis, 301 U.S. 548, 590 (1937)); Samuel R. Bagenstos, "Spending Clause Litigation in the Roberts Court," 58 *Duke L.J.* 345, 355 (2008); Lynn A. Baker and Mitchell N. Berman, "Getting off the *Dole:* Why the Court Should Abandon Its Spending Doctrine, and How a Too-Clever Congress Could Provoke It to Do So," 78 *Ind. L.J.* 459, 467-469 (2003); Lynn A. Baker, "Conditional Federal Spending," 113 n.18.

9. Nat'l Fed'n Indep. Bus. v. Sebelius, 567 U.S. 519, 578-580 (2012); Marty Lederman, "The States' Extraordinary Medicaid Challenge: Claiming a Right Not to Take the Savory with the Sweet (or, . . . All Carrots; No Stick)," Balkinization (blog; Mar. 27, 2012), http://balkin.blogspot.com/2012/03/states-extraordinary-medicaid-challenge .html; *Nat'l Fed'n Indep. Bus.,* 567 U.S. at 580-581.

10. *Id.* at 576, 581.

11. *Id.* at 678-679 (Scalia, J., Kennedy, J., Thomas, J., and Alito, J., dissenting).

12. *Id.* at 576, 581 (majority opinion); *id.* at 682 (Scalia, J., Kennedy, J., Thomas, J., and Alito, J., dissenting); *id.* at 583 (Roberts, C.J.).

13. Kim Phillips-Fein, *Invisible Hands: The Businessmen's Crusade against the New Deal* (2009), 322; George H. Nash, *The Conservative Intellectual Movement in America since 1945,* 3d ed. (2006); T. Marmor, J. Mashaw, and P. Harvey, *America's Misunderstood Welfare State: Persistent Myths, Enduring Realities* (1990), 13; 23 U.S.C. §159 (2012); Michael M. O'Hear, "Federalism and Drug Control," 57 *Vand. L. Rev.* 783, 813–815 (2004); Sandra Guerra, "The Myth of Dual Sovereignty: Multijurisdictional Drug Law Enforcement and Double Jeopardy," 73 *N.C. L. Rev.* 1159, 1180–1190 (1995); No Child Left Behind Act of 2001, Pub. L. No. 107-110, 115 Stat. 1425 (2002) (codified at 20 U.S.C. §§6301–7941 (2012)); James E. Ryan, "The Perverse Incentives of the No Child Left Behind Act," 79 *N.Y.U. L. Rev.* 932, 944–946 (2004); Joseph P. Viteritti, "The Federal Role in School Reform: Obama's 'Race to the Top,'" 87 *Notre Dame L. Rev.* 2087, 2104–2105 (2012).

14. Gary Lawson, *Federal Administrative Law,* 6th ed. (2012), 114.

15. John F. Manning, "Lessons from a Nondelegation Canon," 83 *Notre Dame L. Rev.* 1541, 1551 (2008); Martin H. Redish, *The Constitution as Political Structure* (1995), 136–137; Nat'l Fed'n Indep. Bus. v. Sebelius, 567 U.S. 519, 551 (2012); United States v. Morrison, 529 U.S. 598, 610 (2000); United States v. Lopez, 514 U.S. 549, 559–560 (1995); Terry v. Ohio, 392 U.S. 1, 27 (1967); Katz v. United States, 389 U.S. 347, 351–352 (1967).

16. Somin, "Pandora's Box of Federalism," 495; see Chapter 5.

17. Chris Edwards, CATO Inst., Policy Analysis No. 593, *Federal Aid to the States: Historical Cause of Government Growth and Bureaucracy* (2007), 1, http://www.cato.org/pubs/pas/pa593.pdf; Office of Mgmt. & Budget, *Historical Tables: Budget of the U.S. Government Fiscal Year 2017,* at 272 tbl.12.1 (2017), https://obamawhitehouse.archives.gov/sites/default/files/omb/budget/fy2017/assets/hist.pdf; 42 U.S.C. §§301–1397 (2012); Pub. L. No. 111-5, 123 Stat. 115 (2009); Pub. L. No. 107-110, 115 Stat. 1425 (2002) (codified at 20 U.S.C. §§6301–7941 (2012)); Pub. L. No. 104-193, 110 Stat. 2105 (codified as amended in scattered sections of Titles 8, 21, and 42 of the United States Code).

18. Brief of Amici Curiae Competitive Enter. Inst. et al. in Support of Petitioners (Severability Issue), Nat'l Fed'n Indep. Bus. v. Sebelius, 567 U.S. 519 (2012) (Nos. 11-393, 11-400), 2012 WL 72444; Brief of Chamber of Commerce of the United States of America as Amicus Curiae in Support of Reversal as to the Severability Issue, *Nat'l Fed'n Indep. Bus.,* 567 U.S. 519 (Nos. 11-393, 11-400), 2012 WL 72445; Robert N. Weiner, "Much Ado: The Potential Impact of the Supreme Court Decision Upholding the Affordable Care Act," in *The Health Care Case: The Supreme Court's Decision and Its Implications,* ed. Nathaniel Persily et al. (2013), 69, 70.

19. *See supra* note 12 and accompanying text.

20. U.S. Const. art. 1, §8, cl. 1; sources collected at *supra* note 108; John C. Eastman, "Restoring the 'General' to the General Welfare Clause," 4 *Chap. L. Rev.* 63, 65 (2001); Richard A. Epstein, Foreword, "Unconstitutional Conditions, State Power, and the Limits of Consent," 102 *Harv. L. Rev.* 4, 44–46 (1988). Bagenstos, "Spending

Clause Litigation," 356–363; South Dakota v. Dole, 483 U.S. 203, 207 n.2 (1987); Helvering v. Davis, 301 U.S. 619, 641 (1937).

21. *Dole,* 483 U.S. at 207–208; Baker, *supra* note 100, at 113.

22. *Dole,* 483 U.S. at 212–218 (O'Connor, J., dissenting); Baker, "Conditional Federal Spending," 1963; Bagenstos, "Spending Clause Litigation," 370, 371; Engdahl, "The Spending Power," 57 (paraphrasing Justice O'Connor's proposed test).

23. Steward Mach. Co. v. Davis, 301 U.S. 548, 589–290 (1937); Baker and Berman, "Getting off the *Dole,*" 521.

24. Somin, "Pandora's Box of Federalism," 495.

Separation of Powers

1. *The Executive Branch,* The White House, http://www.whitehouse.gov/1600/executive-branch (last visited Sept. 22, 2017); *Population Clock,* United States Census Bureau, http://www.census.gov/popclock/ (last visited Sept. 22, 2017); Office of Mgmt. & Budget, *Historical Tables: Budget of the U.S. Government, Fiscal Year 2018,* at 367 tbl.3.1, tbl.16.1 (2017), https://www.whitehouse.gov/sites/whitehouse.gov/files/omb/budget/fy2018/hist.pdf; Kenneth F. Warren, *Administrative Law in the Political System* (2011), 35; Jason Webb Yackee and Susan Webb Yackee, "Delay in Notice and Comment Rulemaking: Evidence of Systemic Regulatory Breakdown?," in *Regulatory Breakdown: The Crisis of Confidence in U.S. Regulation,* ed. Cary Coglianese (2012), 163–180; Cynthia R. Farina, "False Comfort and Impossible Promises: Uncertainty, Information Overload, and the Unitary Executive," 12 *U. Pa. J. Const. L.* 357, 398–399 (2010); Soc. Security Admin., *Annual Statistical Supplement to the Social Security Bulletin 2016,* at 2.78 tbl.2.F9 (2016), https://www.ssa.gov/policy/docs/statcomps/supplement/2016/supplement16.pdf; Office of Planning, Analysis, & Tech., U.S. Dep't of Justice, *FY 2016 Statistical Year Book,* at B2 tbl.4 (2013), https://www.justice.gov/eoir/page/file/fysb16/download; Office of the Fed. Register Nat'l Archives and Records Admin., *The United States Government Manual 2017,* at 290–885 (2017), https://www.gpo.gov/fdsys/pkg/GOVMAN-2017-08-02/pdf/GOVMAN-2017-08-02.pdf; United Nations Statistics Division, National Accounts Main Aggregates Database, *GDP and Its Breakdown at Current Prices in US Dollars,* https://unstats.un.org/unsd/snaama/dnlList.asp (last visited Sept. 22, 2017).

2. Gov't Publ'g Office, *United States Government Budget FY 2018—Judicial Branch,* 45–56, https://www.govinfo.gov/content/pkg/BUDGET-2018-APP/pdf/BUDGET-2018-APP.pdf; Office of Mgmt. & Budget, "Historical Tables," at 88 tbl.4.1; U.S. Dep't of Commerce, Bureau of Economic Analysis, "News Release: Gross Domestic Product by Metropolitan Area, 2016," https://www.bea.gov/newsreleases/regional/gdp_metro/2017/pdf/gdp_metro0917.pdf; Adrian Vermeule, *Law's Abnegation: From Law's Empire to the Administrative State* (2016); Eric A. Posner and Adrian Vermeule, *The Executive Unbound: After the Madisonian Republic* (2010); Adrian Vermeule, *Judging under Uncertainty: An Institutional Theory of Legal Interpretation* (2006), 268; David J. Barron and Martin S. Lederman, "The Commander in Chief at the

Lowest Ebb: A Constitutional History," 121 *Harv. L. Rev.* 941 (2008); Neal Kumar Katyal, "Internal Separation of Powers: Checking Today's Most Dangerous Branch from Within," 115 *Yale L.J.* 2314 (2006); Trevor Morrison, "Stare Decisis in the Office of Legal Counsel," 110 *Colum. L. Rev.* 1448 (2010); Deborah N. Pearlstein, "Finding Effective Constraints on Executive Power: Interrogation, Detention, and Torture," 81 *Ind. L.J.* 1255 (2006); Shirin Sinnar, "Protecting Rights from Within? Inspectors General and National Security Oversight," 65 *Stan. L. Rev.* 1027 (2013); Mariah Zeisberg, *War Powers: The Politics of Constitutional Authority* (2013); Steven G. Calbresi and Christopher S. Yoo, *The Unitary Executive: Presidential Power from Washington to Bush* (2008); Gary Lawson, "The Rise and the Rise of the Administrative State," 107 *Harv. L. Rev.* 1231 (1994); Thomas W. Merrill, "Rethinking Article I, Section 1: From Nondelegation to Exclusive Delegation," 104 *Colum. L. Rev.* 2097 (2004); Stephen I. Vladeck, "The Unreviewable Executive: Kiyemba, Maqaleh, and the Obama Administration," 26 *Const. Comment.* 603, 608 (2010).

3. NLRB v. Noel Canning, 573 U.S. (2014); Free Enterprise Fund v. Pub. Co. Accounting Oversight Bd., 130 S. Ct. 3138 (2010); Boumediene v. Bush, 553 U.S. 723, 795 (2008); Hamdan v. Rumsfeld, 548 U.S. 557 (2006). For hopeful reactions, Steven G. Calabresi and Christopher S. Yoo, "Remove *Morrison v. Olson*," 62 *Vand. L. Rev. En Banc* 103, 119 (2009); Harold Hongju Koh, "Setting the World Right," 115 *Yale L.J.* 2350, 2354 (2006). For an opposite view, see Aziz Z. Huq, "Removal as a Political Question," 65 *Stan. L. Rev.* 1 (2013); Eric A. Posner and Cass R. Sunstein, "Chevronizing Foreign Relations Law," 116 *Yale L.J.* 1170 (2007); Eric A. Posner and Adrian Vermeule, "Accommodating Emergencies," 56 *Stan. L. Rev.* 605 (2003); Merrill, "Rethinking Article I, Section 1"; Posner and Vermeule, *The Executive Unbound*.

7. The Nondelegation Doctrine

1. Maeve P. Carey, Cong. Research Serv., R43056, "Counting Regulations: An Overview of Rulemaking, Types of Federal Regulations, and Pages in the Federal Register," 18-19 tbl. 6 (2016), https://fas.org/sgp/crs/misc/R43056.pdf; *Statistics and Historical Comparison,* GovTrack, https://www.govtrack.us/congress/bills/statistics (last visited September 13, 2017); Lisa Schultz Bressman, "Schechter Poultry at the Millennium: A Delegation Doctrine for the Administrative State," 109 *Yale L.J.* 1399, 1403 (2000); Patrick M. Garry, "Accommodating the Administrative State: The Interrelationship between the Chevron and Nondelegation Doctrines," 38 *Ariz. St. L.J.* 921, 928 (2006); Paul Diller, "Habeas and (Non-)Delegation," 77 *U. Chi. L. Rev.* 585, 634 (2010); Sandra B. Zellmer, "The Devil, the Details, and the Dawn of the 21st Century Administrative State: Beyond the New Deal," 32 *Ariz. St. L.J.* 941, 946–957 (2000); John Hart Ely, *Democracy and Distrust* (1980), 132–134; James O. Freedman, *Crisis and Legitimacy: The Administrative Process and American Government* (1978), 93-94; David Schoenbrod, *Power without Responsibility: How Congress Abuses the People through Delegation* (1993), 195-197; Jody Freeman, "The Private Role in

Public Governance," 75 *N.Y.U. L. Rev.* 543, 580-586 (2000); Marci A. Hamilton, "Representation and Nondelegation: Back to Basics," 20 *Cardozo L. Rev.* 807, 809-814 (1999); Julian G. Ku, "The Delegation of Federal Power to International Organizations: New Problems with Old Solutions," 85 *Minn. L. Rev.* 71, 119-120 (2000); Gary Lawson, "Delegation and Original Meaning," 88 *Va. L. Rev.* 327, 351 (2002); Theodore J. Lowi, "Two Roads to Serfdom: Liberalism, Conservatism and Administrative Power," 36 *Am. U. L. Rev.* 295, 295-296 (1987); David Schoenbrod, "The Delegation Doctrine: Could the Court Give It Substance?," 83 *Mich. L. Rev.* 1223, 1254 (1985); J. Skelly Wright, "Beyond Discretionary Justice," 81 *Yale L.J.* 575, 582-587 (1972); Panama Refining Co. v. Ryan, 293 U.S. 388, 430 (1935); A.L.A. Schechter Poultry Corp. v. United States, 295 U.S. 495, 541-542 (1935); Carter v. Carter Coal Co., 298 U.S. 238 (1936); Cass R. Sunstein, "Is the Clean Air Act Unconstitutional?," 98 *Mich. L. Rev.* 303, 330 (1999); Keith E. Whittington and Jason Iuliano, "The Myth of the Nondelegation Doctrine," 165 *U. Pa. L. Rev.* 379, 381 (2017).

2. U.S. Const. art. I, §1 (emphasis added); Whitman v. American Trucking Ass'n, 531 U.S. 457, 472 (2001); Gary Lawson, "The Rise and Rise of the Administrative State," 107 *Harv. L. Rev.* 1231, 1238 (1994); Schoenbrod, "The Delegation Doctrine," 1223, 1227; Cass R. Sunstein, "Constitutionalism after the New Deal," 101 *Harv. L. Rev.* 421, 494 (1987); Eric A. Posner and Adrian Vermeule, "Interring the Nondelegation Doctrine," 69 *U. Chi. L. Rev.* 1721, 1724, 1730 (2002); Whittington and Iuliano, "Myth of the Nondelegation Doctrine," 417 (2017); U.S. Const. art. II, §1, cl. 1 (emphasis added); Mistretta v. United States, 488 U.S. 361, 417 (1989) (Scalia, J., dissenting); Kate Andrias, "The President's Enforcement Power," 88 *N.Y.U. L. Rev.* 1031, 1037 (2013); Patricia L. Bellia, "Faithful Execution and Enforcement Discretion," 164 *U. Pa. L. Rev.* 1753, 1777 (2016); Jack Goldsmith and John F. Manning, "The Protean Take Care Clause," 164 *U. Pa. L. Rev.* 1835, 1864.

3. Wayman v. Southard, 23 U.S. (10 Wheat) 1, 42-43 (1825); Lawson, "Delegation and Original Meaning," 341; Garry, "Accommodating the Administrative State," 926.

4. Marshall Field & Co. v. Clark, 143 U.S. 649, 692 (1892); Richard J. Pierce et al., *Administrative Law and Process,* 4th ed. (2004), 49; Wayman v. Southard, 23 U.S. 1, 43 (1825); Fed. Radio Comm'n v. Nelson Bros. Bond & Mortgage Co., 289 U.S. 266, 284 (1933); N.Y. Cent. Sec. Corp. v. United States, 287 U.S. 12, 25-27 (1932); United States v. Shreveport Grain & Elevator Co., 287 U.S. 77, 85 (1932); J.W. Hampton, Jr. & Co. v. United States, 276 U.S. 394, 406-407 (1928); United States v. Grimaud, 220 U.S. 506, 521 (1911); Buttfield v. Stranahan, 192 U.S. 470 (1904); *Field,* 143 U.S. at 692; Wayman v. Southhard, 10 Wheat. (23 U.S.) 1, 42 (1825); *Aurora,* 11 U.S. at 387-388; Whittington and Iuliano, "Myth of the Nondelegation Doctrine" (empirically documenting the laxity of the doctrine's enforcement in the pre-New-Deal era); *Wayman,* 23 U.S. at 43; *Grimaud,* 220 U.S. 506; *Buttfield,* 192 U.S. 470.

5. 276 U.S. 394, 401, 409 (1928) (emphasis added).

6. 293 U.S. 388, 430 (1935); 295 U.S. 495, 541-542 (1935); Evan J. Criddle, "When Delegation Begets Domination: Due Process of Administrative Lawmaking," 46 *Ga. L. Rev.* 117, 143 (2011); Stephan L. Carter, "From Sick Chicken to *Synar:* The Evolution

and Subsequent De-Evolution of the Separation of Powers," 1987 *B.Y.U. L. Rev.* 719, 729; Garry, "Accommodating the Administrative State," 931–932.

7. Whitman v. American Trucking Ass'ns, 531 U.S. 457 (2001); Loving v. United States, 517 U.S. 748, 768–774 (1996); Touby v. United States, 500 U.S. 160, 167–168 (1991); Skinner v. Mid-America Pipeline Co., 490 U.S. 212, 218–220 (1989); Mistretta v. United States, 488 U.S. 361, 371–379 (1989); Whittington and Iuliano, "Myth of the Nondelegation Doctrine," 380; United States v. Southwestern Cable Co., 392 U.S. 157, 178 (1968); Yakus v. United States, 321 U.S. 414, 427 (1944); Fed. Power Comm'n v. Hope Natural Gas Co., 320 U.S. 591, 600 (1944); Lichter v. United States, 334 U.S. 742, 778 (1948); Diller, "Habeas and (Non-)Delegation," 634; Lawson, "Delegation and Original Meaning," 371; Larry Alexander and Saikrishna Prakash, "Delegation Really Running Riot," 93 *Va. L. Rev.* 1035, 1038 (2007); Elena Kagan, "Presidential Administration," 114 *Harv. L. Rev.* 2245, 2364 (2001); Garry, "Accommodating the Administrative State," 938; Mistretta v. United States, 488 U.S. 361, 416 (Scalia, J., dissenting).

8. City of Arlington v. FCC, 133 S. Ct. 1863, 1879 (2013) (Roberts, C.J., dissenting); Douglas H. Ginsburg, "Delegation Running Riot," 1 *Regulation* 83, 84 (1995); Lawson, "Delegation and Original Meaning"; Whitman v. American Trucking Ass'ns, 531 U.S. 457, 487 (2001) (Thomas, J., concurring); Indus. Union Dep't v. American Petroleum Inst., 448 U.S. 607, 675 (1980) (Rehnquist, J., concurring); De Niz Robles v. Lynch, 803 F.3d 1165, 1171 (10th Cir. 2015) (Gorsuch, J.).

9. Martin H. Redish, *The Constitution as Political Structure* (1995), 135; Posner and Vermeule, "Interring the Nondelegation Doctrine," 1721, 1722; Cynthia R. Farina, "Deconstructing Nondelegation," *Harvard Journal of Law and Public Policy* 33 (2010): 87, 89; *Whitman,* 531 U.S. at 472; Gary Lawson, *Federal Administrative Law,* 6th ed. (2012), 114.

10. John F. Manning, "Lessons from a Nondelegation Canon," 83 *Notre Dame L. Rev.* 1541, 1551 (2008); Redish, *Constitution as Political Structure,* 136–137; Nat'l Fed'r Indep. Bus. v. Sebelius, 132 S. Ct. 2566, 2587 (2012); United States v. Morrison, 529 U.S. 598, 610 (2000); United States v. Lopez, 514 U.S. 549, 559–560 (1995); Terry v. Ohio, 392 U.S. 1, 27 (1967); Katz v. United States, 389 U.S. 347, 351–352 (1967).

11. Philip Hamburger, *Is Administrative Law Unlawful?* (2014), 320; Ginsburg, "Delegation Running Riot"; Hettinga v. U.S., 677 F.3d 471, 480 (D.C. Cir. 2012) (Brown, J., concurring).

12. Office of the Fed. Register Nat'l Archives and Records Admin., *The United States Government Manual 2013* (2013), 97–501, http://www.gpo.gov/fdsys/pkg/GOVMAN -2013-11-06/pdf/GOVMAN-2013-11-06.pdf; Cynthia R. Farina, "False Comfort and Impossible Promises: Uncertainty, Information Overload, and the Unitary Executive," 12 *U. Pa. J. Const. L.* 357, 397; Diller, "Habeas and (Non-)Delegation," 634.

13. Lawson, "Delegation and Original Meaning," at 339; Manning, *supra* note 136, at 1551; Lawson, "Federal Administrative Law," at 11; Mistretta v. United States, 488 U.S. 361, 415 (1989) (Scalia, J., dissenting); Cass R. Sunstein, "Nondelegation Canons," 67 *U. Chi. L. Rev.* 315, 321 (2000).

14. *Id.* at 326–67; *Mistretta,* 488 U.S. at 415 (Scalia, J., dissenting); Sunstein, "Non-delegation Canons," at 326–367; United States v. SW. Cable Co., 392 U.S. 157, 178 (1968).

15. Lee Epstein and Jack Knight, *The Choices Justices Make* (1998); Barry Friedman, *The Will of the People: How Public Opinion Has Influenced the Supreme Court and Shaped the Meaning of the Constitution* (2009); John Ferejohn and Charles Shipan, "Congressional Influence on Bureaucracy," *Journal of Law, Economics, and Organization* 6 (1990), 1.

16. 524 U.S. 417 (1998); *Clinton,* 524 U.S. at 448; Kagan, "Presidential Administration," 2245, 2366; Michael B. Rappaport, "The Selective Nondelegation Doctrine and the Line Item Veto: A New Approach to the Nondelegation Doctrine and its Implications for *Clinton v. City of New York*," 76 *Tul. L. Rev.* 265, 293 (2001).

17. *Clinton,* 524 U.S. at 485 (Breyer, J., dissenting); Rappaport, "The Selective Nondelegation Doctrine," 294, 301; *Clinton,* 524 U.S. at 446–447.

18. Peter B. McCutchen, "Mistakes, Precedent, and the Rise of the Administrative State: Toward a Constitutional Theory of Second Best," 80 *Cornell L. Rev.* 1, 2 (1994).

8. Presidential Administration

1. Thomas O. McGarity, "Avoiding Gridlock through Unilateral Executive Action: The Obama Administration's Clean Power Plan," 7 *Wake Forest J.L. & Pol'y* 141, 197–199 (2017); Richard H. Pildes, Book Review, 125 *Harv. L. Rev.* 1381, 1384 (2012) (reviewing Eric A. Posner and Adrian Vermeule, *The Executive Unbound: After the Madisonian Republic*); Elena Kagan, "Presidential Administration," 114 *Harv. L. Rev.* 2245, 2275–2282 (2001).

2. Free Enter. Fund v. Pub. Co. Accounting Oversight Bd., 561 U.S. 477, 496–498 (2010); Printz v. United States, 521 U.S. 898, 922–923 (1997); Morrison v. Olson, 487 U.S. 654, 710–714 (1988) (Scalia, J., dissenting); Kagan, "Presidential Administration," 2245, 2263–2264; Jeffery Rosen, "The Roberts Court and Executive Power," 35 *Pepp. L. Rev.* 503, 504–506 (2008); Mathew A. Smith, "Delegating Away the Unitary Executive: Reviewing INA §287(G) Agreements through the Lens of the Unitary Executive Theory," 8 *Duke J. Const. L. & Pub. Pol'y* 197, 207 (2013); Steven G. Calabresi and Kevin H. Rhodes, "The Structural Constitution: Unitary Executive, Plural Judiciary," 105 *Harv. L. Rev.* 1153, 1166 (1992).

3. City of Arlington v. FCC, 569 U.S. 290, 315 (2013) (Roberts, C.J., dissenting); Perez v. Mortgage Bankers Ass'n, 135 S. Ct. 1199, 1213 (2015) (Thomas, J., concurring); Gutierrez-Brizuela v. Lynch, 834 F.3d 1142, 1149 (10th Cir. 2016) (Gorsuch, J., concurring); Gary Lawson, "The Rise and the Rise of the Administrative State," 107 *Harv. L. Rev.* 1231, 1231 (1994).

4. Jack M. Beermann, "Congressional Administration," 43 *San Diego L. Rev.* 61, 145–146 (2006); J. R. DeShazo and Jody Freeman, "The Congressional Competition to Control Delegated Power," 81 *Tex. L. Rev.* 1443, 1456–1459 (2003); Aziz Z. Huq, "Removal as a Political Question," 65 *Stan. L. Rev.* 1, 54–62 (2013); Kagan, "Presidential

Administration," 2255–2260; Jonathon R. Macey, "Separated Powers and Positive Political Theory: The Tug of War over Administrative Agencies," 80 *Geo. L.J.* 671, 672–673 (1992); Matthew D. McCubbins et al., "Structure and Process, Politics and Policy: Administrative Arrangements and the Political Control of Agencies," 75 *Va. L. Rev.* 431, 433–435 (1989); Steven G. Calbresi and Christopher S. Yoo, *The Unitary Executive: Presidential Power from Washington to Bush* (2008), 3–9; Steven G. Calabresi and Saikrishna B. Prakash, "The President's Power to Execute the Laws," 104 *Yale L.J.* 541, 570 (1994); Calabresi and Rhodes, "The Structural Constitution," 1156, 1165; Louis Fisher, "The Unitary Executive and Inherent Executive Power," *U. Pa. J. Const. L.* 569, 569–571 (2010); Lawson, "The Rise and the Rise"; Neomi Rao, "Removal: Necessary and Sufficient for Presidential Control," 65 *Ala. L. Rev.* 1205, 1230–1234 (2014); John Yoo, "Unitary, Executive, or Both?," 76 *U. Chi. L. Rev.* 1935, 1939, 1940–1942 (2009); Morrison v. Olson, 487 U.S. 654, 709 (1988) (Scalia, J., dissenting); U.S. Const. art. II, §3.

5. Lawson, "The Rise and the Rise," 1244; Kent H. Barnett, "Avoiding Independent Agency Armageddon," 87 *Notre Dame L. Rev.* 1349, 1387 (2012); Kirti Datla and Richard L. Revesz, "Deconstructing Independent Agencies (and Executive Agencies)," 98 *Cornell L. Rev.* 769, 782 (2013); Lawrence Lessig and Cass R. Sunstein, "The President and the Administration," 94 *Colum. L. Rev.* 1, 106–108 (1994); Neomi Rao, "A Modest Proposal: Abolishing Agency Independence in *Free Enterprise Fund v. PCAOB*," 79 *Fordham L. Rev.* 2541, 2542 (2011); Kevin M. Stack, "Agency Independence after *PCAOB*," 32 *Cardozo L. Rev.* 2391, 2392–2393 (2011); Anthony M. Bottenfield, "Congressional Creativity: The Post-*Chadha* Struggle for Agency Control in the Era of Presidential Signing Statements," 112 *Penn St. L. Rev.* 1125, 1144–1147 (2008); DeShazo and Freeman, "Congressional Competition," 1448, 1456–1458; Thomas O. McGarity, "Administrative Law as Blood Sport: Policy Erosion in a Highly Partisan Age," 61 *Duke L.J.* 1671, 1711–1713 (2012); Administrative Procedure Act, Pub. L. No. 79-404, 60 Stat. 237 (1946) (codified as amended at 5 U.S.C. §§551–559 (2012)); McCubbins et al., "Structure and Process," 442; David B. Spence, "Managing Delegation Ex Ante: Using Law to Steer Administrative Agencies," 28 *J. Legal Stud.* 413 (1999) (providing significant but qualified empirical support for McNollgast model); Jonathan R. Macey, "Organizational Design and the Political Control of Administrative Agencies," *Journal of Law, Economics, & Organization* 8 (1992): 93, 99–101.

6. Hans Bender, "*Free Enterprise Fund v. PCAOB:* Narrow Separation-of-Powers Ruling Illustrates That the Supreme Court Is Not 'Pro-Business,'" 2010 *Cato Sup. Ct. Rev.* 269, 284; Lawson, "The Rise and the Rise," 1241–1246; Morrison v. Olson, 487 U.S. 654, 723 (1988) (Scalia, J., dissenting); *In re* Hennen, 38 U.S. (13 Pet.) 230, 258 (1839) (ex parte); Myers v. United States, 272 U.S. 52, 109–110 (1926); Free Enter. Fund v. Pub. Co. Accounting Oversight Bd., 561 U.S. 477, 518–519 (2010) (Breyer, J., dissenting); PCAOB, 561 U.S. at 483 (quoting Myers v. United States, 272 U.S. 52, 117 (1926)).

7. 272 U.S. 52 (1926); *Myers,* 272 U.S. at 60–61, 134–135, 176; Kagan, "Presidential Administration," 2322.

8. 295 U.S. 602, 618–620 (1935); *Myers,* 272 U.S. at 134–135; *Humphrey's Executor,* 295 U.S. at 627–631.

9. Barnett, "Avoiding Independent Agency Armageddon," 1358; Geoffrey P. Miller, "Independent Agencies," 1986 *Sup. Ct. Rev.* 41, 94.

10. 478 U.S. 714, 720, 726, 736 (1986); *but see* Barnett, "Avoiding Independent Agency Armageddon," 1358.

11. 487 U.S. 654, 660–663, 692 (1998); Fed. Election Comm'n v. NRA Political Victory Fund, 6 F.3d 821, 826 (D.C. Cir. 1993).

12. 561 U.S. 477, 484–486, 514 (2010).

13. *Id.* at 523–526, 530, 536 (Breyer, J., dissenting).

14. *See supra* notes 3–5 and accompanying text.

15. Calabresi and Rhodes, "The Structural Constitution," 1165–1166; Lawson, "The Rise and the Rise," 1244–1245; Free Enter. Fund v. Pub. Co. Accounting Oversight Bd., 561 U.S. 477, 524 (2010) (Breyer, J., dissenting); Richard J. Pierce Jr., "Saving the Unitary Executive Theory from Those Who Would Distort and Destroy It: A Review of *The Unitary Executive* by Steven G. Calabresi and Christopher S. Yoo," 12 *U. Pa. J. Const. L.* 593, 603 (2010).

16. John D. Huber and Charles R. Shipan, *Deliberate Discretion? The Institutional Foundations of Bureaucratic Autonomy* (2002), 16; Lessig and Sunstein, "The President and the Administration," 116; Peter M. Shane, "Legislative Delegation, the Unitary Executive, and the Legitimacy of the Administrative State," 33 *Harv. J.L. & Pub. Pol'y* 103, 104–105.

17. Myers v. United States, 272 U.S. 52 (1926); Steven G. Calabresi and Christopher S. Yoo, "Remove *Morrison v. Olson,*" 62 *Vand. L. Rev. En Banc* 103, 119 (2009); Free Enter. Fund v. Pub. Co. Accounting Bd., 561 U.S. 477, 514 (2010); Morrison v. Olson, 487 U.S. 654, 685–686 (1988); Bowsher v. Synar, 478 U.S. 714, 726 (1986).

18. Office of the Fed. Register Nat'l Archives and Records Admin., *The United States Government Manual 2013, passim,* https://www.gpo.gov/fdsys/pkg/GOVMAN-2013-11-06/pdf/GOVMAN-2013-11-06.pdf; Office of Mgmt. & Budget, *Historical Tables: Budget of the U.S. Government, Fiscal Year 2014,* at 362 tbl.17.1 (2014), https://www.gpo.gov/fdsys/pkg/BUDGET-2014-TAB/pdf/BUDGET-2014-TAB.pdf; *supra* note 5 and accompanying text; *In re Aiken County,* 645 F.3d 428, 438–448 (D.C. Cir. 2011) (Kavanaugh, J., concurring); Calabresi and Yoo, "Remove *Morrison v. Olson,*" 3–4 (emphasis added).

19. Lawson, "The Rise and the Rise," 1244; Barnett, "Avoiding Independent Agency Armageddon," 1358.

20. Bowsher v. Synar, 478 U.S. 714, 726 (1986); Barnett, "Avoiding Independent Agency Armageddon," 1358.

21. 462 U.S. 919 (1983); Immigration & Naturalization Serv. v. Chadha, 462 U.S. 919, 967–969 (1983) (White, J., dissenting); Stephen Breyer, "The Legislative Veto after *Chadha,*" 72 *Geo. L.J.* 785, 786 (1984); Edward H. Stiglitz, "Unitary Innovations and Political Accountability," 99 *Cornell L. Rev.* 1133, 1146–1147 (2014); Immigration & Naturalization Serv. v. Chadha, 462 U.S. 919, 959 (1983).

22. *Chadha,* 462 U.S. at 1002 (White, J., dissenting); Process Gas Consumers Group v. Consumer Energy Council, 463 U.S. 1216 (1983).

23. Fed. Election Comm'n v. NRA Political Victory Fund, 6 F.3d 821, 826 (D.C. Cir. 1993) (Silberman, J.); *Morrison,* 487 U.S. at 689–690; Barnett, "Avoiding Independent Agency Armageddon," 1358.

24. Free Enter. Fund v. Pub. Co. Accounting Bd., 561 U.S. 477, 523, 536–547 (2010) (Breyer, J., dissenting).

25. *Id.* at 522.

26. *In re Aiken County,* 645 F.3d 428, 438–448 (D.C. Cir. 2011) (Kavanaugh, J., concurring); Yoo, "Unitary, Executive, or Both?," 1947.

27. Hosp. Corp. of Am. v. FTC, 807 F.2d 1381, 1392 (7th Cir. 1986).

Individual Rights

1. Admin. Office of the U.S. Courts, Table D-2. U.S. District Courts—Criminal Defendants Filed, by Offense and District (Mar. 31, 2016), http://www.uscourts.gov/sites/default/files/data_tables/fjcs_d2_0331.2016.pdf; Richard A. Posner, *The Federal Courts: Crisis and Reform* (1985), 98; Edward A. Hartnett, "Questioning Certiorari: Some Reflections Seventy-Five Years after the Judges' Bill," 100 *Colum. L. Rev.* 1643, 1726–1728 (2000); Andrew B. Coan, "Judicial Capacity and the Substance of Constitutional Law," 122 *Yale L.J.* 422, 438–439 (2012).

2. Randy E. Barnett, *Restoring the Lost Constitution: The Presumption of Liberty* (2014), 357; Ilya Somin, "A Revival of *Lochner*?," *Jotwell,* June 15, 2015 (reviewing Thomas Colby and Peter J. Smith, "The Return of *Lochner*," 100 *Cornell L. Rev.* 527 (2015)), https://conlaw.jotwell.com/a-revival-of-lochner/; Richard A. Epstein, "Of Citizens and Persons: Reconstructing the Privileges or Immunities Clause of the Fourteenth Amendment," 1 *N.Y.U. J.L. & Liberty* 334 (2005); V. F. Nourse and Sarah A. Maguire, "The Lost History of Governance and Equal Protection," 58 *Duke L.J.* 955, 955–1001 (2009); Melissa L. Saunders, "Equal Protection, Class Legislation, and Colorblindness", 96 *Mich. L. Rev.* 245, 293 (1997); Jack M. Balkin, "Original Meaning and Constitutional Redemption," 24 *Const. Comment.* 427, 450 (2008); Suzanne B. Goldberg, "Equality without Tiers," 77 *S. Cal. L. Rev.* 481, 528 (2004); John Hart Ely, *Democracy and Distrust* (1980), 135; Neil K. Komesar, *Imperfect Alternatives: Choosing Institutions in Law, Economics, and Public Policy* (1994), 251; Toni M. Massaro, "Gay Rights, Thick and Thin," 49 *Stan. L. Rev.* 45, 86 (1996).

3. Komesar, *Imperfect Alternatives,* 258; Jane R. Bambauer and Toni M. Massaro, "Outrageous and Irrational," 100 *Minn. L. Rev.* 281, 317–318 (2015); Robert C. Farrell, "Justice Kennedy's Idiosyncratic Understanding of Equal Protection and Due Process, and Its Costs," 32 *Quinnipiac L. Rev.* 439, 447 (2014).

4. David Schraub, "Unsuspecting," 96 *B.U. L. Rev.* 361, 367 (2016); Komesar, *Imperfect Alternatives,* 251; Catharine A. Mackinnon, *Sexual Harassment of Working Women: A Case of Sex Discrimination* (1979), 106; Richard A. Posner, *Economic Analysis of Law,*

3d ed. (1986), 53; Frank I. Michelman, "Property, Utility, and Fairness: Comments on the Ethical Foundations of 'Just Compensation' Law," 80 *Harv. L. Rev.* 1165, 1258 (1967); Craig R. Habicht, *"Dolan v. City of Tigard:* Taking a Closer Look at Regulatory Takings," 45 *Cath. U. L. Rev.* 221, 245 n.114; Richard A. Epstein, "Physical and Regulatory Takings: One Distinction Too Many," 64 *Stan. L. Rev. Online* 99, 105 (2012); Michael E. Waterstone, "Disability Constitutional Law," 63 *Emory L.J.* 527, 557 (2014); Ilya Somin and Jonathan H. Adler, "The Green Costs of *Kelo:* Economic Development Takings and Environmental Protection," 84 *Wash. U.L. Rev.* 623, 630 (2006); Evan Bernick, "Subjecting the Rational Basis Test to Constitutional Scrutiny," 14 *Geo. J. L. & Pub. Pol'y* 347, 350–351 (2016); Randy E. Barnett, "Keynote Remarks: Judicial Engagement through the Lens of *Lee Optical,*" 19 *Geo. Mason L. Rev.* 845, 860 (2012); Clark Neily, "Litigation without Adjudication: Why the Modern Rational Basis Test Is Unconstitutional," 14 *Geo. J. L. & Pub. Pol'y* 537, 548 (2016); Bambauer and Massaro, "Outrageous and Irrational," 197; 135 S. Ct. 2584 (2015); 135 S. Ct. 2419; Kenji Yoshino, "A New Birth of Freedom? *Obergefell v. Hodges,*" 129 *Harv. L. Rev.* 147, 179 (2015); Ilya Somin, "Two Steps Forward for the 'Poor Relation' of Constitutional Law: Koontz, Arkansas Game & Fish, and the Future of the Takings Clause," *Cato Sup. Ct. Rev.* 215, 216 (2012–2013); Norman A. Dupont, "The Raisins of Wrath: The Court Finds a Fifth Amendment Taking, But Does It Imply Something More?," 47 *ABA Trends* 9, 9 (2016); Calvin Massey, "The New Formalism: Requiem for Tiered Scrutiny?," 6 *U. Pa. J. Const. L.* 945 (2004); Stephen E. Gottlieb, "Tears for Tiers on the Rehnquist Court," 4 *U. Pa. J. Const. L.* 350, 351, 368 (2002); Jeffrey M. Shaman, "Cracks in the Structure: The Coming Breakdown of the Levels of Scrutiny," 45 *Ohio State L.J.* 161 (1984).

5. Nicholas O. Stephanopoulos, "Political Powerlessness," 90 *N.Y.U. L. Rev.* 1527, 1599 (2015); Bertrall L. Ross II and Su Li, "Measuring Political Power: Suspect Class Determinations and the Poor," 104 *Cal. L. Rev.* 323, 382 (2016); Tara Leigh Grove, "Tiers of Scrutiny in a Hierarchical Judiciary," 14 *Geo. J. L. & Pub. Pol'y* 475 (2016).

9. Equal Protection

1. 347 U.S. 483 (1954); Adarand Constructors, Inc. v. Pena, 515 U.S. 200, 240 (1995) (Thomas, J., concurring in part and concurring in the judgment); 347 U.S. 483.

2. Nicholas O. Stephanopoulos, "Political Powerlessness," 90 *N.Y.U. L. Rev.* 1527, 1581 (2015).

3. U.S. Const. Amend. XIV §1; 60 U.S. 393 (1857); U.S. Const. Amend. XIV §1, cl. 5.

4. Melissa L. Saunders, "Equal Protection, Class Legislation, and Colorblindness," 96 *Mich. L. Rev.* 245, 247–248 (1997); V. F. Nourse and Sarah A. Maguire, "The Lost History of Governance and Equal Protection," 58 *Duke L.J.* 955 (2009); David E. Bernstein, "Fifty Years after *Bolling v. Sharpe: Bolling,* Equal Protection, Due Process, and Lochnerphobia," 93 *Geo. L.J.* 1253 (2005); Howard Gillman, *The Constitution Besieged* (1993), 61–100.

5. Strauder v. West Virginia, 100 U.S. 303 (1880) (interpreting the Equal Protection Clause to prohibit racial discrimination in jury selection); Neal v. Delaware, 103 U.S. 370 (1880) (applying *Strauder* to overturn criminal conviction of black defendant); 109 U.S. 3 (1883); Pamela Brandwein, *Rethinking the Judicial Settlement of Reconstruction* (2011), 6, 18; C. Vann Woodward, *Reunion and Reaction: The Compromise of 1877 and the End of Reconstruction* (1951); Charles W. Calhoun, *Conceiving a New Republic: The Republican Party and the Southern Question, 1869–1900* (2006).

6. Nourse and Maguire, "Lost History," 961–962; Bernstein, "Fifty Years After," 1264; Truax v. Corrigan, 257 U.S. 312 (1921); Quaker City Cab Co. v. Pennsylvania, 277 U.S. 389 (1928); David E. Bernstein, "*Lochner* Era Revisionism, Revised: *Lochner* and the Origins of Fundamental Rights Constitutionalism," 92 *Geo. L.J.* 1, 30 (2003); Charles Warren, "The Progressiveness of the United States Supreme Court," 13 *Colum. L. Rev.* 294 (1913).

7. 304 U.S. 144, 152 (1938).

8. Stephen A. Siegel, "The Origin of the Compelling State Interest Test and Strict Scrutiny," 48 *Am. J. Legal Hist.* 355, 398 (2006); Edward Stein, "Immutability and Innateness Arguments about Lesbian, Gay, and Bisexual Rights," 89 *Chi.-Kent L. Rev.* 597, 612 (2014); Adam Winkler, "Fatal in Theory, Strict in Fact?," 59 *Vand. L. Rev.* 793, 794 (2006).

9. Skinner v. Oklahoma ex rel. Williamson, 316 U.S. 535, 541 (1942); Victoria F. Nourse, *In Reckless Hands: Skinner v. Oklahoma and the Near-Triumph of American Eugenics* (2008), 159; Siegel, "Origin of Strict Scrutiny," 355–357, 380; Richard H. Fallon Jr., "Strict Judicial Scrutiny," 54 *UCLA L. Rev.* 1267, 1275–1276, 1281 (2007); 323 U.S. 214, 216 (1944); G. Edward White, "Historicizing Judicial Scrutiny," 57 *S.C. L. Rev.* 1, 75–76 (2005); Michael J. Klarman, "An Interpretive History of Modern Equal Protection," 90 *Mich. L. Rev.* 213 (1991); Gerald Gunther, "The Supreme Court, 1971 Term—Foreword: In Search of Evolving Doctrine on a Changing Court: A Model for a Newer Equal Protection," 86 *Harv. L. Rev.* 1, 8 (1972); Winkler, "Fatal in Theory," 796.

10. Klarman, "An Interpretive History," 254–257, 285; John B. Mitchell, "My Father, John Locke, and Assisted Suicide: The Real Constitutional Right," 3 *Ind. Health L. Rev.* 45, 62 (2006); Neil K. Komesar, *Imperfect Alternatives: Choosing Institutions in Law, Economics, and Public Policy* (1994), 257; John Hart Ely, *Democracy and Distrust* (1980), 59; Adam Winkler, "Fundamentally Wrong about Fundamental Rights," 23 *Const. Comment.* 227 (2006); Gunther, "The Supreme Court," 13; Katie R. Eyer, "Constitutional Crossroads and the Canon of Rational Basis Review," 48 *U.C. Davis L. Rev.* 527, 540 (2014); 429 U.S. 190 (1976); 427 U.S. 307 (1976); Jeb Rubenfeld, "The Anti-Antidiscrimination Agenda," 111 *Yale L.J.* 1141, 1141–1144 (2002); Gerald L. Neuman, "Equal Protection, 'General Equality' and Economic Discrimination from a U.S. Perspective," 5 *Colum. J. Eur. L.* 281, 292 (1999) 292.

11. James E. Fleming, "'There Is Only One Equal Protection Clause': An Appreciation of Justice Stevens's Equal Protection Jurisprudence," 74 *Fordham L. Rev.* 2301, 2311 (2006); Jay D. Wexler, "Defending the Middle Way: Intermediate Scrutiny as Judicial Minimalism," 66 *Geo. Wash. L. Rev.* 298, 326 (1998); David M. Beatty, *The Ultimate*

Rule of Law (2004), 172; Vicki C. Jackson, "Ambivalent Resistance and Comparative Constitutionalism: Opening Up the Conversation on 'Proportionality,' Rights and Federalism," 1 *U. Pa. J. Const. L.* 583 (1999); Andrew M. Siegel, "Equal Protection Unmodified: Justice John Paul Stevens and the Case for Unmediated Constitutional Interpretation," 74 *Fordham L. Rev.* 2339, 2355-2358 (2006); Craig v. Boren, 429 U.S. 190, 211-212 (1976) (Stevens, J., concurring); Dandridge v. Williams, 397 U.S. 471, 508 (1970) (Marshall, J., dissenting); San Antonio Independent Sch. Dist. v. Rodriguez, 411 U.S. 1, 98-99 (1973) (Marshall, J., dissenting); Suzanne B. Goldberg, "Equality without Tiers," 77 *S. Cal. L. Rev.* 481, 518-524 (2004); Kathleen M. Sullivan, "Post-Liberal Judging: The Roles of Categorization and Balancing," 63 *U. Colo. L. Rev.* 293, 296 (1992); e.g., City of Cleburne v. Cleburne Living Ctr., 473 U.S. 432, 464-465 (1985) (Marshall, J., dissenting).

12. Washington v. Davis, 426 U.S. 229, 242 (1976); David A. Strauss, "Discriminatory Intent and the Taming of *Brown*," 56 *U. Chi. L. Rev.* 935, 952 (1989); *Davis,* 426 U.S. at 247-248; Holning Lau, "Identity Scripts and Democratic Deliberation," 94 *Minn. L. Rev.* 897, 965 (2010); Michael C. Dorf, "Equal Protection Incorporation," 88 *Va. L. Rev.* 951, 1014 (2002); Lawrence Gene Sager, "Fair Measure: The Legal Status of Underenforced Constitutional Norms," 91 *Harv. L. Rev.* 1212, 1216 (1978).

13. Maxwell L. Stearns, "*Obergefell, Fisher,* and the Inversion of Tiers," 19 *U. Pa. J. Const. L.* 1043, 1066-1067 (2017); Pamela S. Karlan, "Forward: Loving *Lawrence,*" 102 *Mich. L. Rev.* 1447, 1450 (2004); 539 U.S. 558, 574 (2003); 517 U.S. 620, 632-633 (1996); Russell K. Robinson, "Unequal Protection," 68 *Stan. L. Rev.* 151, 165 (2016); Elizabeth B. Cooper, "The Power of Dignity," 84 *Fordham L. Rev.* 3, 8-9 (2015); 539 U.S. 558 (2003); 517 U.S. 620 (1996); 135 S. Ct. 2584 (2015); Kenji Yoshino, "The New Equal Protection," 124 *Harv. L. Rev.* 747, 763 (2011); Evan Gerstmann, *Same-Sex Marriage and the Constitution,* 2d ed. (2008), 69.

14. Ann L. Schiavone, "Unleashing the Fourteenth Amendment," 2016 *Wis. L. Rev. Forward* 27, 28 (2016); Yoshino, "The New Equal Protection," 776, 792-797; Romer v. Evans, 517 U.S. 620, 633 (1996); Steve Sanders, "Race, Restructurings, and Equal Protection Doctrine through the Lens of *Schuette v. BAMN,*" 81 *Brook. L. Rev.* 1393, 1424 (2016); Pamela S. Karlan, "Equal Protection, Due Process, and the Stereoscopic Fourteenth Amendment," 33 *McGeorge L. Rev.* 473, 488 (2002).

15. Mitchell N. Berman, "Constitutional Decision Rules," 90 *Va. L. Rev.* 1, 82 (2004); Kermit Roosevelt III, "Constitutional Calcification: How the Law Becomes What the Court Does," 91 *Va. L. Rev.* 1649, 1680 (2005); David A. Strauss, "Common Law Constitutional Interpretation," 63 *U. Chi. L. Rev.* 877, 921 (1996); *Slaughterhouse Cases,* 83 U.S. 36, 81 (1872); Howard Gillman, *The Constitution Besieged: The Rise and Demise of Lochner Era Politics Powers Jurisprudence* (2004), 57-60; Nourse and Maguire, "Lost History," 966-980; White, "Historicizing Judicial Scrutiny," 36; Charles W. McCurdy, "The Liberty of Contract; Regime in American Law," in *The State and Freedom of Contract,* ed. Harry N. Scheiber (1998), 165.

16. Bertrall L. Ross II, "Democracy and Renewed Distrust: Equal Protection and the Evolving Judicial Conception of Politics," 101 *Cal. L. Rev.* 1565, 1616-1633 (2013).

17. Ibid., 1581–1582; Stephanopoulos, "Political Powerlessness," 1547; Ely, *Democracy and Distrust*, 84, 103, 146, 148; Komesar, *Imperfect Alternatives*, 223; Jane S. Schacter, "Ely at the Altar: Political Process Theory through the Lens of the Marriage Debate," 109 *Mich. L. Rev.* 1363, 1365 (2011).

18. Stephanopoulos, "Political Powerlessness," 1578; Martin Gilens, *Affluence and Influence: Economic Inequality and Political Power in America* (2012), 81; Frank I. Michelman, "Foreword: On Protecting the Poor through the Fourteenth Amendment," 83 *Harv. L. Rev.* 7, 21 (1969); Daryl J. Levinson, "Foreword: Looking for Power in Public Law," 130 *Harv. L. Rev.* 31, 133 (2016); Yoshino, "The New Equal Protection"; Ely, *Democracy and Distrust*, 135–179.

19. Ross, "Democracy and Renewed Distrust," 1617; William M. Landes and Richard A. Posner, "The Independent Judiciary in an Interest-Group Perspective," *Journal of Law and Economics* 18 (1975): 875, 877; Mancur Olson, *The Logic of Collective Action: Public Goods and the Theory of Groups* (1965), 22–36.

20. *See* Chapters 5–7; California Air Resources Board, "Advanced Clean Car Program: Summary" (parent page last reviewed, Jan. 18, 2017), https://www.arb.ca.gov/msprog /clean_cars/acc%20summary-final.pdf; 29 U.S.C.A. §158(a)(3); Harry H. Wellington, "Union Fines and Workers Rights," 85 *Yale L.J.* 1022, 1046 (1976); 26 U.S.C.A. §1 (a)–(e).

21. Joseph Shapiro, "How Driver's License Suspensions Unfairly Target the Poor," NPR (Jan. 5, 2015), https://www.npr.org/2015/01/05/372691918/how-drivers-license -suspensions-unfairly-target-the-poor; Rand E. Rosenblatt, "Equality, Entitlement, and National Health Care Reform: The Challenge of Managed Competition and Managed Care," 60 *Brook. L. Rev.* 105, 140 (1994); Kimberly Jenkins Robertson, "No Quick Fix for Equity and Excellence: The Virtues of Incremental Shifts in Education Federalism," 27 *Stan. L & Pol. Rev.* 201, 214–215 (2016); *compare* 26 U.S.C.A. §1 (a)–(e) *with* 26 U.S.C.A. §1 (h); 26 U.S.C.A. §26.

22. Ilya Somin, "Closing the Pandora's Box of Federalism: The Case for Judicial Restriction of Federal Subsidies to State Governments," 90 *Geo. L.J.* 461, 495 (2002); see Chapter 5.

23. Klarman, "An Interpretive History"; White, "Historicizing Judicial Scrutiny"; Fallon, "Strict Judicial Scrutiny," 1293–1294; Goldberg, "Equality without Tiers," 485.

24. Reed v. Reed, 404 U.S. 71 (1971); Romer v. Evans, 517 U.S. 620 (1996); Lawrence v. Texas, 539 U.S. 558, 574 (2003) (doing the same in the context of substantive due process); *supra* notes 13–14 and accompanying text; City of Cleburne v. Cleburne Living Ctr., 473 U.S. 432 (1985); *id.* at 451 (Stevens, J., concurring); *id.* at 455 (Marshall, J., concurring).

25. Klarman, "An Interpretive History," 284; White, "Historicizing Judicial Scrutiny," 80; Fallon, "Strict Judicial Scrutiny," 1284.

26. *See supra* notes 16–19 and accompanying text; Stephanopoulos, "Political Powerlessness," 1531; Thomas W. Simon, "Suspect Class Democracy: A Social Theory," 45 *U. Miami L. Rev.* 107, 152 (1990); Nuno Garoupa and Andrew P. Morriss, "The Fable of

the Codes: The Efficiency of the Common Law, Legal Origins, and Codification Movements," 2012 *U. Ill. L. Rev.* 1443, 1466 (2012).

27. *See* Chapter 1.

28. Joseph Tussman and Jacobus tenBroek, "The Equal Protection of the Laws," 37 *Cal. L. Rev.* 341, 343–344 (1949); Vill. of Euclid, Ohio v. Ambler Realty Co., 272 U.S. 365 (1926); Fair Labor Standards Act of 1938, Pub. L. No. 75-718, 52 Stat. 1060 (codified as amended at 29 U.S.C. §213 (2001)); Ariz. Rev. Stat. §13-1406 (person convicted of sexual assault faces 5 to 28 years in prison); *id.* §13-1423 (mandatory life imprisonment for persons convicted of violent sexual assault); *id.* §13-3410 (life imprisonment for persons convicted of serious drug offenses); *id.* §§13-1304, 13-702(D) (first-time kidnapping offender presumptively faces between 5 and 12 years in prison); *id.* §§13-502, 13-707, 13-802, 13-902, 13-2905, 28-701.02 (persons convicted of class 3 misdemeanors—criminal speeding, loitering, criminal trespass in the third degree— subject to a maximum of $500 fine, 12 months' probation, and 30 days in jail); Atchison v. Matthews, 174 U.S. 96, 106 (1899); Timothy Zick, "Angry White Males: The Equal Protection Clause and 'Classes of One,'" 89 *Ky. L.J.* 69, 100 (2000); Andrew Koppelman, "Dumb and Doma: Why the Defense of Marriage Act Is Unconstitutional," 83 *Iowa L. Rev.* 1, 25 n.127 (1997); Michael J. Perry, "Modern Equal Protection: A Conceptualization and Appraisal," 79 *Colum. L. Rev.* 1023, 1068 (1979); Toll v. Moreno, 458 U.S. 1, 39 (1982) (Rehnquist, J., dissenting).

29. Tussman and tenBroek, "Equal Protection," 344; Erwin Chemerinsky, *Constitutional Law* (2016), 726.

30. Patrick E. Tolan Jr., "Government Contracting with Small Businesses in the Wake of the Federal Acquisition Streamlining Act," 44 *A.F. L. Rev.* 75 (1998); Bradley A. Cleveland, "The Last Shall be First: The Use of Localized Socio-Economic Policies in Contingency Contracting Operations," 197 *Mil. L. Rev.* 103, 108 (2008); Harry L. Dorsey et al., *1990 Contract Law Developments—The Year in Review,* 1991 FEB *Army Law.* 3, 65 (1991); Soc. Sec. Admin., *Disability Evaluation under Social Security: Listing of Impairments—Adult Listings (Part A),* https://www.ssa.gov/disability /professionals/bluebook/AdultListings.htm (last visited Nov. 22, 2017); Darien Shanske, "*Engquist* and the Erosion of the Equal Protection Clause: An Attempt to Stop the Creep of Irrational Dicta," 61 *Hastings L.J.* 969, 981 (2010); *compare* U.S. Dep't of Justice, Office of the Deputy Att'y Gen., "Memorandum for all United States Attorneys: Guidance Regarding Marijuana Enforcement" (Aug. 29, 2013), http://www .justice.gov/iso/opa/resources/3052013829132756857467.pdf (announcing the Obama Administration's nonenforcement policy of federal marijuana laws in states that had legalized marijuana) *with* Michael J. Henzey, "Going on the Offensive: A Comprehensive Overview of Internet Child Pornography Distribution and Aggressive Legal Action," 11 *Appalachian J.L.* 1, 38–39 (2011).

31. *See* Chapter 5; Ann Southworth, *Lawyers of the Right: Professionalizing the Conservative Coalition* (2008), 35; Steven M. Teles, *The Rise of the Conservative Legal Movement* (2008), 220; Ilya Somin, "A Revival of *Lochner*?," *Jotwell,* June 15, 2015 (reviewing Thomas Colby and Peter J. Smith, "The Return of *Lochner*," 100 *Cornell L. Rev.* 527 (2015)), https://conlaw.jotwell.com/a-revival-of-lochner/.

32. *See supra* notes 10, 12 and accompanying text; Reva Siegel, "Why Equal Protection No Longer Protects: The Evolving Forms of Status-Enforcing State Action," 49 *Stan. L. Rev.* 1111, 1111 (1997); Charles R. Lawrence III, "The Id, the Ego, and Equal Protection: Reckoning with Unconscious Racism," 39 *Stan. L. Rev.* 317, 319 (1987).

33. Obergefell v. Hodges, 135 S. Ct. 2584, 2608 (2015); *compare* Grutter v. Bollinger, 539 U.S. 306, 353 (2003) (Thomas, J., concurring in part and dissenting in part) *with* Gratz v. Bollinger, 539 U.S. 244, 301 (2003) (Ginsburg, J., dissenting); *compare* Obergefell v. Hodges, 135 S. Ct. 2584, 2608 (2015) (Kennedy, J., majority opinion) *and* Lawrence v. Texas, 539 U.S. 558, 567 (2003) (Kennedy, J., majority opinion) *with* Romer v. Evans, 517 U.S. 620, 636 (1996) (Scalia, J., dissenting) *and Obergefell,* 135 S. Ct. at 2640 (Alito, J., dissenting).

34. Michael C. Dorf, "Incidental Burdens on Fundamental Rights," 109 *Harv. L. Rev.* 1175, 1200 (1996); Gillian E. Metzger, Note: "Unburdening the Undue Burden Standard: Orienting *Casey* in Constitutional Jurisprudence," 94 *Colum. L. Rev.* 2025, 2037 (1994); Lawrence v. Texas, 539 U.S. 558 (2003); Reed v. Reed, 404 U.S. 71 (1971); City of Cleburne v. Cleburne Living Ctr., 473 U.S. 432 (1985).

35. *See supra* note 11 and accompanying text.

36. Komesar, *Imperfect Alternatives,* 253; Tara Leigh Grove, "Tiers of Scrutiny in a Hierarchical Judiciary," 14 *Geo. J. L. & Pub. Pol'y* 475, 489 (2016).

10. Takings

1. U.S. Const. amend. V; Richard A. Epstein, "The Spurious Constitutional Distinction between Takings and Regulation," 11 *Engage: J. Federalist Soc'y Prac. Groups* 11, 13 (2010); Richard A. Epstein, *Takings: Private Property and the Power of Eminent Domain* (1985), 3, 15, 16; William A. Fischel, *Regulatory Takings: Law, Economics, and Politics* (1995), 1.

2. Horne v. Dep't of Agric., 135 S. Ct. 2419, 2428 (2015); Webb's Fabulous Pharmacies, Inc. v. Beckwith, 449 U.S. 155, 155 (1980); Pennsylvania Coal Co. v. Mahon, 260 U.S. 393, 415–416 (1922); *Mahon,* 260 U.S. at 414; Lawrence Blume and Daniel L. Rubinfeld, "Compensation for Takings: An Economic Analysis," 72 *Cal. L. Rev.* 569, 623–624 (1984); Epstein, *Takings,* 143.

3. Mugler v. Kansas, 123 U.S. 623 (1887); Clean Air Act, 42 U.S.C. §§7401–7671q (2012); Fair Labor Standards Act of 1938, 29 U.S.C. §212 (2012); 438 U.S. 104 (1978).

4. Loretto v. Teleprompter Manhattan CATV Corp., 458 U.S. 419, 426 (1982); Lucas v. South Carolina Coastal Council, 505 U.S. 1003, 1019 (1992).

5. Thomas W. Merrill and Henry E. Smith, *The Oxford Introductions to U.S. Law: Property* (2010), 251; F. Patrick Hubbard, "Power to the People: The Takings Clause, Hart's Rule of Recognition, and Populist Law-Making," 50 *U. Louisville L. Rev.* 87, 99 (2011); Robert E. Litan, "Comment on Fischel's Political Economy of Just Compensation," 20 *Harv. J.L. & Pub. Pol'y* 65, 67 (1996); *infra* notes 22–23 and accompanying text.

6. Thomas S. Ulen, "Still Hazy after All These Years," 22 *Law & Soc. Inquiry* 1011, 1012 (1997); Robert Meltz, "Takings Law Today: A Primer for the Perplexed," 34 *Ecology L.Q.* 307, 310 (2007); William Baude, "Rethinking the Federal Eminent Domain Power," 122 *Yale L.J.* 1738, 1738 (2013); Kohl v. United States, 91 U.S. 367 (1875); Chicago, B. & Q.R. Co. v. City of Chicago, 166 U.S. 226 (1897); Jeb Rubenfeld, "Usings," 102 *Yale L.J.* 1077, 1081 (1993); Lingle v. Chevron U.S.A., Inc., 544 U.S. 528, 537 (2005).

7. Baude, "Rethinking," 1785; Mary Massaron Ross, "Public Use: Does *County of Wayne v. Hathcock* Signal a Revival of the Public Use Limit to the Taking of Private Property?," in *Eminent Domain Use and Abuse:* Kelo *in Context,* ed. Dwight H. Merriam and Mary Massaron Ross (2007), 1, 3; Kelo v. City of New London, 545 U.S. 469 (2005); Ilya Somin, *The Grasping Hand: "Kelo v. City of New London" and the Limits of Eminent Domain* (2015), 72; Fischel, *Regulatory Takings,* 6; Christopher Serkin, "The Meaning of Value: Assessing Just Compensation for Regulatory Takings," 99 *Nw. U. L. Rev.* 677, 683 (2005); David L. Callies and Shelley Ross Saxer, "Is Fair Market Value Just Compensation? An Underlying Issue Surfaced in *Kelo,* in *Eminent Domain Use and Abuse: Kelo in Context,* ed. Dwight H. Merriam and Mary Massaron Ross (2007), 142.

8. 260 U.S. 393, 412–416 (1922); *but see* Robert Brauneis, "'The Foundation of Our "Regulatory Takings" Jurisprudence': The Myth and Meaning of Justice Holmes's Opinion in *Pennsylvania Coal Co v. Mahon,*" 106 *Yale L.J.* 613 (1996).

9. Bruce A. Ackerman, *Private Property and the Constitution* (1977), 156; Carol M. Rose, "*Mahon* Reconstructed: Why the Takings Issue Is Still a Muddle," 57 *S. Cal. L. Rev.* 561–562 (1984); Joseph L. Sax, "Takings, Private Property and Public Rights," 81 *Yale L.J.* 149, 149 (1971); Ulen, "Still Hazy," 1013; Hodel v. Irving, 481 U.S. 704 (1987); Kaiser Aetna v. United States, 444 U.S. 164, 178 (1979); Gregory S. Alexander, "Ten Years of Takings," 46 *J. Legal Educ.* 586, 590 (1996).

10. 458 U.S. 419 (1982); 505 U.S. 1003, 1027 (1992) (emphasis added); *Lucas,* 505 U.S. at 1030; John R. Nolon, "Land Use and Climate Change: Lawyers Negotiating above Regulation," 78 *Brook. L. Rev.* 521, 558 (2013).

11. 438 U.S. 104, 116, 124 (1978).

12. Adam Winkler, *Fundamentally Wrong about Fundamental Rights* (2006), 233; Richard J. Lazarus, "The Measure of a Justice: Justice Scalia and the Faltering of the Property Rights Movement within the Supreme Court," 57 *Hastings L.J.* 759, 804 (2006); Eduardo Moisés Peñalver, "Regulatory Taxings," 104 *Colum. L. Rev.* 2182, 2194 (2004); James E. Krier and Steward E. Sterk, "An Empirical Study of Implicit Takings," 58 *Wm. & Mary L. Rev.* 35, 62–64 (2016).

13. 544 U.S. 528, 544 (2005); Krier and Sterk, "An Empirical Study," 87; *but see* Hodel v. Irving, 481 U.S. 704, 717 (1987).

14. John J. Costonis, "Presumptive and Per Se Takings: A Decisional Model for the Taking Issue," 58 *N.Y.U. L. Rev.* 465, 529 (1983); Murr v. Wisconsin, 137 S. Ct. 1933, 1945 (2017); Merrill and Smith, *The Oxford Introductions,* 255, 257; *Loretto,* 458 U.S. at 441; Krier and Sterk, "An Empirical Study," 57; *id.,* 56–58, 59–62; Richard A. Posner, "The Supreme Court, 2004 Term—Leading Cases: Public Use—Economic

Development," 119 *Harv. L. Rev.* 287, 293 n.59 (2005); *compare* Loretto v. Tele-prompter Manhattan CATV Corp., 458 U.S. 419 (1982) *with* Yee v. City of Escon-dido, 503 U.S. 519 (1992).

15. 483 U.S. 825 (1987); 512 U.S. 374 (1994); Lingle v. Chevron U.S.A., Inc., 544 U.S. 528, 530; David A. Dana and Thomas W. Merrill, *Property: Takings* (2002), 213.

16. *Dolan,* 512 U.S. at 386–387, 391; *id.,* at 387, 395; David A. Dana, "Land Use Regula-tion in an Age of Heightened Scrutiny," 75 *N.C. L. Rev.* 1243, 1245 (1997); Krier and Sterk, "An Empirical Study," 48.

17. Mark Fenster, "Takings Formalism and Regulatory Formulas: Exactions and the Consequences of Clarity," 92 *Cal. L. Rev.* 609, 653 (2004); J. David Breemer, "The Evolution of the 'Essential Nexus': How State and Federal Courts Have Applied *Nollan* and *Dolan* and Where They Should Go from Here," 59 *Wash. & Lee L. Rev.* 373, 337 (2002); Lee Anne Fennell and Eduardo M. Peñalver, "Exactions Creep," 2013 Sup. Ct. Rev. 287, 329 (2014); Dolan v. City of Tigard, 512 U.S. 374, 384 (1994); Nollan v. California Coastal Comm'n, 483 U.S. 825, 831 (1987); Lingle v. Chevron U.S.A., Inc., 544 U.S. 528, 548 (2005); Mark Fenster, "Regulating Land Use in a Constitutional Shadow: The Institutional Contexts of Exactions," 58 *Hastings L.J.* 729, 731 n.20 (2007); Merrill and Smith, *The Oxford Introductions,* 255.

18. 133 S. Ct. 2586 (2013); Dana and Merrill, *Property: Takings,* 211; Gus Bauman and William H. Ethier, "Development Exactions and Impact Fees: A Survey of American Practices," 50 *Law & Contemp. Probs.* 51, 56 (1987); 133 S. Ct. at 2593; *but see id.* at 2604 (Kagan, J., dissenting).

19. Fennell and Peñalver, "Exactions Creep," 298, 300; Dana and Merrill, *Property: Tak-ings,* 69; Peñalver, "Regulatory Taxings," 2200; Koontz v. St. Johns River Water Mgmt. Dist., 133 S. Ct. 2586, 2601–2602 (2013); *id.* at 2603–2604. (Kagan, J., dis-senting); John D. Echeverria, "*Koontz:* The Very Worst Takings Decision Ever?," 22 *N.Y.U. Envtl. L.J.* 1, 46 (2014).

20. *Id.* at 2599, 2603; Fennell and Peñalver, "Exactions Creep," 351; Echeverria, "*Koontz*"; Antonio M. Elias, Note, "*Koontz v. St. Johns River Water Management District* Was Not a Big Deal," 34 *Va. Envtl. L.J.* 457, 482 (2016); Westlaw Keycite, Westlaw Next, https://1.next.westlaw.com.

21. John F. Hart, "Land Use Law in the Early Republic and the Original Meaning of the Takings Clause," 94 *Nw. U. L. Rev.* 1099, 1101–1103 (2000); William Michael Treanor, "The Original Understanding of the Takings Clause and the Political Process," 95 *Colum. L. Rev.* 782, 782–784 (1995); Michael B. Rappaport, "Originalism and Regu-latory Takings: Why the Fifth Amendment May Not Protect against Regulatory Tak-ings, but the Fourteenth Amendment May," 45 *San Diego L. Rev.* 729, 731 (2008); Lucas v. South Carolina Coastal Council, 505 U.S. 1003, 1019 (1992); William Mi-chael Treanor, "Jam for Justice Holmes: Reassessing the Significance of *Mahon,*" 86 *Geo. L.J.* 813, 816 (1998); Pennsylvania Coal Co. v. Mahon, 260 U.S. 393, 426 (1922); Brauneis, "Foundation," 64; *but see* Murr v. Wisconsin, 137 S. Ct. 1933, 1957 (2017) (Thomas, J., dissenting).

22. Brannon P. Denning and Michael B. Kent Jr., "Anti-Evasion Doctrines in Constitu-tional Law," 2012 *Utah L. Rev.* 1773, 1792–1793 (2012); Penn Cent. Transp. Co. v. City

of New York, 438 U.S. 104, 116 (1978); John D. Echeverria, "Making Sense of *Penn Central*," 39 *Envtl. L. Rep. News & Analysis* 10471, 10472 (2009); Neil K. Komesar, *Imperfect Alternatives: Choosing Institutions in Law, Economics, and Public Policy* (1994), 235; Abraham Bell and Gideon Parchomovsky, "Takings Reassessed," 87 *Va. L. Rev.* 277, 314 (2001); Richard A. Epstein, "Physical and Regulatory Takings: One Distinction Too Many," 64 *Stan. L. Rev. Online* 99, 101 (2012).

23. Stewart E. Sterk, "The Federalist Dimension of Regulatory Takings Jurisprudence," 114 *Yale L.J.* 203, 205 (2004); Rubenfeld, "Usings," 1081; Andrea L. Peterson, "The Taking Clause: In Search of Underlying Principles Part I—A Critique of Current Takings Clause Doctrine," 77 *Cal. L. Rev.* 1299, 1304 (1989); Rose, "*Mahon* Reconstructed," 566; Marc R. Poirier, "The Virtue of Vagueness in Takings Doctrine," 24 *Cardozo L. Rev.* 93, 97 (2002); James E. Krier, "The Takings-Puzzle Puzzle," 38 *Wm. and Mary L. Rev.* 1143, 1143 (1997).

24. Dana and Merrill, *Property: Takings,* 9.

25. Bradley C. Karkkainen, "The Police Power Revisited: Phantom Incorporation and the Roots of the Takings 'Muddle,'" 90 *Minn. L. Rev.* 826, 911 (2006); Treanor, "The Original Understanding," 875; Barton H. Thompson Jr., "Judicial Takings," 76 *Va. L. Rev.* 1449, 1492 (1990); Ilya Somin and Jonathan H. Adler, "The Green Costs of *Kelo*: Economic Development Takings and Environmental Protection," 84 *Wash. U.L. Rev.* 623, 626 (2006); Bowen v. Gilliard, 483 U.S. 587, 609–634 (1987) (Justice Brennan, joined by Justice Marshall, dissenting from the majority's holding that no regulatory taking occurred); Hodel v. Irving, 481 U.S. 704, 718 (1987) (Justices Brennan and Marshall joining the majority opinion holding that a regulatory taking occurred); Ruckelshaus v. Monsanto Co., 467 U.S. 986 (1984) (Justices Brennan and Marshall joining the majority's finding of a taking); Texaco, Inc. v. Short, 454 U.S. 516, 540–554 (1982) (Justices Brennan and Marshall dissenting from the majority's finding of no taking) (1984); Webb's Fabulous Pharmacies, Inc., v. Beckwith, 449 U.S. 155 (1980) (Justices Brennan and Marshall joining the majority opinion holding that a taking had occurred); *but* Nollan v. California Coastal Comm'n, 483 U.S. 825, 842–864 (1987) (Justices Brennan and Marshall dissenting from the majority's holding that imposition of a public access requirement on otherwise private beachfront property constitutes a taking); Frank I. Michelman, "Property, Utility, and Fairness: Comments on the Ethical Foundations of 'Just Compensation' Law," 80 *Harv. L. Rev.* 1165, 1167 (1967); Dana and Merrill, *Property: Takings,* 36–37; Komesar, *Imperfect Alternatives,* 233–234; Ilya Somin, "Why Robbing Peter Won't Help Poor Paul: Low-Income Neighborhoods and Uncompensated Regulatory Takings," 117 *Yale L.J. Pocket Part* 72, 72 (2007); David E. Bernstein, "Roots of the 'Underclass': The Decline of Laissez-Faire Jurisprudence and the Rise of Racist Labor Legislation," 43 *Am. U. L. Rev.* 85, 136 (1993).

26. Carol M. Rose, "What Federalism Tells Us about Takings Jurisprudence," 54 *UCLA L. Rev.* 1681, 1698 (2006); Michael A. Bailey and Forrest Maltzman, *The Constrained Court: Law, Politics, and the Decisions Justices Make* (2011), 98.

27. *See* Chapter 5.

28. *See supra* notes 12–13 and accompanying text.

29. *See supra* note 6 and accompanying text; Joseph L. Sax, "Takings and the Police Power," 74 *Yale L.J.* 36, 62–63 (1964); Fischel, *Regulatory Takings,* 253–288; *supra* note 9 and accompanying text.

30. Koontz v. St. Johns River Water Mgmt. Dist., 133 S. Ct. 2586, 2599 (2013); *Koontz,* 133 S. Ct. at 2608 (Kagan, J., dissenting); *see supra* note 22 and accompanying text.

31. *See* Chapter 1.

32. Rose, "What Federalism Tells Us," 1688; Komesar, *Imperfect Alternatives,* 239; Epstein, *Takings,* 281 (emphasis added); *id.* at 3397–3398 (emphasis in original).

33. Americans with Disabilities Act of 1990 (ADA), 42 U.S.C. §§12101–12213 (2013) (amended 2008); Civil Rights Act of 1964, Pub. L. No. 88-352, 78 Stat. 241 (codified as amended in scattered sections of 2 U.S.C., 28 U.S.C., and 42 U.S.C.); Endangered Species Act of 1973, Pub. L. No. 93-205, 87 Stat. 884 (codified as amended at 16 U.S.C. §§1531–1544 (2000)); Controlled Substances Act (CSA), 21 U.S.C. §§801–904 (2000); Sherman Antitrust Act of 1890, 26 Stat. 209 (codified as amended at 15 U.S.C. §§1–7); Lanham Act, Pub. L. No. 79-489, 60 Stat. 427 (codified at 15 U.S.C. §§1051–1141); Federal Aviation Act of 1958 (FAA), Pub. L. No. 85-726, 72 Stat. 731 (codified at 49 U.S.C.A. §§40101–41741); Fair Labor Standards Act of 1938, 29 U.S.C. §§201–219 (2012); Epstein, *Takings,* 95 (emphasis in original).

34. Epstein, *Takings,* 96, 111–112; Komesar, *Imperfect Alternatives,* 236–237; Rose, "What Federalism Tells Us," 1688; Sterk, "Federalist Dimension," 271.

35. James L. Huffman, "The Past and Future of Environmental Law," 30 *Envtl. L.* 23, 29–30 (2000); Ann Southworth, *Lawyers of the Right: Professionalizing the Conservative Coalition* (2008), 35; Steven M. Teles, *The Rise of the Conservative Legal Movement* (2008), 220; Institute for Justice, *Economic Liberty,* at http://ij.org/issues/economic-liberty/ (last visited Sept. 19, 2017).

36. *See supra* notes 12, 14 and accompanying text.

37. Murr v. Wisconsin, 137 S. Ct. 1933 (2017) (5–3 decision: Kennedy, Ginsburg, Breyer, Sotomayor, and Kagan in the majority; Roberts, Thomas, and Alito in dissent); Koontz v. St. Johns River Mgmt. Dist., 133 S. Ct. 2586 (2013) (5–4 decision: Alito, Roberts, Scalia, Thomas, and Kennedy in majority; Kagan, Ginsburg, Breyer, and Sotomayor in dissent); Kelo v. City of New London, 545 U.S. 469 (2005) (5–4 decision: Stevens, Souter, Kennedy, Ginsburg, and Breyer in majority; O'Connor, Scalia, Rehnquist, and Thomas in dissent); Murr. V. Wisconsin, 137 S. Ct. 1933, 1951 (2017) (Roberts, C.J., dissenting); Dolan v. City of Tigard, 512 U.S. 374, 396 (1994) (Rehnquist, C.J.) (internal citations omitted); Nollan v. California Coastal Comm'n, 483 U.S. 825, 831 (1987) (Scalia, J., majority) (internal citations and quotations omitted); Kelo v. City of New London, 545 U.S. 469, 483 (2005) (Stevens, J., majority); Nollan v. California Coastal Comm'n, 483 U.S. 825, 848 (1987) (Brennan, J., dissenting); Koontz v. St. John's River Management District, 133 S. Ct. 2586, 2612 (2014) (Kagan, J., dissenting).

38. Lynn E. Blais, "Urban Revitalization in the Post-*Kelo* Era," 34 *Fordham Urb. L.J.* 657, 683 (2007); Dana and Merrill, *Property: Takings,* 178–179; Merrill and Smith, *The Oxford Introductions,* 241; Thomas E. Roberts, "Facial Takings Claims under *Agins-Nectow:* A Procedural Loose End," 24 *U. Haw. L. Rev.* 623, 623 n.2 (2002); Fennell

and Peñalver, "Exactions Creep," 324; Carol M. Rose, "Takings, Federalism, Norms," 105 *Yale L.J.* 1121, 1034 (1996).

39. Ulen, "Still Hazy," 1012; "50 State Statutory Surveys: Real Property: Eminent Domain: Procedures for Acquisition of Property," 0130 SURVEYS 3 (West 2016); *e.g.,* Ariz. Rev. Stat. §28-7098 (2002).

40. *See supra* note 14 and accompanying text; Krier and Sterk, "An Empirical Study," 62-63.

41. Rose, "*Mahon* Reconstructed," 566; Ackerman, *Private Property,* 235 n.2; Michelman, "Property, Utility, and Fairness," 1214-1215, 1230, 1250.

42. Komesar, *Imperfect Alternatives,* 237-238; Rose, "What Federalism Tells Us," 1696, 1699.

43. Fischel, *Regulatory Takings,* 140; Michelman, "Property, Utility, and Fairness," 1230; Komesar, *Imperfect Alternatives,* 237-238; Rose, "What Federalism Tells Us," 1696, 1699.

44. Dana and Merrill, *Property: Takings,* 225-226; Fennell and Peñalver, "Exactions Creep," 296; John G. Sprankling, "Property and the Roberts Court," 65 *U. Kan. L. Rev.* 1, 20 (2016); Krier and Sterk, "An Empirical Study," 68; Anne E. Carlson and Daniel Pollak, "Takings on the Ground: How the Supreme Court's Takings Jurisprudence Affects Local Land Use Decisions," 35 *U.C. Davis L. Rev.* 103, 106-108 (2001).

45. Krier and Sterk, "An Empirical Study," 68-69; Elias, "*Koontz,*" 482-483; Nollan v. California Coastal Comm'n, 483 U.S. 825, 846 (1987) (Brennan, J., dissenting); Dolan v. City of Tigard, 512 U.S. 374, 405 (1994) (Stevens, J., dissenting); Koontz v. St. John's River Management District, 133 S. Ct. 2586, 2604 (2014) (Kagan, J., dissenting).

46. Elias, "*Koontz,*" 482-483.

47. Echeverria, "*Koontz,*" 1, 3; Fischel, *Regulatory Takings,* 346; *Koontz,* S. Ct. at, 2610 (2013) (Kagan, J., dissenting).

48. Elias, "*Koontz,*" 475-476, 480, 482, 488; Richard A. Epstein, *Bargaining with the State* (1993), 183; Vicki Been, "'Exit' as a Constraint on Land Use Exactions: Rethinking the Unconstitutional Conditions Doctrine," 91 *Colum. L. Rev.* 473, 511-528 (1991); Fennell and Peñalver, "Exactions Creep," 316.

49. *Koontz,* 133 S. Ct. at 2597 (2013); *but see* Elias, "*Koontz,*" 469.

11. Judicial Capacity and the Constitutional Choice Set

1. R. G. Lipsey and R. K. Lancaster, "The General Theory of Second Best," *Review of Economic Studies* 24 (1956): 11; Adrian Vermeule, "Foreword: System Effects and the Constitution," 123 *Harv. L. Rev.* 4, 17 (2009).

2. Adrian Vermeule, *The Constitution of Risk* (2014), 52-53; Albert O. Hirschman, *The Rhetoric of Reaction* (1991), 43.

3. Philip Hamburger, *Is Administrative Law Unlawful?* (2014).

4. United States v. Lopez, 514 U.S. 549, 559-561 (1995); United States v. Morrison, 529 U.S. 598, 615-618, 620 (2000).

5. Jack M. Balkin, "Commerce," 109 *Mich. L. Rev.* 1, 43 (2010); Robert D. Cooter and Neil S. Siegel, "Collective Action Federalism: A General Theory of Article I, Section 8," 63 *Stan. L. Rev.* 115, 164 (2010); *Morrison,* 529 U.S. at 617.

6. Andrew Coan, "Implementing Enumeration," 57 *Wm. & Mary L. Rev.* 1985, 2007–2009 (2016); Abigail R. Moncrieff, "Safeguarding the Safeguards: The ACA Litigation and the Extension of Indirect Protection to Nonfundamental Liberties," 64 *Fla. L. Rev.* 639, 684–685 (2012).

7. Hamburger, *Is Administrative Law Unlawful?,* 31–32, 508; Gary Lawson, "The Return of the King: The Unsavory Origins of Administrative Law," 93 *Tex. L. Rev.* 1521, 1522 (2015); Adrian Vermeule, "No," 93 *Tex. L. Rev.* 1547, 1566 (2015) (reviewing Hamburger, *Is Administrative Law Unlawful?*); Wayman v. Southard, 23 U.S. (10 Wheat.) 1, 43 (1825).

8. Cynthia R. Farina, "False Comfort and Impossible Promises: Uncertainty, Information Overload, and the Unitary Executive," 12 *U. Pa. J. Const. L.* 357, 397 and n.168 (2010); *Code of Federal Regulations: Page Breakdown—1975 through 2013,* Federal Register (Oct. 29, 2014), https://www.federalregister.gov/uploads/2014/04/CFR-Actual-Pages-published1-2013.pdf (spanning 200 volumes and 175,000 pages); Hamburger, *Is Administrative Law Unlawful?,* 492.

9. Vermeule, *The Constitution of Risk,* 1553.

10. PHH Corp. v. CFPB, 839 F.3d 1, 7 (D.C. Cir. 2016), *vacated, reh'g en banc granted,* Order Granting Petition for Rehearing En Banc, No. 15-1177 (Feb. 16, 2017).

11. Seven-Sky v. Holder, 661 F.3d 1, 17 (D.C. Cir. 2011); Thomas More Law Ctr. v. Obama, 651 F.3d 529, 561 (6th Cir. 2011); Mark A. Hall, "Commerce Clause Challenges to Health Care Reform," 159 *U. Pa. L. Rev.* 1825, 1836 (2011); Corey Rayburn Yung, "The Incredible Ordinariness of Federal Penalties for Inactivity," 2012 *Wis. L. Rev.* 841, 842.

12. Lawrence Lessig, "Translating Federalism: *United States v. Lopez,*" 1995 *Sup. Ct. Rev.* 125, 174; Randy J. Kozel, "Settled versus Right: Constitutional Method and the Path of Precedent," 91 *Tex. L. Rev.* 1843, 1855–1859 (2013).

13. Glenn H. Reynolds and Brannon P. Denning, "Lower Court Readings of *Lopez,* or What If the Supreme Court Held a Constitutional Revolution and Nobody Came?," 2000 *Wis. L. Rev.* 369, 378–379; Andrew Coan, "Judicial Capacity and the Substance of Constitutional Law," 122 *Yale L.J.* 422, 446–452 (2012).

12. Judicial Capacity and Judicial Competence

1. Cass R. Sunstein and Adrian Vermeule, "Interpretations and Institutions," 101 *Mich. L. Rev.* 885 (2003); John Yoo, "Courts at War," 91 *Cornell L. Rev.* 573, 597–600 (2006); Hamdi v. Rumsfeld, 542 U.S. 507, 578 (2004) (Scalia, J., dissenting); United States v. Armstrong, 517 U.S. 456, 465 (1996); Rostker v. Goldberg, 453 U.S. 57, 65 (1981); Gilligan v. Morgan, 413 U.S. 1, 10 (1973); Brief for Appellants at 18, Florida v. U.S. Dep't. of Health and Human Services, 643 F.3d 1235 (11th Cir. 2011) (Nos. 11-11021, 11-11067), 2011 WL 1461593, at 18, *aff'd in part sub. nom.* Nat'l Fed'n. of Indep.

Bus. v. Sebelius, 567 U.S. 519 (2012); Brief for the United States at 18, Free Enter. Fund v. Pub. Co. Accounting Oversight Bd., 561 U.S. 477 (2010) (No. 08-861), 2009 WL 3290435, at 18; Brief for the United States, at 38, United States. v. Morrison, 529 U.S. 598 (2000) (Nos. 99-5, 99-29), 1999 WL 1037259, at 38.

2. John F. Manning, "The Nondelegation Doctrine as a Canon of Avoidance," 2000 *Sup. Ct. Rev.* 223, 241–242; Cass R. Sunstein, "Nondelegation Canons," 67 *U. Chi. L. Rev.* 315, 321; Aziz Z. Huq, "Removal as a Political Question," 65 *Stan L. Rev.* 1, 6; Peter Strauss, "*Free Enterprise Fund v. Public Company Accounting Oversight Board,*" 62 *Vand. L. Rev. En Banc* 51, 54–55 (2009); Richard H. Pildes, "Free Enterprise Fund, Boundary-Enforcing Decisions, and the Unitary Executive Branch Theory of Government Administration," 6 *Duke J. Const. L. & Pub. Pol'y* 1, 11–12 (2010); Free Enterprise Fund v. Pub. Co. Accounting Oversight Bd., 561 U.S. 477, 523 (2010) (Breyer, J., dissenting); *e.g.,* Patsy v. Bd. of Regents of Fla., 457 U.S. 496, 513 (1982); United States v. Gainey, 380 U.S. 63, 67 (1965); Butz v. Glover Livestock Comm'n. Co., Inc., 411 U.S. 182, 185 (1972).

3. *PCAOB,* 561 U.S. at 523 (Breyer, J., dissenting); Neil Komesar, *Imperfect Alternatives: Choosing Institutions in Law, Economics, and Public Policy* (1994), 137, 139, 251–252; Huq, "Removal," 72; Adrian Vermeule, *Judging under Uncertainty: An Institutional Theory of Legal Interpretation* (2006), 268; Andrew Coan, "Judicial Capacity and the Substance of Constitutional Law," 122 *Yale L.J.* 422, 450–451; Douglas Laycock, "A Syllabus of Errors," 105 *Mich. L. Rev.* 1169, 1172–1177 (2007); Cass R. Sunstein, "The Most Knowledgeable Branch," 164 *U. Pa. L. Rev.* 1607, 1609–1610 (2016); Neil K. Komesar, *Law's Limits: The Rule of Law and the Supply and Demand of Rights* (2001), 59–75; Einer R. Elhauge, "Does Interest Group Theory Justify More Intrusive Judicial Review?," 101 *Yale L.J.* 31, 89 (1991); Thomas W. Merrill, "Institutional Choice and Political Faith," 22 *Law & Soc. Inquiry* 959 (1997); Jason Webb Yackee and Susan Webb Yackee, *A Bias toward Business? Assessing Interest Group Influence On the U.S. Bureaucracy,* 68 J. Pol. 128 (2006).

4. Coan, "Judicial Capacity," 446.

5. Harold Hongju Koh, "Why the President (Almost) Always Wins in Foreign Affairs: Lessons of the Iran-Contra Affair," 97 *Yale L.J.* 12551316; Eric. A. Posner and Cass R. Sunstein, "Chevronizing Foreign Relations Law," 116 *Yale L.J.* 1170, 1193 (2007).

6. *See* Chapter 4.

7. Richard A. Posner, "The Rise and Fall of Judicial Self-Restraint," 100 *Cal. L. Rev.* 519 (2012); Pamela S. Karlan, "Foreword: Democracy and Disdain," 126 *Harv. L. Rev.* 1, 68; Aziz Z. Huq, "When Was Judicial Self-Restraint?," 100 *Cal. L. Rev.* 579 (2012); Michael A. Bailey and Forrest Maltzman, *The Constrained Court: Law, Politics, and the Decisions Justices Make* (2011), 83.

8. Sunstein, "Nondelegation Canons," 315, 321, 326–327; John F. Manning, "Lessons from a Nondelegation Canon," 83 *Notre Dame L. Rev.* 1541, 1551 (2008); John F. Manning, "The Nondelegation Doctrine as a Canon of Avoidance," 2000 *Sup. Ct. Rev.* 223, 241–242; Martin H. Redish, *The Constitution as Political Structure* (1995), 136–137; NFIB v. Sebelius, 132 S. Ct. 2566, 2587 (2012); United States v. Morrison, 529 U.S. 598, 610 (2000); United States v. Lopez, 514 U.S. 549, 559–560 (1995); Peter H.

Aranson et al., "Theory of Legislative Delegation," 68 *Cornell L. Rev.* 1, 58 (1982); Theodore J. Lowi, "Two Roads to Serfdom: Liberalism, Conservatism, and Administrative Power," 36 *Am. U. L. Rev.* 295, 297 (1986); Komesar, *Imperfect Alternatives,* 90–97.

9. Miguel Poiares Maduro, "In Search of a Meaning and Not in Search of the Meaning: Judicial Review and the Constitution in Times of Pluralism," 2013 *Wis. L. Rev.* 541, 559 (2013); Adrian Vermeule, "Judicial Review and Institutional Choice," 43 *Wm. & Mary L. Rev.* 1557 (2002); Henry M. Hart Jr. and Albert M. Sacks, *The Legal Process: Basic Problems in the Making and Application of Law* (The Foundation Press, 1994 ed., prepared from 1958 tentative ed.), 113; Komesar, *Imperfect Alternatives,* 3; Komesar, *Law's Limits,* 23.

10. Komesar, *Imperfect Alternatives,* 50; Komesar, *Law's Limits,* 20–21; Vermeule, *Judging under Uncertainty,* 64; John Rappaport, "Second-Order Regulation of Law Enforcement," 103 *Cal. L. Rev.* 205, 236 (2015); Laycock, "A Syllabus of Errors," 1172–1177 (2007); Erwin Chemerinsky, "The Supreme Court 1998 Term—Foreword: The Vanishing Constitution," 103 *Harv. L. Rev.* 43, 83–87 (1989); Abram Chayes, "The Role of the Judge in Public Law Litigation," 89 *Harv. L. Rev.* 1281 (1976).

11. Rappaport, "Second-Order Regulation," 232; Cass R. Sunstein, "The Most Knowledgeable Branch," 164 *U. Pa. L. Rev.* 1607, 1616 (2016); Komesar, *Imperfect Alternatives,* 126, 128; Frederick Schauer, "Do Cases Make Bad Law?," 73 *U. Chi. L. Rev.* 883, 894 (2006).

12. Nicholas O. Stephanopoulos, "Political Powerlessness," 90 *N.Y.U. L. Rev.* 1527, 1556 (2015); Michael E. Waterstone, "Disability Constitutional Law," 63 *Emory L.J.* 527, 557 (2014); Thomas P. Crocker, "Envisioning the Constitution," 57 *Am. U. L. Rev.* 1, 31 (2007); Rappaport, "Second-Order Regulation," 232–236; Chemerinsky, "The Vanishing Constitution," 85–86; Laycock, "A Syllabus of Errors," 1175–1176; Rappaport, 233.

13. Judicial Capacity and Judicial Independence

1. 135 S.Ct. 2584 (2015); 133 S.Ct. 2612 (2013); *Obergefell,* 135 S.Ct. at 2624 (Roberts, C.J., dissenting); *id.* at 2629 (Scalia, J., dissenting); *Shelby Cty.,* 133 S.Ct. at 2648 (Ginsburg, J., dissenting); *Obergefell,* 135 S.Ct. at 2605; *Shelby Cty.,* 133 S.Ct. at 2631; Transcript of Oral Argument at 21–22, *Shelby Cty.,* 133 S.Ct. 2612 (No. 12-96); Alexander Bickel, *The Least Dangerous Branch: The Supreme Court at the Bar of Politics* (1962); John Hart Ely, *Democracy and Distrust: A Theory of Judicial Review* (1980); Barry Friedman, *The Will of the People: How Public Opinion Has Influenced the Supreme Court and Shaped the Meaning of the Constitution* (2009); Larry D. Kramer, *The People Themselves: Popular Constitutionalism and Judicial Review* (2004); James B. Thayer, "The Origin and Scope of the American Doctrine of Constitutional Law," 7 *Harv. L. Rev.* 129, 156 (1893).

2. Friedman, *The Will of the People,* 9–16; Gerald Rosenberg, *The Hollow Hope: Can Courts Bring About Social Change?,* 2d ed. (2008); Keith E. Whittington, *Political*

Foundations of Judicial Supremacy: The Presidency, the Supreme Court, and Constitutional Leadership in U.S. History (2007); Richard Pildes, "Is the Supreme Court a Majoritarian Institution?," 2010 *Sup. Ct. Rev.* 103, 114–154; Raoul Berger, *Government by Judiciary: The Transformation of the Fourteenth Amendment* (1977).

3. Mark Tushnet, *Why the Constitution Matters* (2010), 16–17; Friedman, *The Will of the People,* 376; Pildes, "Majoritarian Institution?," 126–142, 157–158; Jack M. Balkin and Sanford Levinson, "Understanding the Constitutional Revolution," 87 *Va. L. Rev.* 1045, 1066–1083 (2001); Michael A. Bailey and Forrest Maltzman, *The Constrained Court: Law, Politics, and the Decisions Justices Make* (2011), 2; Adrian Vermeule, "The Short-Run Inelasticity of Constitutional Law," Jotwell, December 5, 2011 (reviewing Pildes, "Majoritarian Institution?"), https://conlaw.jotwell.com/the-short -run-inelasticity-of-constitutional-law.

4. 347 U.S. 483 (1954); Engel v. Vitale, 370 U.S. 421 (1962); Abington School District v. Schempp, 374 U.S. 203 (1963); 410 U.S. 113 (1973); Friedman, *The Will of the People*; Rosenberg, *The Hollow Hope*, 82–87; Heather D. Boonstra and Elizabeth Nash, "A Surge of State Abortion Restrictions Puts Providers—And the Women They Serve— in the Crosshairs," *Guttmacher Policy Review* 17 (2014): 1, 9.

5. *See* Chapter 5.

6. Bailey and Maltzman, *The Constrained Court,* 98; Friedman, *The Will of the People,* 375; Lee Epstein and Jack Knight, *The Choices Justices Make* (1997).

7. *See supra* note 3; Pamela S. Karlan, "Foreword: Democracy and Disdain," 126 *Harv. L. Rev.* 1 (2012); Richard A. Posner, "The Rise and Fall of Judicial Self-Restraint," 100 *Cal. L. Rev.* 519 (2012); *but see* Aziz Huq, "When Was Judicial Restraint?," 100 *Cal. L. Rev.* 579 (2012).

8. Friedman, *The Will of the People*; Gary Lawson, "The Rise and Rise of the Administrative State," 107 *Harv. L. Rev.* 1231 (1994); Adrian Vermeule, "Beard & Holmes on Constitutional Adjudication," 29 *Const. Comment.* 457, 473 (2014).

9. *See supra* note 6; Bailey and Maltzman, *The Constrained Court,* 14; Friedman, *The Will of the People,* 376.

10. Tom Ginsburg and James Melton, *The Endurance of National Constitutions* (2009), 101; Andrew Coan and Anuj Desai, "Difficulty of Amendment and Interpretive Choice," 1 *J. Inst. Stud.* 201, 209 (2015); Nathaniel Persily et al., eds., *Public Opinion and Constitutional Controversy* (2008), 14; Gregory A. Caldeira and James L. Gibson, "The Etiology of Public Support for the Supreme Court," *American Journal of Political Science* 36 (1992): 640; Pildes, "Majoritarian Institution?," 129, 131, 139; Robert McCloskey and Sanford Levinson, *The American Supreme Court,* 6th ed. (2016), 117; Jeff Shesol, *Supreme Power: Franklin Roosevelt vs. the Supreme Court* (2010), 305; Tara Leigh Grove, "The Structural Safeguards of Federal Jurisdiction," 124 *Harv. L. Rev.* 869, 889–917 (2011).

11. John Sides and Daniel J. Hopkins, *Political Polarization in American Politics* (2015); Nathaniel Persily, ed., *Solutions to Political Polarization in America* (2015); Richard H. Pildes, "Why the Center Does Not Hold: The Causes of Hyperpolarized Democracy in America," 99 *Cal. L. Rev.* 273 (2011); Marc J. Hetherington and Thomas J. Rudolph, *Why Washington Won't Work: Polarization, Political Trust, and*

the Governing Crisis (2015); Marc J. Hetherington, *Why Trust Matters: Declining Political Trust and the Demise of American Liberalism* (2006); *The Oxford Handbook of Social and Political Trust,* ed. Eric Uslaner (2017); "Public Trust in Government Remains Near Historic Lows as Partisan Attitudes Shift," Pew Res. Ctr. (May 3, 2017), http://www.people-press.org/2017/05/03/public-trust-in-government-remains-near -historic-lows-as-partisan-attitudes-shift/.

12. *See* Chapter 11.

13. Pildes, "Majoritarian Institution?," 129–130; Shesol, *Supreme Power,* 169; Chapter 5 *supra;* McNollgast, "Politics and the Courts: A Positive Theory of Judicial Doctrine and the Rule of Law," 68 *S. Cal. L. Rev.* 1631, 1672 (1995).

14. Friedman, *The Will of the People,* 232; McCloskey and Levinson, *The American Supreme Court,* 117; William E. Leuchtenburg, "FDR's Court-Packing Plan: A Second Life, a Second Death," 1985 *Duke L.J.* 673, 673 (1985); Barry Cushman, *Rethinking the New Deal Court: The Structure of a Constitutional Revolution* (1998); Daniel E. Ho and Kevin M. Quinn, "Did a Switch in Time Save Nine?," 2 *J. Legal Analysis* 69, 69 (2010).

15. Jeremy Waldron, "The Core of the Case against Judicial Review," 115 *Yale L.J.* 1346, 1389–1390 (2006) (posing this question); Ely, *Democracy and Distrust,* 103; Friedman, *The Will of the People,* 369–370; Pildes, "Majoritarian Institution?," 104.

16. Bickel, *The Least Dangerous Branch;* Ely, *Democracy and Distrust;* Alon Harel and Tsvi Kahana, "The Easy Core Case for Judicial Review," 2 *J. Legal Anal.* 227 (2010); Reva B. Siegel, "Constitutional Culture, Social Movement Conflict and Constitutional Change: The Case of the De Facto Era," 94 *Cal. L. Rev.* 1323 (2006); Waldron, "Core of the Case"; Friedman, *The Will of the People,* 370; Pildes, "Majoritarian Institution?," 116.

17. *Id.;* 558 U.S. 310 (2010); 570 U.S. 2 (2013); 567 U.S. 519 (2012); 133 S.Ct. 2675 (2013); Karlan, "Democracy and Disdain," 13; Marc Spindelman, "Obergefell's Dreams," 77 *Ohio St. L.J.* 1039, 1064 (2016); *supra* note 1 and accompanying text; David A. Strauss, "We the People, They the People, and the Puzzle of Democratic Constitutionalism," 91 *Tex. L. Rev.* 1969, 1971 (2013); e.g., Linda Greenhouse, Opinion, "Will Politics Tarnish the Supreme Court's Legitimacy?," *New York Times,* Oct. 26, 2017, https://www .nytimes.com/2017/10/26/opinion/politics-supreme-court-legitimacy.html; Ariana de Vogue, "Conservatives Prepare for Justice Anthony Kennedy's Retirement," CNN (May 2, 2017, 7:37 a.m.), http://www.cnn.com/2017/05/01/politics/justice-anthony -kennedy-retirement-rumors/index.html; Joseph P. Williams, "All Eyes Are on Justice Anthony Kennedy's Retirement Plans," *U.S. News & World Report* (July 10, 2017, 9:13 a.m.), https://www.usnews.com/news/national-news/articles/2017-07-10/all-eyes-are-on -justice-anthony-kennedys-retirement-plans.

18. *See* Chapter 6.

19. Jack M. Balkin, "Commerce," 109 *Mich. L. Rev.* 1, 23 (2010); Reuel E. Schiller, "The Era of Deference: Courts, Expertise, and the Emergence of New Deal Administrative Law," 106 *Mich. L. Rev.* 399, 425–428 (2007) (collecting and recounting New-Deal era critiques); Sylvia A. Law, "In the Name of Federalism: The Supreme Court's Assault on Democracy and Civil Rights," 70 *U. Cin. L. Rev.* 367 (2002); Saikrishna B. Prakash

and John C. Yoo, "The Puzzling Persistence of Process-Based Theories of Federalism," 79 *Tex. L. Rev.* 1459, 1521 (2001); John C. Yoo, "The Judicial Safeguards of Federalism," 70 *S. Cal. L. Rev.* 1311, 1313 (1997).

20. 347 U.S. 483 (1954); Berger, *Government by Judiciary*, 145; "The Southern Manifesto," Strom Thurmond Institute, Clemson, SC (2013), http://sti.clemson.edu /component/content/article/192-general-info/790-1956-qsouthern-manifestoq; Obergefell v. Hodges, 135 S.Ct. 2584, 2627 (2015) (Scalia, J., dissenting); *id.* at 2611–2612 (Roberts, J., dissenting); Romer v. Evans, 517 U.S. 620, 636 (1996); United States v. Virginia, 518 U.S. 515, 567 (1996); United States v. Carolene Prods. Co., 304 U.S. 144, 152 n.4 (1938); Jesse H. Choper, *Judicial Review and the National Political Process: A Functional Reconsideration of the Role of the Supreme Court* (1980), 127; Ely, *Democracy and Distrust,* 31; Jane S. Schacter, "Ely at the Altar: Political Process Theory through the Lens of the Marriage Debate," 109 *Mich. L. Rev.* 1363, 1407, 1409–1410 (2011); Chemerinsky, "The Vanishing Constitution," 103 *Harv. L. Rev.* 43, 74 (1989); Lawrence H. Tribe, "The Puzzling Persistence of Process Based Constitutional Theories," 89 *Yale L.J.* 1063, 1073 (1980); Corinna Barrett Lain, "Upside-Down Judicial Review," 101 *Geo. L.J.* 113, 116 (2012); David Strauss, "The Modernizing Mission of Judicial Review," 76 *U. Chi. L. Rev.* 859, 862 (2009); Robert Post and Reva Siegel, "Popular Constitutionalism, Departmentalism, and Judicial Supremacy," 92 *Cal. L. Rev.* 1027, 1036 (2004).

21. *See* Chapter 9.

22. Brown v. Bd. of Educ., 347 U.S. 483 (1954); Florida *ex rel.* Hawkins v. Bd. of Control, 350 U.S. 413 (1956); Turner v. City of Memphis, 369 U.S. 350 (1962); United States v. Virginia, 518 U.S. 515, 554 (1996); Craig v. Boren, 429 U.S. 190 (1976); Frontiero v. Richardson, 411 U.S. 677 (1973); Obergefell v. Hodges, 135 S.Ct. 2584 (2015).

23. City of Cleburne v. Cleburne Living Ctr., 473 U.S. 432 (1985); Jane R. Bambauer and Toni M. Massaro, "Outrageous and Irrational," 100 *Minn. L. Rev.* 281, 285–287 (2015).

Appendix

1. Derek Beach and Rasmus Brun Pedersen, *Causal Case Study Methods: Foundations and Guidelines for Comparing, Matching, and Tracing* (ebook 2016); John Gerring, *Case Study Research: Principles and Practices: Strategies for Social Inquiry* (2016).

2. Gary Goertz, "Multimethod Research, Causal Mechanisms, and Case Studies," unpublished manuscript (2017), 76; Beach and Pedersen, *Causal Case Study Methods,* 91–92, 425, 1979, 1990–1991; Gary Goertz and James Mahoney, *A Tale of Two Cultures: Qualitative and Quantitative Research in the Social Sciences* (2012); Alexander L. George and Andrew Bennett, *Case Studies and Theory Development in the Social Sciences* (2005); Goertz and Mahoney, *A Tale of Two Cultures;* James Mahoney, "Toward a Unified Theory of Causality," 41 *Comparative Political Studies* (2008): 412.

3. Goertz, "Multimethod Research," 57, 182; Beach and Pedersen, *Causal Case Study Methods,* 2005, 4894.

4. Beach and Pedersen, *Causal Case Study Methods,* 5805.

5. *Id.,* at 3575; Gerring, *Case Study Research,* 6281.

6. Frank B. Cross et al., "A Positive Political Theory of Rules and Standards," 2011 *Ill. L. Rev.* 101 (2011); Russell B. Korobkin, "Behavioral Analysis and Legal Form: Rules vs. Standards Revisited," 79 *Or. L. Rev.* 23, 25–30 (2000); Eric A. Posner and Adrian Vermeule, "Accommodating Emergencies," 56 *Stan. L. Rev.* 605, 608–09 (2003); Jonathan Masur, "A Hard Look or a Blind Eye: Administrative Law and Military Deference," 56 *Hastings L.J.* 441, 442 (2005).

7. Chapters 2 and 4 *supra;* Lawrence Lessig, "Translating Federalism: *United States v. Lopez,*" 1995 *Sup. Ct. Rev.* 125, 171 (1995); Frederick Schauer, "Legal Realism Untamed," 91 *Tex. L. Rev.* 749, 769 (2013).

8. Beach and Pedersen, *Causal Case Study Methods,* 2414; *id.,* 2409.

9. Lee Epstein and Jack Knight, "Reconsidering Judicial Preferences," 16 *Ann. Rev. Pol. Sci.* 11, 26 (2013); Lawrence Baum, *The Puzzle of Judicial Behavior* (1997), 128.

Acknowledgments

The first words of this book were dictated in conversation with Anuj Desai along the path circumscribing Lake Mendota in Madison, Wisconsin, in October 2011. The final words were written in my writing studio overlooking the Catalina Mountains north of Tucson, Arizona, in May 2018. Needless to say, my thinking evolved considerably over the course of these seven years, I hope for the better. I certainly benefited enormously from the generous engagement of scores of friends and colleagues during that time.

I will not attempt to name them all here, but a few deserve special mention. At Wisconsin, Anuj Desai and David Schwartz provided years of enthusiastic encouragement, leavened by wonderfully constructive criticism. At Arizona, Dave Marcus and Toni Massaro listened to me drone on about judicial capacity for more hours than I suspect any of us could count—time they will never get back but for which I will always be grateful. All four of them read every page of this manuscript and offered deeply insightful feedback. The final product is much better for their input. Without their support and friendship, it might not exist at all.

In late 2017, David Fontana volunteered to read a complete draft of this book and followed through with timely and incisive comments. This gesture was made all the more generous by the slightness of our prior acquaintance. Frank Michelman and Carol Rose supplied expert and extremely helpful guidance on regulatory takings. Howie Erlanger and Sergio Puig did the same on empirical methods. Richard Posner asked productively skeptical questions at various stages of the project and kindly introduced me to Michael Aronson at Harvard University Press, whose wise counsel, I am certain, was instrumental to the acceptance of my proposal. After Michael's retirement, Thomas LeBien and James Brandt supplied equally helpful guidance at later stages of the editorial process.

The original germ of an idea for this project first came into focus during my Constitutional Law class at the University of Wisconsin in the spring of 2011. My students that semester greatly helped me to formulate this idea more fully and coherently. In later semesters, my constitutional theory seminar students were similarly helpful as I refined and expanded it.

A veritable army of students contributed invaluable research assistance over the years, beginning with Bob Hammond, Dan Walters, Chelsey Metcalf, and Courtney Lanz at the University of Wisconsin. Jayme Weber, Esther Sanchez-Gomez, and Lindsey Huang took up the baton at the University of Arizona. Julie Pack, Casey Grove, and Aaron Green provided capable, timely, and tireless support during the final stretch. Sections of this book build on ideas first discussed in "Judicial Capacity and the Substance of Constitutional Law," *Yale Law Journal* 122: 422–458 (2012). Chapters 7 and 8 reprint text originally published as "Judicial Capacity and Executive Power," written with Nicholas Bullard and published in the *Virginia Law Review* 102: 765–831 (2016). Portions of Chapter 6 were first published as "Judicial Capacity and the Conditional Spending Paradox," *Wisconsin Law Review* 339: 349–381 (2013).

Looking back, I feel incredibly fortunate to have begun my academic career at two extraordinary institutions, the University of Wisconsin Law School and the University of Arizona's James E. Rogers College of Law. The resources and support I received at both places, from administration, staff, and colleagues, were all one could ask for. Among those colleagues was my friend Neil Komesar, to whom this book owes its greatest intellectual debt. In the peculiar economy of scholarly influence, I hope the book itself will serve as partial repayment.

Since this is a first book, I also need to thank my parents. My mother taught me to read, and my father taught me to write. Both my parents lovingly nursed me through a malignant brain tumor when I was nine years old. My father also provided numerous stylistic and organizational suggestions for this book and served countless hours as a sounding board while I clarified my thoughts out loud. When I needed to significantly cut back and reformat the endnotes, he spent most of a day writing several tricky macros to automate this process, saving me dozens of hours of tedious work.

Finally, and above all, I am grateful to my wife, Lori, and my children, Sabina, Sonali, and Ezra. Their love, patience, and good humor sustained me during the many stretches when I doubted whether this book could or would or should be completed. The answer to the first two of those questions was obviously yes. The third I leave readers to answer for themselves.

Index